Hiking through History
Virginia

HELP US KEEP THIS GUIDE UP TO DATE

Every effort has been made by the author and editors to make this guide as accurate and useful as possible. However, many things can change after a guide is published—trails are rerouted, regulations change, techniques evolve, facilities come under new management, and so on.

We would appreciate hearing from you concerning your experiences with this guide and how you feel it could be improved and kept up to date. While we may not be able to respond to all comments and suggestions, we'll take them to heart, and we'll also make certain to share them with the author. Please send your comments and suggestions to the following address:

Globe Pequot Press
Reader Response/Editorial Department
PO Box 480
Guilford, CT 06437

Or you may e-mail us at: editorial@GlobePequot.com

Thanks for your input, and happy trails!

Hiking through History
Virginia

Exploring the Old Dominion's Past by Trail

Johnny Molloy

FALCONGUIDES

GUILFORD, CONNECTICUT
HELENA, MONTANA

AN IMPRINT OF GLOBE PEQUOT PRESS

To buy books in quantity for corporate use
or incentives, call **(800) 962-0973**
or e-mail **premiums@GlobePequot.com.**

FALCONGUIDES®

FalconGuides is an imprint of Globe Pequot Press.
Falcon, FalconGuides, and Outfit Your Mind are registered trademarks of Morris Book Publishing, LLC.

Interior photos by Johnny Molloy

Text design: Sheryl P. Kober
Project editor: Lauren Szalkiewicz / Julie Marsh
Layout: Sue Murray
Maps by Alena Joy Pearce © Morris Book Publishing, LLC

Library of Congress Cataloging-in-Publication Data

Molloy, Johnny, 1961-
Hiking through history Virginia : exploring the Old Dominion's past by trail / Johnny Molloy.
    pages cm
Includes index.
ISBN 978-0-7627-8662-6
1. Hiking–Virginia–Guidebooks. 2. Historic sites–Virginia–Guidebooks. 3. Virginia–Guidebooks. I. Title.
GV199.42.V8M66 2014
917.5504–dc23

                                                                            2014004139

Printed in the United States of America

10 9 8 7 6 5 4 3 2 1

This book is for our forebearers in the Old Dominion who made the history
and to those who strived to preserve it.

A tranquil section of trail belies the battlefield's violent past (hike 14).

Contents

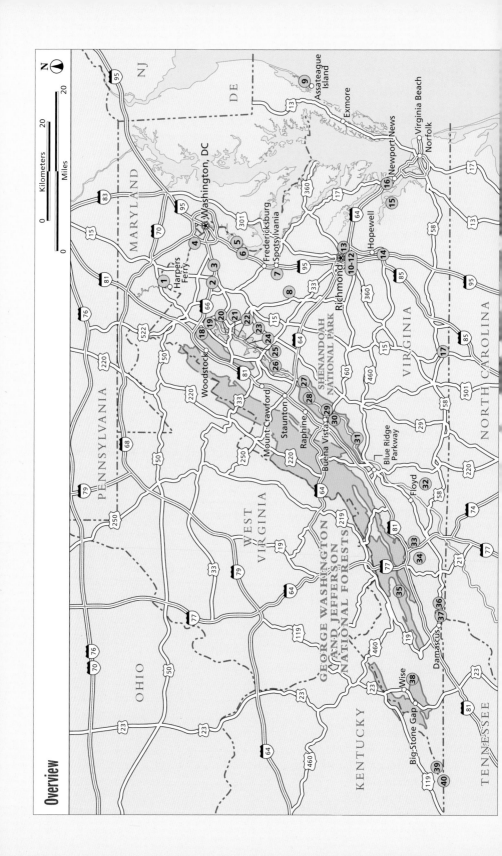

ACKNOWLEDGMENTS

Thanks to all the people who preserved history before we ever got here. Thanks to DeLorme for the fine GPS that was used to create maps for this book. Thanks to Sierra Designs for providing me with great tents, sleeping bags, and clothing for the outdoors. Thanks also to the folks at FalconGuides.

Most of all thanks to my wife Keri Anne for accompanying me on the trail and at home.

INTRODUCTION

What a pleasure it has been to pen this guide to Virginia's historic hikes. Using Virginia's rich past as a backdrop, I have selected forty hikes that are scattered throughout the Old Dominion, taking you to the most fascinating places where Virginia's past can be experienced by trail. These historic hiking destinations include Belle Isle, a menagerie of history on the James River in Richmond; Manassas Battlefield on the outskirts of Washington, DC; Shenandoah National Park, where vestiges of forgotten pioneer lifeways can be explored; and Cumberland Gap National Historical Park, where Daniel Boone himself led settlers into what was then the uncharted West.

And there is more, like hiking to see a nineteenth-century lighthouse on Assateague Island astride the Atlantic Ocean, strolling the Virginia Creeper Trail—an old railroad grade-turned-path deep in a mountain fastness—or walking through Chippokes Plantation, a 400-year-old working farm in the Tidewater. The book includes trails of varied lengths and difficulties, as well as different types of destinations, from sites visited by George Washington himself, such as the Great Falls of Virginia, to places like the Shot Tower, where musket balls were made on the frontier, to Raven Cliff Furnace in the Jefferson National Forest, where iron was processed from raw ore.

Virginia is one of the most history-laden states in the Union. Being a writer of outdoor guidebooks and a student of American history, I tackled this project with great enthusiasm. When preparing this book I realized that readers, even those going on historic hikes, want to know the basics: how to get to the trailhead, how far the hike is, information about hike difficulty, when to go, what they are going to see along the way, and where they are within reason at any given moment of the hike. This book covers those essentials, yet differentiates itself from other hiking guides by emphasizing trailside history.

Let's face it: In our rush-rush electronic world, we are hurriedly looking for an authority, "someone who knows" to help us pursue our goal of hiking through Virginia's history. This is my approach: Imagine you and I relaxing around a campfire, and you ask about the best historic hikes in Virginia. I tell you as one friend would to another, in story fashion, rather than reading, like a dry, dull textbook. Virginia's history is too captivating for that! This guide conveys concise, organized information to help busy people make the most of their limited and precious outdoor recreation time, and provides an opportunity to experience the mosaic of history that can be had in the Old Dominion.

While contemplating the historical hikes in this guide, Richmond—Virginia's capital city—comes to mind first. Not only does Belle Isle, with its physical representations of the past, stand out, but the nearby downtown Canal Walk provides insight into early Richmond, waterpower, and how times have changed. The Floodwall/ Slave Trail took me to a darker era, when men traded for other men, human chattel brought to riverside docks. Just north of town, Cold Harbor Battlefield's Bloody Run ran red with men who gave their lives fighting to end slavery.

Richmond pulses with the Old Dominion's past, yet many other historic hiking locales are scattered throughout the state. Occoneechee Plantation State Park recalls the Old South and lifeways of the Virginia planter. More modest homestead reflections can be found hiking to the Johnson Farm, a preserved homestead high atop the Blue Ridge, among the Peaks of Otter, where generations of highlanders found homes amid mountain majesty. Of course, aboriginal Virginians had already discovered that life in the Blue Ridge was nothing if not beautiful. The Hensley Settlement, straddling the Virginia-Kentucky border, contains an entire community of homes and other farm buildings, even a school, providing a snapshot of rural life in the early 1900s.

Stuarts Knob, at Fairy Stone State Park, unveils layers of early industry, from iron-ore seekers digging with a pick and shovel in the 1700s to shaft mining around which a company town quickly rose and fell with the iron market. The Virginia Highlands—the Old Dominion's rooftop—also holds layers of time, from the long hunters who hounded bear in primeval spruce-fir forests, to the day of the loggers, to the home-steaders who tried to live in the harsh uplands, to the cattle grazers that followed, to today's Appalachian Trail hikers that clamber through mile-high meadows and forests.

Around Washington, DC, you can visit the Great Falls of Virginia and see how a canal around the magnificent falls was commissioned by none other than George Washington himself. Hike to Leesylvania Plantation, where George Washington vis-ited the plantation of Henry Lee II, grandfather of Robert E. Lee. Other area hikes include Manassas Battlefield and the Assateague Coast Guard Station and Lighthouse, where you can tramp along the Atlantic Ocean to visit an oceanfront preserved build-ing and an operational lighthouse.

How fortunate we are to have preserved lands laced with trails that contain Vir-ginia's past. At Shenandoah National Park we can visit and even overnight in an authentic pioneer cabin, or see Camp Hoover, the first presidential retreat. However, it was not only national parks that held history within their bounds but also state parks such as Occoneechee Plantation and city parks like Newport News Park, where you can walk miles of earthworks from the Battle of Dam No. 1, as the Rebels fought the relentless and ultimately successful crushing of the Confederacy.

The foresight of creating historical parks and building trails within them benefits us greatly, lending a tangible link to what has transpired in the past. These destina-tions also harbor the natural beauty for which Virginia is known, from the mountains to the sea. May the hikes presented in this book help you explore, understand, and appreciate the natural and human history of the Old Dominion. Enjoy.

Weather

Virginia experiences all four seasons in their entirety, and given the state's elevations—from over 5,700 feet to sea level—the state could be experiencing them all at the same time. Summer can be warm, with occasional downright hot spells in the eastern low-lands. The mountains will be cooler. Morning hikers can avoid heat and the common afternoon thunderstorms. A mobile device equipped with Internet access allows hikers to monitor storms as they arise. Hikers are drawn outdoors in increasing numbers when the first northerly fronts of fall sweep cool, clear air across the Old Dominion. Crisp mornings, great for vigorous treks, give way to warm afternoons, more conducive to family strolls. Fall is drier than summer. Winter will bring frigid subfreezing days, chilling rains, and snows, especially in the mountains. There are also fewer hours of daylight. However, a brisk hiking pace and smart time management will keep you warm and walking while the sun is still above the horizon. Each cold month has a few days of mild weather. Make the most of them. Spring will be more variable. A warm day can be followed by a cold one. Extensive spring rains bring regrowth but also keep hikers indoors. But any avid hiker will find more good hiking days than they will have time to hike in spring and every other season. A good way to plan your hiking is to check monthly averages of high and low temperatures and average rainfall for each month in Lynchburg, roughly in the center of the state. Elevation and specific location will lead to different exact temperatures. Below is a table showing each month's averages for Lynchburg. This will give you an estimate of what to expect each month.

Month	Average High (°F)	Average Low (°F)	Precipitation (inches)
January	45	25	3.1
February	49	27	3.0
March	58	34	3.6
April	68	43	3.3
May	75	51	3.7
June	83	60	3.6
July	87	64	4.4
August	85	63	3.3
September	78	56	3.9
October	69	44	3.1
November	59	35	3.4
December	48	27	3.2

Flora and Fauna

The natural landscape of Virginia, inextricably intertwined with its human history, offers everything from a maze of hills and hollows in the far west to the mile-high mountains of the Blue Ridge to rolling midlands of the Piedmont, where big rivers carve bigger valleys, to the gentle Tidewater and onward to the Eastern Shore, abutting the mighty Atlantic Ocean. A wide variety of wildlife calls these dissimilar landscapes home.

Deer will be the land animal you most likely will see hiking Virginia's historic trails. They can be found in every Virginia county. Deer in some of the parks are remarkably tame and may linger on or close to the trail as you approach. A quiet hiker may also witness bears, turkeys, raccoons, or even a coyote. Bears can be found throughout most of Virginia, save for the easternmost Tidewater and the Eastern

Shore. They occur in greatest numbers in the western mountains and eastern swamps. Do not be surprised if you observe beavers, muskrats, or a playful otter along streams and lakes. If you feel uncomfortable when encountering any critter, keep your distance and they will generally keep theirs.

Overhead, many raptors will be plying the skies for food, including hawks, falcons, and owls. Depending on where you are, other birds you may spot range from kingfishers to woodpeckers. Look for waterfowl in lakes and tidal waters. Songbirds are abundant throughout the state.

Virginia's flora offers just as much variety, especially with such a range of elevation and transitioning aquatic environments, from mountain streams to saltwater seas. Along the trails you will find evergreen forests, hardwoods coloring autumn's landscapes, even spartan beach environments. Wildflowers will be found in spring, summer, and fall along watercourses and in drier site-specific situations.

Wilderness / Land Use Restrictions / Regulations

Virginia's historical hikes are accomplished primarily in city, state, and federal parks, plus national forests and wildlife refuges. Each operates with its own system of rules, and we are responsible for knowing them. Since these hikes do travel to historical destinations, there is always a layer of Virginia's past overlain upon each park. For example, though Newport News Park, a city park, does have multiple forms of outdoor recreation, from camping to golf, the preserved battle site—on the National Register of Historic Places—is managed with an emphasis on preservation. Same goes for places like Fairy Stone State Park, where traditional park activities such as swimming, fishing, and bicycling are undertaken, yet the historic trails circling Stuarts Knob at Fairy Stone are also an intregal part of the park experience. National parks often offer a mix of preservation and recreation to visitors. At the Johnson Farm on the Blue Ridge Parkway in the Peaks of Otter, historical, recreational, and nature trails are all interconnected with facilities including a visitor center, campground, and lodge. At Cumberland Gap National Historical Park, emphasis is on history first. So, in the end, it depends on the managing body and the mission of the park in terms of how the preserved past is treated.

Also, no matter where you go to hike through Virginia's past, consider adding other recreational opportunities while you are there, whether you strap on a backpack and overnight in the back of beyond or take a guided tour, go on a bike ride, or spend the night in a cozy cabin. The important thing is to get out there and connect with history on your own terms.

HOW TO USE THIS GUIDE

Take a close enough look and you'll find that this guide contains just about everything you'll ever need to choose, plan for, enjoy, and survive a historical hike in Virginia. Stuffed with useful area information, *Hiking through History Virginia* features forty mapped and cued hikes. Here's an outline of the book's major components:

Each hike listed starts with a short summary of the hike's highlights. These quick overviews give you a taste of the hiking adventures and the history contained within. You'll learn about the trail terrain and what surprises each route has to offer. Following the overview, you'll find the hike specs: quick, nitty-gritty details of the hike. Most are self-explanatory, but here are some details:

Distance: The total distance of the recommended route—one-way for loop hikes, the round-trip on an out-and-back or lollipop hike, point-to-point for a shuttle. Options are additional.

Hiking time: The average time it will take to cover the route. It is based on the total distance, elevation gain, and the condition and difficulty of the trail. Your fitness level will also affect your time.

Difficulty: Each hike has been assigned a level of difficulty. The rating system was developed from several sources and personal experience. These levels are meant to be a guideline only and may prove easier or harder for different people depending on ability and physical fitness.

Easy—Five miles or less total trip distance in one day, with minimal elevation gain and paved or smooth-surfaced dirt trail.

Moderate—Up to 10 miles total trip distance in one day, with moderate elevation gain and potentially rough terrain.

Difficult—More than 10 miles total trip distance in one day, strenuous elevation gains, and rough and/or rocky terrain.

Trail surface: General information about what to expect underfoot.

Best season: General information on the best time of year to hike.

Other trail users: Such as horseback riders, mountain bikers, inline skaters, etc.

Canine compatibility: Know the trail regulations before you take your dog hiking with you. Dogs are not allowed on several trails in this book.

Land status: City park, state park, national park or forest, etc.

Fees and permits: Whether you need to carry any money with you for park entrance fees and permits.

Maps: This is a list of other maps to supplement the maps in this book. USGS maps are the best sources for accurate topographical information, but the local park map may show more-recent trails. Use both.

Trail contacts: This is the location, phone number, and website for the local land manager(s) in charge of all the trails within the selected hike. Before you head out, get trail access information, or contact the land manager after your visit if you see problems with trail erosion, damage, or misuse.

Piers of a forgotten bridge front downtown Richmond (hike 10)

Finding the trailhead: Dependable driving directions to parking.

The Hike is the meat of the chapter. Detailed and honest, it is a carefully researched impression of the trail and the history along the way, both natural and human.

Under **Miles and Directions,** mileage cues identify all turns and trail name changes, as well as points of interest. Options are also given for many hikes to make your journey shorter or longer depending on the amount of time you have. Do not feel restricted to the routes and trails that are mapped here. Be adventurous and use this guide as a platform to discover new routes for yourself.

Tips are quick, interesting facts about the locale.

A **sidebar** is included with nearly each hike. This often expounds on a particular aspect of the area's past or better ways to enjoy your historical hiking experience. These sidebars may pique your interest to research beyond the history given here.

Enjoy your outdoor exploration of Virginia's past, and remember to pack out what you pack in.

How to Use the Maps

Overview map: This map shows the location of each hike in the area by hike number.

Route map: This is your primary guide to each hike. It shows all of the accessible roads and trails, historical points of interest, water, landmarks, and geographical features. It also distinguishes trails from roads, and paved roads from unpaved roads. The selected route is highlighted, and directional arrows point the way.

TRAIL FINDER

Hikes	Best Hikes for Stories of People	Best Hikes for Civil War Buffs	Best Hikes for Industrial History	Best Hikes for History-Loving Dogs	Best Hikes for History-Loving Children	Best Hikes for Nature Lovers	Best Hikes for Backpacking History Buffs
1. Split Rock		●	●			●	
2. Bull Run Mountains Conservancy	●	●	●				
3. First Manassas	●	●			●		
4. Great Falls of the Potomac	●		●	●	●	●	
5. Leesylvania State Park	●	●				●	
6. Prince William Forest Park			●	●		●	
7. Spotsylvania History Trail				●	●		
8. Lake Anna State Park			●		●	●	
9. Assateague Coast Guard Station and Lighthouse					●	●	
10. Belle Isle	●	●	●		●	●	
11. Canal Walk at Richmond	●	●	●	●			
12. Floodwall/Slave Trail	●	●	●	●			
13. Cold Harbor Battlefield Loop		●			●	●	
14. Petersburg National Battlefield	●	●			●		
15. Chippokes Plantation	●				●	●	

TRAIL FINDER

Hikes	Best Hikes for Stories of People	Best Hikes for Civil War Buffs	Best Hikes for Industrial History	Best Hikes for History-Loving Dogs	Best Hikes for History-Loving Children	Best Hikes for Nature Lovers	Best Hikes for Backpacking History Buffs
16. Battle of Dam No. 1 at Newport News Park	●	●				●	
17. Occoneechee Plantation	●			●	●	●	
18. Elizabeth Furnace	●		●	●	●		
19. Fox Hollow Snead Farm Loop	●			●		●	
20. Thornton River Loop	●	●				●	●
21. Corbin Cabin Loop	●					●	●
22. Skyland	●		●		●	●	
23. Rose River Loop			●	●	●	●	●
24. Rapidan Camp	●				●	●	●
25. Pocosin Mission	●				●	●	
26. Browns Gap	●	●		●		●	●
27. Humpback Rocks	●				●	●	
28. Saint Marys Wilderness			●	●		●	●
29. Brown Mountain Creek	●			●	●	●	●

TRAIL FINDER

Hikes	Best Hikes for Stories of People	Best Hikes for Civil War Buffs	Best Hikes for Industrial History	Best Hikes for History-Loving Dogs	Best Hikes for History-Loving Children	Best Hikes for Nature Lovers	Best Hikes for Backpacking History Buffs
30. Bluff Mountain	•					•	•
31. Johnson Farm	•			•	•	•	
32. Stuarts Knob at Fairy Stone State Park			•		•		
33. Shot Tower via New River Trail	•		•		•		
34. Raven Cliff Furnace			•	•	•	•	
35. Burkes Garden from Chestnut Knob	•					•	•
36. Virginia Highlands Circuit	•					•	•
37. Virginia Creeper Trail			•		•	•	•
38. Guest River Gorge	•		•	•	•	•	
39. Hensley Settlement	•					•	•
40. Cumberland Gap	•	•	•	•	•		

Map Legend

Symbol	Description	Symbol	Description
81	Interstate Highway	✪	Capital
460	US Highway	—	Dam
671	State Highway		Gate
FR520	County/Forest Road		Lighthouse
	Local Road		Lodging
	Railroad	P	Parking
	Featured Trail	✕	Pass/Gap
	Trail	▲	Peak/Summit
	State Line		Picnic Area
	Small River or Creek	∥	Rapids
	Intermittent Stream		Restaurant/Dining
	Body of Water		Restrooms
	National Forest/Park		Scenic View/Viewpoint
	National Wilderness Area	⊄	Spring
	State/County Park		Tower
	Miscellaneous Park	○	Town
	Boat Ramp	①	Trailhead
	Bridge	⊢——⊣	Tunnel
■	Building/Point of Interest	?	Visitor/Information Center
⋀	Campground		Waterfall
▲	Campsite		

Greater Washington, DC, and the Eastern Shore

Outcrop on the Bull Run Mountains provides view of the Blue Ridge.

1 Split Rock

This hike heads to an overlook known as Split Rock. Look over the majestic scene where the Potomac and Shenandoah Rivers meet, where Virginia, West Virginia, and Maryland all come together, with the town of Harpers Ferry, West Virginia, lying below. This hike's beginning is home to Harpers Ferry National Historical Park, where you can step back in time to early American manufacturing, railroad history, and Civil War drama.

Start: Shenandoah Street off US 340
Distance: 6.2-mile balloon loop
Hiking time: About 3.5-4.5 hours
Difficulty: More difficult due to distance and elevation gain
Trail surface: Natural, except for bridge crossing
Best season: Whenever the skies are clear
Other trail users: None

Canine compatibility: Leashed dogs permitted
Land status: National historical park
Fees and permits: Parking fee required
Schedule: 24/7/365
Maps: Loudon Heights Trails; USGS Harpers Ferry
Trail contact: Harpers Ferry National Historical Park, PO Box 65, Harpers Ferry, WV 25425; (304) 535-6029; www.nps.gov/hafe

Finding the trailhead: From Berryville, Virginia, take US 340 north into West Virginia and stay with it, passing Charles Town and continuing into Harpers Ferry, West Virginia. Once in Harpers Ferry, look for the left turn onto Shenandoah Street just before crossing the bridge over the Shenandoah River. Follow Shenandoah Street just a short distance, then come to a fee parking area on your right, part of Harpers Ferry National Historical Park. Trailhead GPS: N39 19.2894' / W77 44.6448'

The Hike

This hike starts in an old town. Harpers Ferry was part of the colony of Virginia when founded in 1751 by Robert Harper. He saw the potential value of the area as a strategic transportation corridor as well as a source for ample waterpower, and garnered 125 acres at the peninsula where the Shenandoah River meets the Potomac River. The Virginia General Assembly officially recognized the place as "Shenandoah Falls at Mr. Harpers Ferry." The town grew, and today, parts of the town's historic area are protected as a national historical park.

The beauty of the place was undeniable then and remains so today. Thomas Jefferson himself came to Harpers Ferry in October of 1783. He described it as thus: "the passage of the Potomac through the Blue Ridge is perhaps one of the most stupendous scenes in nature. . . ." It wasn't long after Jefferson's visit that the United States Armory and Arsenal was established in 1799. Harpers Ferry transformed from riverside village to industrial town. For the next six decades, up until the Civil War, more than 600,000 firearms were produced. Waterpower was very important to

Looking downstream on the Potomac River from Split Rock

manufacturing here, but the real industrial breakthrough came when John Hall first undertook manufacturing using interchangeable firearm parts, allowing rifles to be manufactured by machine rather than by hand. Other manufacturing followed the same idea. In the 1800s Virginius Island, located very near the trailhead for this hike, was an industrial powerhouse. Here, an iron foundry, tannery, machine shop, flour mill, and sawmill were all operating using the latest technology of the time. An interconnected network of nature trails explores this intriguing area.

Being at the confluence of two rivers and a mountain passage, it was not long before the canals and railroads made their way to Harpers Ferry. As the east pushed west and commerce needed a route through the mountains, the Chesapeake and Ohio Canal came through as well as the Baltimore and Ohio Railroad. These enhanced Harpers Ferry's place as a manufacturing center.

The Civil War changed everything though. Being an important industrial, transportation, and arms-manufacturing locale, both sides prized Harpers Ferry. The town ended up changing hands between North and South eight times during the Civil War. Before that, as soon as Virginia seceded from the Union, Yankee soldiers protecting the arsenal set fire to it, preventing the Rebels from obtaining the armory. Back and forth the battling went. Stonewall Jackson captured more than 12,000 Union soldiers at one time in Harpers Ferry, the largest such capturing of the enemy in the entire Civil War. The town finally ended up in Union hands, and the Northerners used it as a base to raid the Shenandoah Valley.

This hike starts near the historic manufacturing base of Harpers Ferry before crossing a bridge over the Shenandoah River. The route uses the Appalachian Trail (AT) to climb Loudon Heights, the second-highest mountain above Harpers Ferry. The top of this mountain drops nearly 900 feet to the Potomac River. You will follow the AT to the Virginia/West Virginia state line, then take the Loudon Heights Trail (aka Blue Trail) along the state line to Split Rock. During the Battle of Harpers Ferry, Confederate soldiers drug cannons to the top of Loudon Heights and pounded Union positions. Interestingly, after the Union army recaptured Harpers Ferry, they established a series of campgrounds for soldiers on Loudon Heights despite its extremely sloped nature as well as its decided lack of water. It was a miserable existence. Later, Loudon Heights was abandoned by both sides.

John Brown and the Civil War

During the year 1859 the rhetoric was rising about slavery throughout the United States. The incident at Harpers Ferry was arguably the fuse that led to the Civil War's beginning. A fellow named John Brown decided to lead a revolt intended to free American slaves. He started his revolt in Harpers Ferry. His plan was to seize the weapons located at the United States Arsenal and Armory in town, arm the slaves, and use the labyrinthine hills and hollows of the Blue Ridge Mountains for guerrilla warfare. Brown led a group of twenty-one men, first seizing the armory and other places in town. The US Marines pursued John Brown, and the raid was over within thirty-six hours.

John Brown was then brought to trial and convicted of murder, conspiring with slaves to rebel, and treason against the United States. He was hung for his crimes but became a martyr, as this incident heightened national discussion of the morality of slavery. Both sides sharpened their rhetoric, deciding to settle their differences with blood and gunpowder.

Split Rock

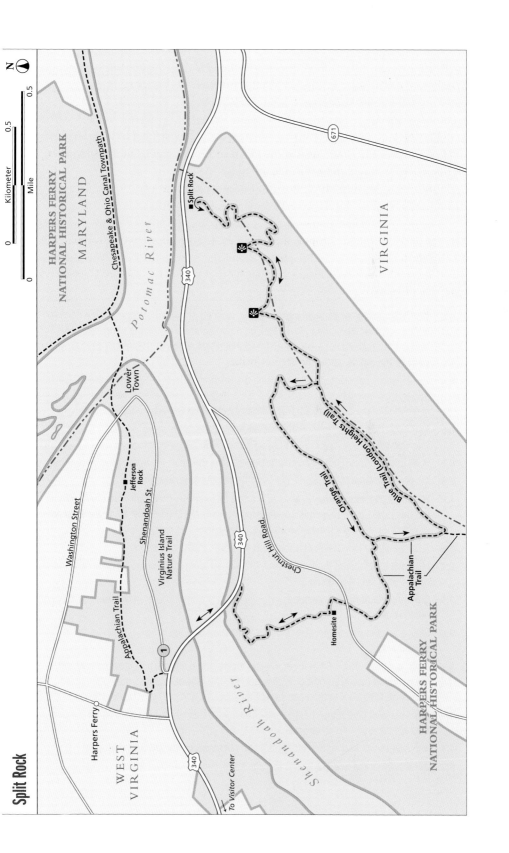

But for modern-day hikers, Loudon Heights is a worthy goal. It now features resplendent forests growing among the rocky soils. Your vistas from Split Rock present views into three states—West Virginia, Virginia, and Maryland—as well as views of Harpers Ferry, the confluence of the Shenandoah and Potomac Rivers, and finally of the Chesapeake and Ohio Towpath running across the waters. And the view downstream on the Potomac ain't too bad either!

▶ **Thomas Jefferson described the view of the confluence of the Potomac and Shenandoah Rivers at Harpers Ferry as "being worth a voyage across the Atlantic."**

While you are here, be sure to visit Lower Town, the historic district in Harpers Ferry, as well as Virginius Island and the national historical park visitor center. There is a lot of history right here at the confluence of the Shenandoah and Potomac Rivers.

Miles and Directions

0.0 From the parking lot on Shenandoah Street, walk up Shenandoah Street to the US 340 bridge over the Shenandoah River. Pick up the AT southbound on the bridge walkway across the Shenandoah River. (The AT northbound takes you into Harpers Ferry.) Soak in views of the rapids below and Virginius Island.

0.4 The AT leaves left on steps after crossing the Shenandoah River. Cut under the US 340 bridge, then emerge south of US 340. Pass through a small clearing, then work up the south side of the Shenandoah River in rocky woods. Cruise along bluffs above the river.

0.6 Turn away from the Shenandoah River, angling up the north slope of Loudon Heights in hardwoods.

0.9 Pass through an old homesite just before crossing Chestnut Hill Road. Keep ascending.

1.3 Intersect the Orange Trail. Stay right (south), with the Appalachian Trail.

1.5 Reach the crest of Loudon Heights and a trail intersection. Leave left from the AT, joining the much-less-used Blue Trail (Loudon Heights Trail). Travel northeast along the boundary of West Virginia and Virginia. The walking is easy here.

1.8 Pass the stone foundation of a forgotten ridgetop structure. Descend.

2.1 Meet the other end of the Orange Trail. This will be your return route. Continue right (east) on the Blue Trail, descending.

2.4 Come near a power-line clearing and walk out to a warm-up view of the rivers and mountains below.

2.6 Pass a second power-line view of the Tri-State area of Harpers Ferry. Continue downhill on switchbacks.

3.1 Open onto Split Rock. From here, you can look at the confluence of the Potomac and Shenandoah Rivers, Maryland Heights and the C&O Towpath across the Potomac, and an extensive valley view to the east, as well as a look at Harpers Ferry. Backtrack.

4.1 Meet the east end of the Orange Trail, leave right, descending, then level off on a mountainside bench. Head southwest.

4.9 Intersect the AT. Turn right, northbound, and backtrack for the US 340 bridge.

6.2 Arrive back at the Shenandoah Street trailhead, completing the hike.

2 Bull Run Mountains Conservancy

This hike adds a scenic overlay to the history contained within. Start at the south end of the Bull Run Mountains, first passing ruins of a tavern, then coming to huge Chapman's Mill, once a thriving operation. From there, climb to an open rock outcrop with extensive views west to the Blue Ridge. Finally, backtrack to pass a hand-dug linear quarry and a family cemetery.

Start: Trailhead on Beverly Mill Drive
Distance: 4.7-mile loop
Hiking time: About 2.5-3.5 hours
Difficulty: Moderate; does have 1 extensive climb
Trail surface: Natural surfaces
Best season: When the skies are clearest
Other trail users: None
Canine compatibility: Leashed dogs permitted

Land status: Private conservancy
Fees and permits: No fee; liability waiver required
Schedule: Open daily year-round
Maps: *Bull Run Mountains Conservancy Trail Map; USGS Thoroughfare Gap*
Trail contact: Bull Run Mountains Conservancy Inc., PO Box 210, Broad Run, VA 20137; (703) 753-2631; brmconservancy.org

Finding the trailhead: From exit 40 on I-66 (Haymarket/Leesburg), take US 15 south for 0.3 mile to VA 55 west. Turn right and join VA 55 west for 2.6 miles to turn right on Turner Road. Cross over I-66 (no access) and then immediately turn left on Beverly Mill Drive. Follow Beverly Mill Drive 0.6 mile to the Bull Run Mountains Conservancy trailhead, just a little west of the Stone House. (The direct access for Chapman's Mill is a little beyond the conservancy trailhead.) Trailhead GPS: N38 49.482'/W77 42.378'

The Hike

Broad Run cuts a narrow passage between the Bull Run Mountains to the north and the Pond Mountains to the south. This opening, known as Thoroughfare Gap, lies between the Blue Ridge and the Shenandoah Valley to the west and the Piedmont and the ocean to the east. Thoroughfare Gap has been a natural travel corridor door for as long as animals and aboriginal Virginians have been migrating. Since Virginia was an English possession, colonists have used the gap. As early as the 1600s, settlers and soldiers, traders and explorers have all made their way through this mountain passage. Today, I-66 links Washington, DC, to points west, passing through Thoroughfare Gap.

With that in mind, it is no surprise that history was made in this neck of the woods. And Virginians and visitors alike are fortunate that the Bull Run Mountains Conservancy stepped in in 1995 to protect the Bull Run Mountains and the history at Thoroughfare Gap. Add to that the additional layer of protection provided by those restoring Chapman's Mill. (More about that later.) The Bull Run Mountains Conservancy manages 800 acres of the greater 2,486-acre Bull Run Mountains Natural Area Preserve.

Hiker peers into an ice storage well

After leaving the trailhead our hike takes us past the Chapman Mansion and ice-house. You can peer into the rock-lined pit where ice was stored for summertime use and look down upon the old Chapman Mansion. It was built by Jonathan Chapman, the same man whose family built the seven-story Chapman's Mill, which you will soon see. The mansion is now mere stone walls.

Then you'll come to Chapman's Mill. Strategically located in Thoroughfare Gap, the mill capitalized on trade between the agriculturally prolific Shenandoah Valley and cities to the east such as Alexandria, where agricultural products could be shipped by boat to other points in the United States and beyond to other continents.

Times were good and they only got better when the Manassas Gap Railroad started passing through Thoroughfare Gap in 1852. This rail transportation sped up the process of getting grain to the mill and finished product to markets in the East. Chapman's Mill was enlarged and brought up to seven stories in height. It is currently believed to be the tallest stone structure in the United States.

During the Civil War the Confederate Army turned the mill into a meat-curing warehouse and distribution center. Here, animals were processed and turned into meat rations for the Rebels. However, after the First Battle of Manassas, the Rebels burned the mill to prevent Yankee access. Next, during the Battle of Thoroughfare Gap on August 28, 1862, the mill changed hands three times. Soldiers climbed up the mill and shot out from its windows at the opposition. The Confederacy ultimately won the battle, allowing General Robert E. Lee to march east through Thoroughfare Gap and join the rest of the Rebels for the Second Battle of Manassas, which they also won.

> Chapman's Mill provided cornmeal and flour for American troops for seven wars: the French and Indian, Revolutionary, War of 1812, Civil War, Spanish-American War, World War I, and World War II.

In the 1870s the Beverly family restored Chapman's Mill to operation. The mill took on their name. They stayed in business until 1951. Unfortunately, the mill burned in 1998, but attempts are being made at restoring the historic structure. A campaign known as Turn the Mill Around is under way to repair the site, which is listed on the National Register of Historic Places. For more information on this, visit chapmansmill.org.

Next, you will visit the remains of another, smaller mill, known as the Upper Mill. From there, take the Fern Hollow Trail up to a gap. Then join the Chestnut Ridge Trail as it leads to the crest of the Bull Run Mountains. From here, walk through oaks, pines, and rocks aplenty atop the ridgeline. Leave conservancy property using an easement to access a large rock outcrop framed with Table Mountain pines, presenting a stellar view toward points west.

The Bull Run Mountains Conservancy

The private, philanthropic Bull Run Mountains Conservancy was established in 1995. They protect the most easterly mountain chain in Virginia's mountains, which contains rare plant communities, especially along its quartz outcrops. Additionally, the historic layer located within has been protected. The Bull Run Mountains Conservancy also runs numerous environmental programs for adults and kids, emphasizing local history as well as environmental education. They work to get kids outdoors, an endeavor that is sorely needed today. And when they do, the conservancy emphasizes having fun out there. They also run nature camps, and hikes for adults and families are led throughout the year. The conservancy also partners with other groups and schools for field research. The organization is dependent on membership and volunteerism to keep it thriving. Consider joining this group and supporting their efforts. For more information, visit brmconservancy.org.

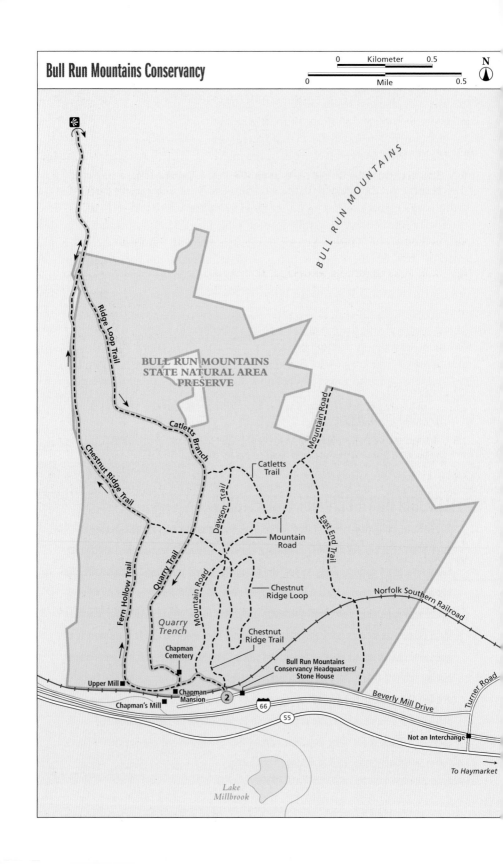

Descend from this high perch, eventually joining the Quarry Trail. Here you will visit a hand-dug linear trench from which rock was extracted to build the mill and house for the Chapmans. Finally, stop by the historic Chapman Cemetery, then return to the trailhead.

Miles and Directions

0.0 Start by crossing the railroad tracks just a little west of the Stone House. Be sure to deposit your liability waiver, which you can print and fill out at home from the BRMC website. Immediately come to an intersection. Here, the Chestnut Ridge Trail leads right. Stay left.

0.1 Come to another intersection. Here Mountain Road leads right. Stay straight, curving around a ridge rising to your right.

0.2 Come to the connector to the Chapman Cemetery and the Quarry Trail. This will be your return route. For now, stay straight and shortly pass the ice pit and ruins of the Chapman Mansion. A fence borders the pit. Pass the overlook of Chapman's Mill. The huge stone walls are impressive. I-66 roars in the background. Broad Run flows below.

0.4 Pass the ruins of the Upper Mill. It also has newer relics, including a refrigerator. Turn up Fern Hollow, leaving the railroad, interstate, and Broad Run behind.

0.5 Pass a cool spring enclosed in a concrete box on your left. Continue up the wooded vale.

0.9 Reach a gap and join the Chestnut Ridge Trail. Head left on a broad path through oaks.

1.3 Make the crest of Bull Run Mountain. A spur trail leads left; stay with the main, wide official path northbound.

1.8 Intersect the Ridge Loop Trail. For now, keep straight and follow a conservation easement, a doubletrack trail, on private land heading toward the vista. Ascend.

2.3 Come to the signed overlook, which splits west from the main easement. A wide panorama opens to the farms, fields, and forests below, and the Blue Ridge and mountains beyond. Look around at the ragged rock ramparts below the overlook. Backtrack.

3.5 Come alongside Catletts Branch, gurgling to your left.

3.7 Meet the Catletts Trail. Stay straight on the Quarry Trail.

3.9 Come to a four-way intersection. Keep straight here, ascending on the Quarry Trail.

4.3 Come to the Quarry Trench. Here, cross the hand-dug rock vein used to build Chapman's Mill and home.

4.5 Reach the Chapman Cemetery, enclosed in stone and wrought iron. Descend just a bit to complete the loop. Backtrack.

4.7 Reach the trailhead, completing the hike.

3 First Manassas

Make a circuit through the eastern half of Manassas Battlefield, where the first clash of the Civil War took place in July of 1861. A blazed trail takes you from the park visitor center through the woods and fields of the preserved historical locale. Visit the Stone Bridge, homesites, and the only two buildings that were there when both the First Manassas and Second Manassas battles took place.

Start: Park visitor center
Distance: 5.2-mile loop
Hiking time: About 3–3.5 hours
Difficulty: Moderate
Trail surface: Gravel, grass, natural surfaces
Best season: Year-round
Other trail users: None
Canine compatibility: Leashed dogs permitted

Land status: National battlefield park
Fees and permits: Entrance permit required
Schedule: Open daily year-round
Maps: *Manassas National Battlefield Park Trail Guide; USGS Gainesville*
Trail contact: Manassas National Battlefield Park, 12521 Lee Hwy., Manassas, VA 20109; (703) 361-1339; www.nps.gov/mana

Finding the trailhead: From exit 47 on I-66, west of Washington, DC, take Sudley Road (VA 234) north for 0.7 mile, then turn right and dead-end at the visitor center. The First Manassas Trail starts at the east end of the visitor center parking lot. Trailhead GPS: N38 48.772'/W77 31.260'

The Hike

At times it seemed as if the Civil War was inevitable. At other times it looked as if the North and South could compromise their way into a conflict-free future. However, the issues of slavery, states' rights, and the industrial-versus-rural lifeways of the regions simply could not be overcome. Although the Civil War officially began in April of 1861 at Fort Sumter, South Carolina, the armies of the Confederate States of America and the United States of America first clashed here at Manassas in July of 1861.

Our nation's leaders feared this day. Southerners longed to throw the cloak of Yankee piety and self-righteousness from an agrarian economy built around slavery. Northerners tired of prideful states' rights advocates wishing to keep the national government as weak as possible. In 1830 President Andrew Jackson stated in his famous toast, "Our Federal Union, it must be preserved."

▶ The Stone House was restored to its Civil War condition in 1960. Most of the exterior remains as it was in the 1860s.

It was not to be. Nobody knew exactly where or when the first battle would take place. Both the Yankees and the Confederates were sure of their causes and equally sure of a quick victory. The residents of Washington, DC, treated this Battle of First Manassas almost like a picnic. Along with congressmen, many locals took

The Stone House served as a field hospital during both battles here.

carriages and horses out to the battle site. Manassas was important because it was the junction of two railroads, the Orange and Alexandria Railroad and the Manassas Gap Railroad. Both sides knew that whoever controlled these railroads could easily make their way to and from the Confederate capital in Richmond.

Recruits on both sides were full of pomp and bluster, ready to defend their noble causes. Higher-ups, from officers to politicians, as well as the average citizen, believed the War Between the States would be short and quick. Both sides had plenty of veteran officers, yet the carnage that was to take place during the Civil War would shock all. And the first blow came here at Manassas. Just five days earlier 35,000 freshly mustered Union soldiers, signed up as ninety-day volunteers, headed south to go capture Richmond.

Of course, the Confederates had other plans. They realized the rail junction at Manassas would be a Yankee target, and the two sides undertook their battle near a stream named Bull Run before dawn on July 21. A feint by the Union army at the Stone Bridge over Bull Run only temporarily threw off the Rebels. Their defensive line was collapsing and they made a stand at Henry Hill. This is where Thomas J. Jackson, Confederate general, held the line against the Federals, causing a fellow soldier

Inside the Stone House

to remark, "There stands Jackson like a stone wall! Rally behind the Virginians!" A Southern hero was born: Stonewall Jackson.

After a lull in the battle, both sides resumed their attempt to take Henry Hill. Finally, with fresh Confederate recruits, the Southerners overwhelmed the Union. The Yankees began to withdraw toward Washington. To their surprise, the road to the capital was clogged with the battle onlookers who left Manassas after witnessing the carnage and seeing that war was no picnic. The raw Union recruits fell into a panicked retreat. The Battle of First Manassas was over. The Confederates, with President Jefferson Davis on hand, celebrated. However, both sides surmised the Civil War was likely to be a long and deadly one.

It would be thirteen months later before the Union and Confederate armies would meet again at Manassas. This hike follows the First Manassas Trail, which focuses on the Battle of First Manassas. The trail is blue blazed as it follows grassy tracks through fields and dirt pathways through the woods. You will start near the battlefield visitor center and head east. The trail takes you by the Van Pelt Homesite and on to the Stone Bridge, where the Yankees tried to trick the Rebels into bringing

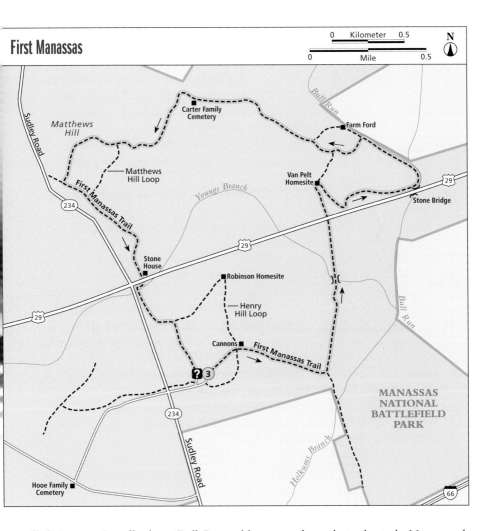

all their men. A walk along Bull Run adds a natural touch to the trek. Next, work your way to Matthews Hill, where outstanding views to the south reveal the battlefield. Work your way to Buck Hill, where more battlefield vistas await. Stop by the Stone House, where a tavern keeper and his wife rode out the conflict. Ultimately, wounded soldiers coalesced in the structure. The Stone House also saw the hordes of retreating Yankee soldiers pass by in humiliating defeat.

Finally, you climb to Henry Hill and visit the Henry House, another building intact from that time. View the grave of Mrs. Judith Carter Henry, the only civilian killed in the Battle of First Manassas. The frail 85-year-old woman refused to leave her home—and perhaps was unable to—and was struck by artillery. Beyond the Henry House it is but a short jaunt back to the battlefield visitor center.

Miles and Directions

0.0 Start on the First Manassas Trail, heading east on a grassy track through a field. Pass a line of cannons and the Henry Hill Loop Trail. It was here on Henry Hill where most of the fighting occurred in the Battle of First Manassas. Pass through a mix of field and forest.

0.5 Come to a trail intersection. Head left, northbound, on the doubletrack path, staying with the blue blazes of the First Manassas Trail, toward the Stone Bridge. Cedars border the path. A horse trail (not shown on the map) runs parallel to the doubletrack path.

0.9 Stay with the First Manassas Trail as it splits left and bridges Youngs Branch. Open onto a field.

1.3 Come to and carefully cross US 29. The First Manassas Trail continues north, climbing a tree-lined lane.

1.4 Reach a hilltop and the Van Pelt Homesite and farm known as "Avon." Abraham Van Pelt, the Union supporter from New Jersey, was finally run out of the area by Confederate loyalists. From here, turn acutely right, heading southeast toward the Stone Bridge. Another trail heads northeast and shortcuts the loop, bypassing the Stone Bridge.

1.7 Reach a long boardwalk spanning a wetland after topping a hill. Places like this are where battlefield preservation inadvertently can protect natural plant communities.

1.9 Come to the Stone Bridge. Note that it has been restored. During the Battle of First Manassas, the center was destroyed to prevent use by the opposition. Turn north upstream on Bull Run through floodplain forest. Do not cross the Stone Bridge.

2.3 Come to a trail intersection. Here, a short loop goes past Farm Ford. Turn left here with the blue-blazed First Manassas Trail. Climb away from Bull Run.

2.5 Reach another intersection. Here, a path leads left back to the Van Pelt Homesite. Stay right here, with the First Manassas Trail, heading northwest through a field. Enjoy good views of the battlefield to the west.

2.6 Pass the other end of the loop coming from the Farm Ford.

3.1 Come to the site of Pittsylvania Plantation and the spur trail leading left to the Carter Family Cemetery.

3.7 Stay right past the first intersection with the Matthews Hill Loop.

4.0 Come to a T trail intersection on a grassy hill. Head left, southbound. The right turn goes to parking on Sudley Road. Pass cannon emplacements and enjoy long views south of the battlefield.

4.2 Pass the second intersection with the Matthews Hill Loop. Dip south, then surmount Buck Hill and drop toward the Stone House.

4.6 Reach the Stone House, a significant landmark for soldiers in both Manassas battles. During the warm season the house is open for tours. Cross US 29 at the traffic light. Cross Youngs Branch on a bridge, then climb toward Henry Hill.

4.9 Stay straight for the Henry House as the Henry Hill Loop heads left.

5.1 Come to the Henry House.

5.2 Reach the north side of the visitor center, ending the hike.

4 Great Falls of the Potomac

Have you ever seen the Great Falls of the Potomac? The crashing whitewater wonder is truly a natural highlight of the Old Dominion. The area's history is nearly as impressive. George Washington himself commissioned a system of canals and locks to allow barge traffic to navigate around this extensive whitewater froth that crashes through Mather Gorge. On your hike visit the falls, locks, canals, and even the ghost town of Matildaville, built for the men tending the lock and canal system and their families.

Start: Great Falls Park Visitor Center
Distance: 4.7-mile loop
Hiking time: About 2.5–3.5 hours
Difficulty: Moderate; there is a 150-foot climb
Trail surface: Gravel, natural surfaces
Best season: Year-round
Other trail users: Horses on some sections, joggers
Canine compatibility: Leashed dogs permitted

Land status: National park
Fees and permits: Entrance fee required
Schedule: Open daily year-round
Maps: *Great Falls Park; USGS Vienna, Falls Church*
Trail contact: Great Falls Park, 9200 Old Dominion Dr., McLean, VA 22102; (703) 285-2965; www.nps.gov/grfa

Finding the trailhead: From exit 44 on I-495, west of Washington, DC, take VA 193 west (Georgetown Pike) for 4.3 miles to turn right at a traffic light onto Old Dominion Drive. Follow Old Dominion Drive for 0.9 mile to enter Great Falls Park. Park near the visitor center. Trailhead GPS: N38 59.847'/W77 15.317'

The Hike

Hiking at Great Falls Park is a lesson in human and natural history. The Great Falls are just that—great—and a sight to see. Young George Washington, as he traveled the Potomac and surveyed interior lands of the Ohio River valley, saw this crashing cascade, admired its beauty, yet decided the Potomac River would only prosper as an essential trade corridor if the Great Falls and other, lesser rapids could be bypassed. So the idea was born: Create a canal system on the Potomac River.

What became the Patowmack Canal took a long time to build. Washington's dream, this canal system linking the Potomac River valley with its access to the Atlantic Ocean and the Ohio River Valley to the west, would bind these two regions economically, strengthening a fragile-yet-expanding United States.

Nevertheless, the rapids of the Potomac River would prove formidable, especially here at the Great Falls. Along this point the Potomac descends 70 feet in a mile, dropping from the Piedmont to

▶ The lock and canal system skirting around Great Falls, commissioned by George Washington, took seventeen years to complete.

The Great Falls of the Potomac roar on a hot summer morning.

the Atlantic coastal plain through a rugged gorge of exposed bedrock. In addition, remember, this canal was dug using 1700s technology that meant backbreaking labor, although crude and dangerous blasting with powder was used. The canal system was developed not only here at Great Falls but also at other places along the river. In some cases canals were used, but the riverbed was also dredged and scoured to deepen it for boat traffic.

As the Great Falls canals were being built and after they were in operation, the town of Matildaville came to life. Developed by Revolutionary War hero Henry "Light Horse" Lee, Matildaville was a classic company town—with its company store, superintendent's house, mill, foundry, and employees dwellings.

Yet after all this labor and developing of the canal transportation system, the Patowmack Company never realized a profit. They could not even pay the interest on their debt, which was huge due to the exorbitant costs of building the canals and locks around the Great Falls. The fluctuations in the river levels rendered the canals operable only a month or two each year. After being in operation from 1802 to 1830, the Patowmack Canal was abandoned. Its assets were turned over to the Chesapeake

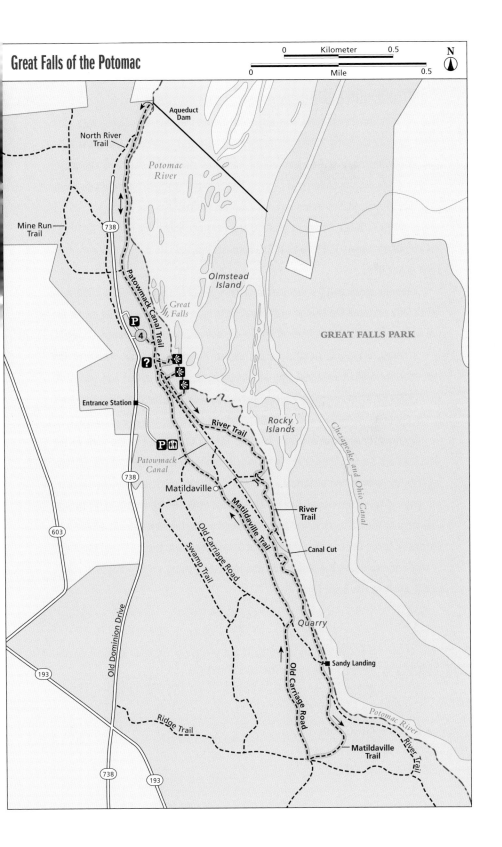

Great Falls of the Potomac

0 Kilometer 0.5
0 Mile 0.5
N

Aqueduct
Dam

North River
Trail

*Potomac
River*

Mine Run
Trail

738

Patowmack Canal Trail

*Olmstead
Island*

*Great
Falls*

P

4

GREAT FALLS PARK

Entrance Station

River Trail

*Rocky
Islands*

P

*Patowmack
Canal*

738

Matildaville

Matildaville Trail

River
Trail

603

Old Carriage Road

Swamp Trail

Canal Cut

Chesapeake and Ohio Canal

Quarry

193

Old Dominion Drive

Old Carriage Road

Sandy Landing

Potomac River

Ridge Trail

Matildaville
Trail

River Trail

738

193

Waterfalls and Carousels

It is strange how sometimes two dissimilar things become associated with each other. Back in the early 1900s, an amusement park was located at the Great Falls. One of the pastimes at this amusement park was riding the carousel. The music from this ride drew in children of all ages. The carousel featured forty animals on its revolving circuit. Riders would pick their favorite critter and go 'round and 'round, smiles on their faces. However, in 1936 the Potomac River flooded and destroyed the carousel's organ. The owners of the carousel jumped into action and were soon back in business.

Then the music and the carousel stopped again at the Great Falls. In 1952 Fairfax County acquired the land around Great Falls for a park. The carousel owner did not want to become an employee of the county and dismantled the Denzel Carousel.

Visitors to the park longed for the music, the rides, and the memories the carousel provided. A carousel was purchased from Rhode Island and moved to Great Falls Park. Once again, children laughed as they sat atop the various animals in the carousel.

However, changes were afoot. In 1965 Fairfax County ceded the park to the National Park Service. The national park people wondered if the carousel was in keeping with the natural and historical aspects of the Great Falls. However, the carousel was allowed to continue operation by the National Park Service after a letter-writing campaign by the citizenry. Nevertheless, the end of the carousel came in 1972 when Hurricane Agnes flooded the Potomac and Great Falls Park. It simply cost too much to repair the carousel. The iconic ride was removed, ending seven decades of riding to the music by the Great Falls.

and Ohio Canal Company. They were to build a successful canal running parallel to the Potomac just across the river on the Maryland side.

After the Patowmack Canal was abandoned, so was Matildaville. The lessons learned in building this canal lock system were used in other projects such as the Chesapeake and Ohio Canal. Today, we can see the leftover relics of both the town and this transportation system standing astride the natural beauty of the Great Falls.

Miles and Directions

0.0 Start by walking downhill from the corner of the parking area near the visitor center, which will be to your right. Immediately meet a gravel trail going left and right and go left on the Patowmack Trail, upstream along the Potomac River. Great Falls roars through the trees to your right. Pass along the Patowmack Canal to your right.

0.2 Pass a spur leading left to the Mine Run Trail. Keep straight. River views open to your right.

0.7 Meet the North River Trail. Keep straight. The North River Trail deteriorates just before coming to the Aqueduct Dam, constructed in the 1950s to provide water to Washington, DC. Backtrack to the park visitor center.

1.5 Walk out the spur to Overlook #1 after getting south of the visitor center. Impressive views open of the Great Falls from rough outcrops. Walk back out to Overlook #2.

1.8 Soak in the view from Overlook #2.

1.9 Overlook #3 delivers a great panorama both upstream and downstream. Return to the Patowmack Trail and head south.

2.0 Split left on the River Trail. A picnic area and the canal remains are off to your right. Begin traversing through incredible boulder gardens, heading down the Mather Gorge.

2.3 A spur leads right to the Patowmack Canal Trail. Stay left on the River Trail and cross a bridge through a rocky mini-gorge.

2.6 Cross the Patowmack Canal, then turn left. Pass a lock. Follow the mini-loop dropping left to the Canal Cut. Continue downstream along rocky Mather Gorge, with bluff views.

3.0 Intersect the spur leading left to Sandy Landing. Stay straight with the River Trail.

3.1 Reach an intersection. The River Trail leaves left. Head right on the Matildaville Trail. Climb from the river.

3.4 Come to another intersection. Turn right here, and follow a very short connector trail, then join the wide Old Carriage Road, heading for the visitor center.

3.8 Return to the Matildaville Trail. Keep straight on it toward the visitor center. The other direction on the Matildaville Trail takes you past the quarry used to obtain stone to build the Patowmack Canal.

4.2 Come to the heart of Matildaville. The ruins of the superintendent's house are located here and a lock of the canal is just downhill. Look around for other ruins.

4.3 The Old Carriage Road comes in on your left. Keep straight, bridging a stream, then reach a restroom building and alternate parking on your left. Pass through scattered picnic tables and resting benches.

4.6 Come to the south side of the visitor center. This is a good time to head in to learn more about the park.

4.7 Reach the parking area, completing the hike.

5 Leesylvania State Park

This hike travels hills above the tidal Potomac River. Leave the scenic shore—ideal for a picnic—to climb to Freestone Point and a Civil War battery featuring a stellar view of the river and Maryland beyond. From there, visit the site of Fairfax, a home from the early 1800s. More woodland winding leads up to the historic Lee homesite, Leesylvania, dating back to before the United States was a country. Pass the Lee home garden and cemetery amid more hilly mature forest, then return to the riverside picnic area.

Start: Freestone Point Picnic Area
Distance: 1.6-mile figure-eight double loop
Hiking time: About 1.5–2 hours
Difficulty: Easy; does have hills
Trail surface: Natural surfaces
Best season: Any time the skies are clear for views
Other trail users: None
Canine compatibility: Leashed dogs permitted

Land status: Virginia state park
Fees and permits: Parking permit required
Schedule: Open daily year-round
Maps: Leesylvania State Park; USGS Indian Head, Quantico
Trail contact: Leesylvania State Park, 201 Daniel K. Ludwig Dr., Woodbridge, VA 22191; (703) 730-8205; virginiastateparks.gov

Finding the trailhead: From exit 152 on I-95, south of Washington, DC, take VA 234 south for 0.4 mile to a traffic light and US 1 (Jefferson Davis Highway). Turn left on US 1 north and follow it 2.6 miles to a traffic light. To the left is Cardinal Drive and to the right is Neabsco Road. Turn right on Neabsco Road and follow it for 1.4 miles to the right turn into Leesylvania State Park. Follow Daniel K. Ludwig Drive through the state park for 2.2 miles to reach a traffic circle and the Freestone Point Picnic Area. Parking is on the right, just before the traffic circle. The Lees Woods Trail begins on the left-hand side of the traffic circle. Trailhead GPS: N38 35.472' / W77 14.895'

The Hike

Talk about packing history into a hike. The Lees Woods Trail, a figure-eight double loop, may have more history per foot than any other trail in this guide. For starters, George Washington is involved. More about that later. Leesylvania Plantation, located on a fertile peninsula overlooking the Potomac, was valuable not only agriculturally but perhaps even more so due to its strategic location on the river: Crops and other valuables—as well as landowners themselves—could be transported by water on the river. This part of the Old Dominion was lightly populated (hard to believe compared to now). Even the best of roads were rough, muddy, and dangerous. Having water transportation gave a planter a huge advantage.

Two story brick chimney of the Fairfax home

Henry Lee II saw this advantage. He built his hilltop house, Leesylvania, with an eye not only for a commanding view of his grounds and fields, but also to access the river and its shipping possibilities. He could send his products upstream to the Falls of the Potomac or down to the Atlantic Ocean, enabling him to trade throughout colonial America or even with the mother country, England, across the sea.

▶ Henry Lee II, who established the first plantation in what is now Leesylvania State Park, was the great grandfather of Confederate General Robert E. Lee.

It was by water that America's first son, George Washington, would come and go on his visits to Henry Lee and Leesylvania Plantation. See, Henry and George were friends, fellow planters with a bent for discussing current events, whether they were the latest agricultural practices or an impending national revolution. Therefore, when you visit the Lee homesite, Leesylvania, remember that George Washington slept there too. Imagine the site as bordered by fields, with many working hands about. The hilltop homesite is wooded now and is harder to visualize in its former grandeur.

Therefore it happens that this piece of ground in Prince William County, now nearly engulfed by the Washington metroplex, was one of the earlier estates in the Old Dominion. Later, Alfred Lee, grandson of Henry Lee and father of Robert E. Lee, sold the Leesylvania Plantation site (the plantation house had burned down in 1790) to Captain Henry Fairfax. He bought the 2,000-acre plantation in 1825. Fairfax then built his own brick structure, the remains of which you can see on the hike. Fairfax's manse was built about a half mile from the Lee residence. Fairfax resided there for twenty-two years, raising seven offspring on the site. And what a site it is. Set on a hill, the original house had a wide porch overlooking the Potomac. A yard sloped down to the water, where a landing and beach lay. Even today, park visitors walk themselves and their dogs and play along this shore. The Fairfaxes and Lees saw the economic and aesthetic value, whereas today we hold dear the land for its natural, recreational—and historical—value. The home remained in the Fairfax family until 1908, when the home was burned. The brick foundation, walls, and chimneys are all that remain of the Fairfax home.

Later on the hike, you will visit the cemetery where the Fairfaxes and Lees are buried, though the headstones of the Lees were stolen and the Fairfaxes' removed.

More Than Just a Trail

Leesylvania State Park is a fine destination with much to do in addition to hiking. Have a picnic and walk along the river on the Potomac Trail. Head out to the fishing pier to see what is biting. Launch your boat and motor or paddle the shoreline. There is also a gift shop, a campground, and other hiking trails on the west side of the park.

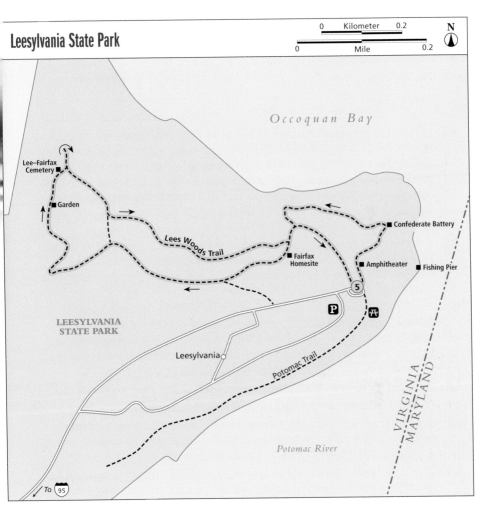

Leesylvania State Park

0 — Kilometer — 0.2

0 — Mile — 0.2

N

Occoquan Bay

Lee–Fairfax Cemetery ■

■ Garden

Lees Woods Trail

■ Confederate Battery

■ Fairfax Homesite

■ Amphitheater

■ Fishing Pier

5

P

⛺

LEESYLVANIA STATE PARK

Leesylvania

Potomac Trail

VIRGINIA
MARYLAND

Potomac River

To 95

History happens right out of the blocks on this hike. You will first pass the site of a 1920s hunting lodge, the Freestone Point Hunt Club, from back when this was a sleepy rural area. It was built by New York businessmen with a liking for waterfowl hunting on the Potomac as well as easy access to the lodge by rail. Time marched on and the two-story rustic lodge passed through other hands. Urban encroachment and unregulated hunting did in the waterfowl and the lodge was eventually taken down.

Ahead you will find the site of a Confederate battery that was erected in September 1861, with three cannons and a commanding view of Occoquan Bay and the Potomac River. It was not but a few days before they skirmished with Union boats on the Potomac. The cannons are gone but the majestic panorama remains.

Next in order are the homesite of Fairfax, then the Leesylvania Plantation site. Beyond are the Leesylvania Plantation gardens, then the cemetery, as discussed above. Lastly, take a spur trail to a ravine and a spot where the Alexandria and Fredericksburg Railroad was put through in the 1870s. The steep hills required deep cuts in the hills. Landslides occurred much too frequently, however, and the rail line eventually was abandoned.

Miles and Directions

0.0 Start on the signed Lees Woods Trail, located on the traffic circle and the end of the park road. You will see a footpath, broken by wooden-and-earth steps, leading uphill toward the park amphitheater. Do not take the gated gravel road uphill from the traffic circle. And do not take the trail leading toward the park fishing pier through the picnic area. Immediately pass the park amphitheater. It was built on the site of an old hunting lodge—the Freestone Point Hunt Club—built in the 1920s. The fireplace still stands. Continue climbing through mature forest of oak, holly, and pawpaw.

0.1 Reach Freestone Point Battery and an overlook of the Potomac River and Occoquan Bay. Soak in long-range vistas and check out the earthworks protecting the cannons stationed here. The trail circles away from the overlook and cruises through forest on the edge of the bluff above Occoquan Bay, shaded by regal oaks.

0.3 Come to a trail intersection. Here, stay right, then head left for the Fairfax Homesite. View the remains of the brick building, which was built in 1825 and burned down in 1909. Check out the two-story chimney. Note the old well nearby, used by the Fairfaxes for drinking water. Continue walking a wide track that was part of the access road used by the Fairfaxes.

0.5 A spur trail comes in on the left, leading down to the main park road. Stay straight.

0.7 A fire road leaves right and shortcuts the Lees Woods Trail. Stay left.

0.9 Reach the site of Leesylvania after climbing a hill. This is where Henry Lee II resided and George Washington visited. The home was built in the 1750s. Leave the homesite, passing by the gardens of Leesylvania. A short mini-loop circles the garden site. Walk through hills.

1.0 Come to the Lee-Fairfax Cemetery, enclosed by a wrought-iron fence. The headstones are missing. Head left from here and shortly reach an interpretive sign overlooking a ravine. Here, a now-defunct railroad line was put through. Backtrack to the cemetery and continue the loop.

1.1 Pass the other end of the fire road bisecting the loop. Keep straight on a narrow ridge.

1.5 Return to the trail intersection near the Fairfax Homesite. Turn left here, downhill, then split right. Descend on a wide track, passing near the park amphitheater.

1.6 Emerge at the trailside traffic circle near the picnic area, ending the hike.

6 Prince William Forest Park

Even the founding of this woodland haven outside Washington, DC, is historic. Established as a demonstration work camp built by the Civilian Conservation Corps during the Great Depression, Prince William Forest Park offers a chance to see the trails, camps, and buildings of the area, as well as explore a pyrite mine operated along Quantico Creek. Also, view some eye-pleasing cascades along the streams in addition to one of the largest preserved tracts of Piedmont forest in the Old Dominion.

Start: Pine Grove Picnic Area near the park visitor center
Distance: 7.1-mile balloon loop
Hiking time: About 3.5–4.5 hours
Difficulty: Moderate to difficult due to distance
Trail surface: Natural surfaces
Best season: Year-round
Other trail users: None
Canine compatibility: Leashed dogs permitted

Land status: National park
Fees and permits: Entrance permit required
Schedule: Open daily year-round
Maps: *Prince William Forest Park;* *USGS Quantico*
Trail contact: Prince William Forest Park, 18100 Park Headquarters Rd., Triangle, VA; (703) 221-7181; www.nps.gov/prwi

Finding the trailhead: From exit 150B on I-95, south of Washington, DC, take VA 619 (Joplin Road) west just a short distance and reach the entrance to Prince William Forest Park. Turn right onto the entrance road and follow it 0.4 mile to the Pine Grove Picnic Area, near the park visitor center. Trailhead GPS: N38 33.585' / W77 20.863'

The Hike

The very establishment of Prince William Forest Park has a historic bent about it. In the 1930s, with the United States deep into economic woes, President Franklin Delano Roosevelt instituted a taxpayer-sponsored work program known as the Civilian Conservation Corps (CCC). The program's goals were to reduce unemployment and teach job skills. Young men enrolled in the CCC were chosen to develop parks throughout the United States. Some parks to be established were known as Recreational Demonstration Areas, designed to transform marginal farmland into recreation destinations.

Negligible farmland located on Quantico and Chopawamsic Creeks was purchased by the United States to establish the Chopawamsic Recreational Demonstration Area. The CCC went to work developing a "camp for low income, inner-city children and families to get away and experience the great outdoors." Since this camp was close to the capital, it

▶ From 1942 to 1945 the cabin camps of the park were turned into "spy camps," training centers for armed forces personnel to learn the subterfuge business.

Hiker poses amid ruin of pyrite mine.

was to be a showcase for the CCC. By the summer of 1936, the Chopawamsic RDA was open for business, with nearby city dwellers learning the ways of the woods. The CCC continued to work, building cabins, bridges, dams, and roads. Three major camps were located within the park and more than 2,000 CCC enrollees mustered through the ranks over a seven-year period.

Then World War II came along. The CCC was simply defunded and potential enrollees instead went into the armed forces. The park went into war mode as well and was transformed into a military installation—including a secret camp to train spies. The southern end of Chopawamsic RDA became a training area for the Office of Strategic Services, the forerunner to the CIA. They stayed in some of the cabin camps developed by the CCC and trained as spies. This spy tradition continues to this day. Much of the park along Chopawamsic Creek, located south of current-day Prince William Forest Park, became part of the Quantico military reservation.

That is how Prince William Forest Park and Quantico came to be. The establishment of the Cabin Branch Mine that you will see on this hike occurred earlier. In 1889 the Cabin Branch Mining Company was established. Set along the banks of Quantico Creek, the mine's objective was pyrite, commonly known as fool's gold.

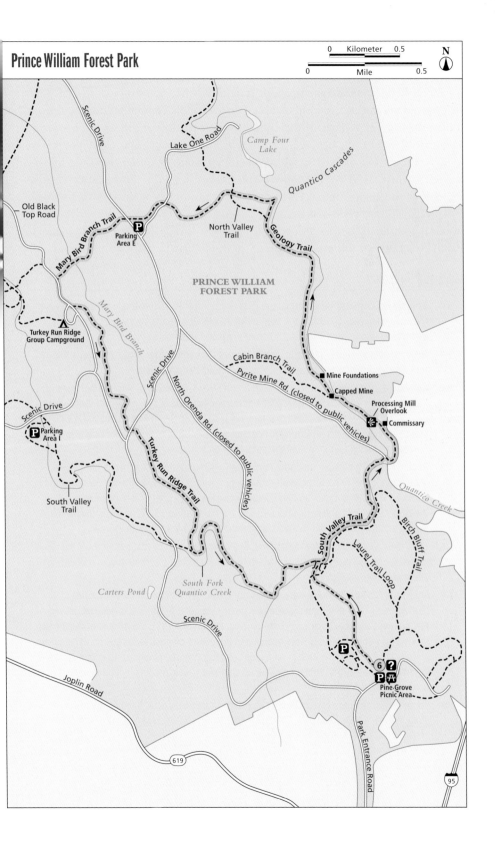

Prince William Forest Park

0   Kilometer   0.5

0   Mile   0.5

N

Scenic Drive

Lake One Road

Camp Four Lake

Quantico Cascades

Old Black Top Road

Mary Bird Branch Trail

P Parking Area E

North Valley Trail

Geology Trail

PRINCE WILLIAM FOREST PARK

Mary Bird Branch

Turkey Run Ridge Group Campground

Scenic Drive

Cabin Branch Trail

Pyrite Mine Rd. (closed to public vehicles)

■ Mine Foundations

■ Capped Mine

Processing Mill Overlook

■ Commissary

Scenic Drive

P Parking Area I

North Orenda Rd. (closed to public vehicles)

Turkey Run Ridge Trail

South Valley Trail

Quantico Creek

South Valley Trail

Birch Bluff Trail

Laurel Trail Loop

Carters Pond

South Fork Quantico Creek

Scenic Drive

P

6 **?**

P **⛺** Pine Grove Picnic Area

Joplin Road

619

Park Entrance Road

95

Though it sparkles, pyrite has no aesthetic value. It is, however, used in making paper, gunpowder, and soap.

A full-fledged operation was built here, from the mineshafts to the rail lines that moved the mineral, to a large processing area and a community for the miners. Today, we can see vestiges of this industrial past nestled in the woods bordering Quantico Creek.

Interestingly, the trail system we use to visit the mine and other places was initially laid out by the CCC. The Pine Grove Picnic Shelter, located at the trailhead, is a good example of the many structures built during that time. They all share the commonality of being rustic wood-and-stone buildings in the pioneer style commonly seen in our national park system (Prince William Forest Park is operated by the National Park Service). Enjoy this preserved legacy of the 1930s.

Miles and Directions

0.0 Start by walking northwest through the Pine Grove Picnic Area from the historic Pine Grove Picnic Shelter. Pass by picnic and play areas, as well as a restroom building. Other trails and alternate parking are located south of the picnic area.

0.2 Begin the actual Laurel Trail Loop, a path leaving the corner of the picnic area as a signed trail. Descend through rich woods of pine, dogwood, oak, and beech.

0.5 Come to a major trail intersection. South Orenda Road, closed to public cars but open to bicyclers and hikers, comes in on your left. The continuation of the Laurel Trail loop leaves right. Keep straight and descend to a footbridge spanning South Fork Quantico Creek. Meet the South Valley Trail. Turn right, heading downstream with South Fork Quantico Creek flowing to your right. Enjoy mountain laurel blossoms in spring.

1.3 Reach a trail intersection after passing through wooded bottoms and over a bluff. Pyrite Mine Road leaves left. You, however, cross Quantico Creek just above its confluence with South Fork Quantico Creek and immediately turn left, away from private property, joining the North Valley Trail. The bridge crossed was built in the late 1800s and was part of the mining effort. Cruise an old roadbed upstream, with Quantico Creek to your left.

1.5 Enter the Cabin Branch Mine area. Come to a concrete structure, the remnants of the former miner commissary. The many pines in the area indicate disturbance. Join a boardwalk crossing former mine tailings.

1.6 Reach the Old Mill Overlook. Here, across the creek, was the main mine-processing location. For more than thirty years, pyrite was processed here. The area was denuded of vegetation and Quantico Creek was compromised. However, in 1995 the mine was reclaimed. Mines were capped, tailings were buried, and trees were planted. Today, barren ground now harbors plant life and the area is on a long-term recovery. The stream is no longer absorbing sulfur and other pollutants. Continue up Quantico Creek, passing a capped mine bordered by a fence.

1.8 Bridge Quantico Creek and meet the Cabin Branch Trail. Stay right, heading upstream along the North Valley Trail.

1.9 Pass the foundations of mine buildings, including an engine room, boiler room, and machine shop, elements of a mining operation that extend beyond the actual mine. Continue up Quantico Creek, leaving the greater pyrite mine area. Soak in the natural beauty of this Piedmont woodland.

2.7 Intersect the Geology Trail. Stay right along Quantico Creek on the Geology Trail. Pass through a narrow gorge with a series of cascades pouring over rock.

2.9 The trail dead-ends at a second series of cascades and open rock slabs on Quantico Creek. Do not continue upstream on a user-created trail. Backtrack just a short distance, then ascend away from Quantico Creek.

3.1 Meet the North Valley Trail. Stay straight on the Geology Trail.

3.4 Come to Lake One Road. Turn left and join the doubletrack path south.

3.5 Leave right from Lake One Road on a singletrack path leading to Parking Area E. Pass through a pretty picnic area with parking. Cross Scenic Drive, then join the Mary Bird Branch Trail.

4.0 Come to bottomland and Mary Bird Branch. Cross the bottom on a boardwalk, then bridge Mary Bird Branch. Climb away from the valley.

4.1 Come to the Old Black Top Road. Turn left and walk past a gate, coming to the Turkey Run Ridge Ranger Station, group campground, and trailhead parking area. Keep south along the paved Turkey Run Ridge Access Road, passing a parking area on your right.

4.2 Leave left on the singletrack Turkey Run Ridge Trail. Roller-coaster south on the ridge, running parallel to Scenic Drive.

5.0 Cross Scenic Drive.

5.6 Meet the South Valley Trail after descending to South Fork Quantico Creek. Head left. Enjoy streamside hiking after climbing a bluff.

6.4 Meet North Orenda Road. Stay right on the roadbed and keep downstream along South Fork Quantico Creek.

6.6 Return to the bridge crossing South Fork Quantico Creek and complete the loop portion of the hike. From here, cross the bridge and backtrack south on the Laurel Trail Loop.

7.1 Return to the trailhead after passing through the Pine Grove Picnic Area, finishing the hike.

7 Spotsylvania History Trail

This hike makes a circuit through the Spotsylvania Court House Battlefield, where Robert E. Lee and Ulysses S. Grant clashed as Grant doggedly pushed for Richmond in the Civil War's latter stages. A marked path takes you to significant battle sites and homesites of the time, cushioned among the gently rolling hills of Spotsylvania County. The mix of eye-appealing forest and field, important earthworks, and interpretive information makes for a rewarding historic hike.

Start: Spotsylvania Battlefield Exhibit Shelter
Distance: 4.3-mile loop
Hiking time: About 3-3.5 hours
Difficulty: Moderate
Trail surface: Grass, natural surface, some asphalt
Best season: May, to coincide with battle time
Other trail users: None
Canine compatibility: Leashed dogs permitted

Land status: National military park
Fees and permits: None
Schedule: Sunrise-sunset
Maps: *Spotsylvania History Trail—A Walking Tour; USGS Spotsylvania*
Trail contacts: Fredericksburg and Spotsylvania County Battlefields Memorial National Military Park, 120 Chatham Ln., Fredericksburg, VA 22405; (540) 373-6122; www.nps.gov/frsp

Finding the trailhead: From Fredericksburg, take VA 208 west toward Spotsylvania. Join the Courthouse Bypass toward Lake Anna, then reach VA 613 (Brock Road) at a traffic light. Turn right on Brock Road and follow it 1.3 miles to the right turn into the Spotsylvania battlefield at Grant Drive West, where a sign indicates SPOTSYLVANIA COURTHOUSE BATTLEFIELD EXHIBIT SHELTER. Trailhead GPS: N38 13.141'/W77 36.844'

The Hike

The bucolic beauty of the battlefield in its current state belies its horrific past. Nearly one in three combatants—more than 30,000—were injured, killed, or missing in action. Much of the fighting was at close range, both with gunfire and hand-to-hand combat. Bayonets were flying too. As testament to the close-range struggling, a 22-inch-wide oak tree stump stands in the Smithsonian Institution, felled by bullets fired from the opposing sides. At a spot called the Bloody Angle, dead soldiers were literally heaped upon one another, as Grant sought to break through Lee's defensive lines that defended strategic crossroads, presenting the most direct route to Richmond, at Spotsylvania Court House.

▶ More than 3,000 Confederate soldiers and twenty cannons were captured by the Union during the Battle of Spotsylvania Courthouse, the largest single capturing of Confederate soldiers during the Civil War.

Today, the battlefield offers an oasis of greenery as Fredericksburg fans outward and Lake Anna's popularity continues to grow. The

Spotsylvania Court House Battlefield

trail, marked with paint blazes and signs, alternately traces grassy hills, quiet roadways within the battlefield, and slender tracks winding through hardwoods and evergreens. Blooming dogwoods and mountain laurel have supplanted ragged, cutover forests, sawed down to construct miles of earthworks that once threaded this locale. Before beginning your hike, soak in the interpretive information at the exhibit shelter. It will help you understand the battlefield through which you will walk. The shelter has restrooms. In addition, a shaded picnic area is located just north of the exhibit shelter.

After passing some monuments you will join Hancock Road, along which the Union trenches of Warren's Line lie. The path then turns into woods and travels south toward the top of Laurel Hill. Here, Confederate trenches protected the roads leading toward Spotsylvania. The loop hike then comes along a series of earthworks the South also used in defending the crossroads. These trenches were hastily dug as the Yankees had penetrated the original Rebel fortifications. You will also find a fascinating reconstructed earthwork that shows what the defenses would have looked like in 1864 versus the rounded and timeworn earthworks that remain 150 years later, bloodied and muddied when they were new.

Location, Location, Location

Spotsylvania County and the town of Fredericksburg lie in the greater Rapidan and Rappahannock River valleys. The agriculturally rich terrain was well suited for farms large and small. The area was also located roughly halfway between the Confederate States of America capital of Richmond and the United States of America capital in Washington. Being where it was left more bloodstains on this American soil than any-where else any time—no fewer than four significant and deadly conflicts took place on this parcel of the Old Dominion, more than 105,000 casualties on both sides.

The first Fredericksburg / Spotsylvania County clash occurred in December 1862. The Confederates, led by Stonewall Jackson, made a smashing victory and weakened Union public sentiment about fighting their Southern brethren. This bloody land saw another Rebel win at Chancellorsville in April of 1863. Some say the Grim Reaper won at the Battle of the Wilderness in May of 1864, with 30,000 troops killed, wounded, or missing. The May 1864 clash where this historic hike takes place—Spotsylvania Court House—saw intense hand-to-hand combat that continued to wear down the Confederates. Ultimately, the superior Union war machine trod south through Fredericksburg and Spotsylvania County, situated between the oppos-ing capitals, ending the war and leaving its mark on this strategic location.

Just as the trenches have changed over time, so has the Harrison House. Once a quiet farm dwelling swept into the center of our Civil War, all that remains of the site are scattered bricks and part of a stone foundation. The next major stop comes at the McCoull House Site, with its very few remnants. However, more than 1,500 Union soldiers are buried nearby, along with an unknown number of Confederate interred.

The hike then saddles along "the Muleshoe," as this curved shape of the Confed-erate fortifications became known. This is where Grant probed and ultimately pen-etrated the Rebel lines. Lee realized the position could not be held, and sent waves of soldiers into the Union fighters, buying time to construct more defensible earth-works a quarter mile distant. For twenty hours the carnage continued. This battle area drew the moniker "Bloody Angle." Eventually, the Southerners withdrew to their new earthworks. Grant tried to take this new line, but the gallant Confederates held.

It was only three days later that both armies headed south to fight again. The wreckage of the Battle of Spotsylvania Courthouse was left to time, now healed over and preserved in Virginia history.

Spotsylvania History Trail

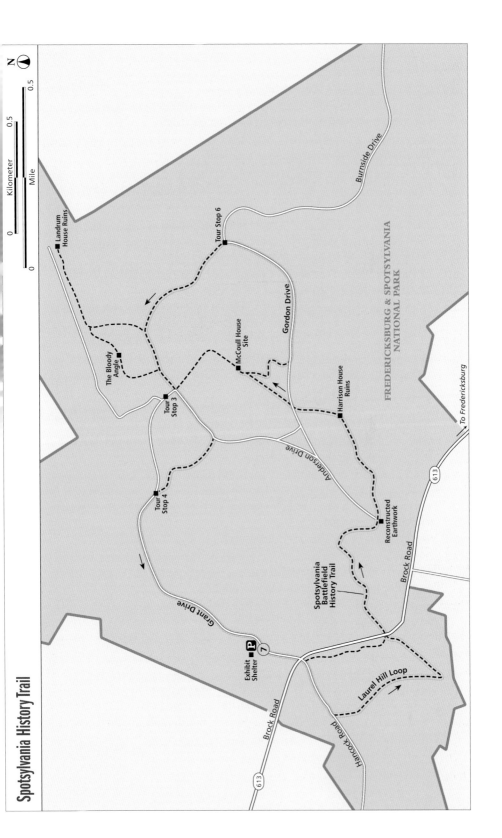

Miles and Directions

0.0   Start at the Spotsylvania Battlefield Exhibit Shelter parking area. Leave south on grass to the intersection of Grant Drive West, Brock Road, and Hancock Road. Cross Brock Road, then follow gravel Hancock Road, joining the Laurel Hill Loop.

0.3   Leave Hancock Road left into pines, oaks, and dense brush on a singletrack path. Emerge into the edge of a field, then head south through the field on a mown track.

0.5   A mown spur trail leads right to an interpretive sign explaining the fighting at Laurel Hill.

0.7   Come to a monument at the south end of Laurel Hill. Turn back northeast toward Brock Road.

0.8   Reach and cross Brock Road as the main hiking loop trail comes in on your left as a mown path. The path shortly enters cedar, oak, and some of the largest holly trees in the Old Dominion. Soon you'll come to more Confederate trenches.

1.3   Find the reconstructed earthwork at the south end of Anderson Drive. Head northeast through forest and field to the Harrison House ruins.

1.6   Reach the Harrison House ruins, located amid a few locust trees atop a hill. From here, head north toward Gordon Drive, crossing an iron-tinted spring.

1.8   Cross Gordon Drive. Walk parallel to the road leading to the McCoull House Site.

2.0   Reach the McCoull House Site. Here, the main loop cuts acutely right (southeast). If you want to shortcut the loop, follow the gravel track past the McCoull House Site, then turn left (northwest) on a footpath.

2.2   Turn left on Gordon Drive. Walk along the wooded asphalt battlefield road. Confederate trenches run along the south side of Gordon Drive.

2.6   Come to auto Tour Stop #6, East Face of Salient. Here, the loop hike leaves Gordon Drive and travels alongside more earthworks.

3.0   Reach a bridge crossing trenches and a spur trail leading right. This spur makes a small circuit through the Bloody Angle. Keep straight on the main loop, coming under oaks. Pass by a few monuments. In this area the infamous 22-inch-diameter oak tree was felled by bullets and bullets alone.

3.1   Pass the other end of the loop trail circling the Bloody Angle. Keep straight.

3.2   Come to and cross Anderson Drive. Auto Tour Stop #3, Bloody Angle, is off to your right. Do not take the footpath leading left into woods—it heads to the McCoull House Site. Walk south along the right-hand side of Anderson Drive.

3.4   Leave right from Anderson Drive at a sign indicating a Confederate counterattack. Pass through a meadow and soon enter forest.

3.6   Come to Grant Drive and auto Tour Stop #4. Head west along the wooded lane. Descend.

3.9   Cross over a tributary at a low point. Keep southwest in woods, walking along Grant Drive.

4.3   Reach the battlefield exhibit shelter and the hike's end after passing the battlefield picnic area.

8 Lake Anna State Park

Set along the shore of Virginia's most popular impoundment, this hike at Lake Anna State Park explores woods, streams, and Lake Anna, while visiting the site of Glenora Plantation and a pre-lake settler's homesite before returning to the trailhead. A well-timed visit will also avail ranger-led tours of the park's gold mines.

Start: Main Lake Anna State Park trailhead parking area
Distance: 4.5-mile loop
Hiking time: About 2.5–3.5 hours
Difficulty: Moderate
Trail surface: Natural surface
Best season: Year-round
Other trail users: Bicyclers, equestrians
Canine compatibility: Leashed dogs permitted

Land status: State park
Fees and permits: Entrance fee required
Schedule: Open daily year-round
Maps: *Lake Anna State Park Trails; USGS Lake Anna West*
Trail contact: Lake Anna State Park, 6800 Lawyers Rd., Spotsylvania, VA 22551; (540) 854-5503; virginiastateparks.gov

Finding the trailhead: From exit 118 on I-95, south of Fredericksburg, take VA 606 west for 4 miles to Snell, and intersect VA 208. Keep straight, joining VA 208 west for 11 miles to Lawyers Road (VA 601). Turn right on VA 601 and follow it 3.3 miles to the state park entrance on your left. Enter the state park, passing the contact station, and continue for 1.7 miles to the park office. Turn left just past the park office and follow this road leading toward the park cabins for 0.2 mile to the trailhead on your right. Trailhead GPS: N38 7.004' / W77 49.129'

The Hike

What comprises the 2,000 acres of Lake Anna State Park is valuable land, especially as the popularity of Lake Anna continues to grow. Today, the worth of the land is directly related to its proximity to Lake Anna. Waterfront property can go for big bucks. The original holders of this terrain along the North Anna River, centuries before Lake Anna was dammed, were the Mannahoak Sioux. After seeing tribes to the east being defeated by the English, the Mannahoaks simply fled west to the Ohio River valley, their ancestral lands. Slowly, the westward white migration continued, and Virginia became part of the United States. Settlers were filtering into the North Anna River basin, establishing simple farms.

Then gold was found by settlers in the early 1800s. The shiny stuff reposited along streamside gravel beds, there for the taking. Experienced miners came in and placer-mined. Imagine a ramped-up version of traditional gold panning, where streamside sediment is processed—filtered if you will—to uncover gold. Here in

▶ Lake Anna was impounded in 1971 to provide a reliable water source for cooling the nearby Dominion Power nuclear plant.

Old metal bed frame at the Taylor Homestead

the Lake Anna area, gold was fine and flaky. At one time no fewer than twenty-three placer-mining operations were in operation here in Spotsylvania County.

During this period, in the early 1800s, the land's value was tied to the minerals reposing in the soil. Values rose when the heirs of James Goodwin recorded a deed for "the right to search for gold." By 1835 Virginia's first gold rush—albeit minor—was under way along the streams flowing into the North Anna River. From 1830 to 1850 Virginia was the third-largest gold-producing state in the country.

Let it be known that some men can resist gold fever. John Jerdone was one such man. In the 1830s this wealthy planter built Pigeon Plantation, named after nearby Pigeon Run, the epicenter of gold mining in the North Anna River valley. Jerdone was financed by family money. His grandfather Francis was a successful merchant who later established iron foundries in the Old Dominion. On Pigeon Plantation John Jerdone grew tobacco, wheat, and corn. Interestingly, in 1829 Jerdone wrote

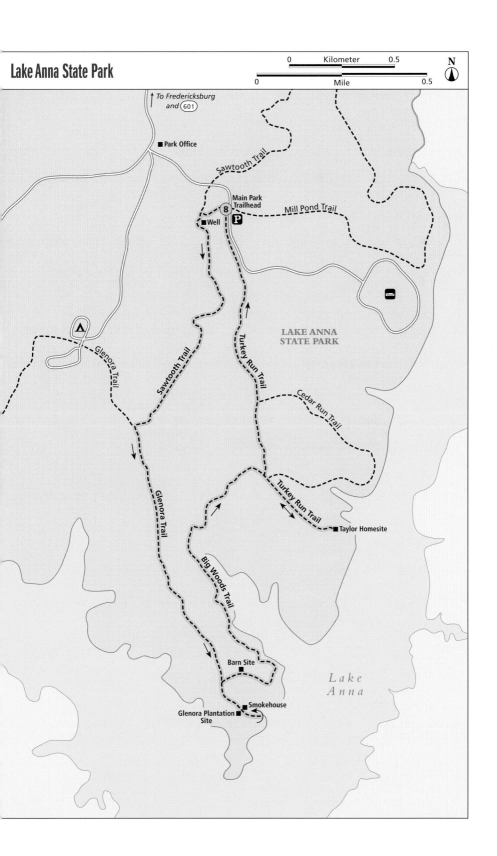

Lake Anna State Park

0   Kilometer   0.5

0   Mile   0.5

N

↑ To Fredericksburg
and 601

■ Park Office

Sawtooth Trail

Main Park
Trailhead

8

■ Well   P

Mill Pond Trail

LAKE ANNA
STATE PARK

Turkey Run Trail

Glenora Trail

Sawtooth Trail

Cedar Run Trail

Turkey Run Trail

Glenora Trail

■ Taylor Homesite

Big Woods Trail

■ Barn Site

Lake
Anna

■ Smokehouse

Glenora Plantation ■
Site

his father, also named Francis, of an interest in digging for gold but doubted actually finding any. Pigeon Plantation grew to over 3,000 acres. With the Civil War looming, Jerdone sold the plantation. The plantation was renamed Glenora by a new owner. The land and buildings went through many hands until the tract was bought as one of many parcels comprising Lake Anna State Park. Unfortunately, the main house had fallen into disrepair and was torn down in 2000. However, one outbuilding—the smokehouse—was saved.

Our historic hike leads us to the scenic site of Glenora. Ironically, the site of Glenora, on a peninsula surrounded on three sides by Lake Anna, with quick and easy water access, has incredible value. Maybe not as much as a successful gold mine, but real value, due to its lakefront location.

Major gold mining did occur on Pigeon Run, at the Goodwin Mine. A shaft was dug. Steam engines powered rock-crushing machinery. The shaft delved near 100 feet down. The mining peaked in the 1880s. Today, on the park tours, you can see this mining area, along with stone walls and mounts for machinery. The open mine and other unsafe facets of this deep excavation are why visitors are permitted at the gold mine only with park rangers. I hope that unbridled public access will be allowed in the future. However, an advantage of ranger-led tours is the personal narrative given by park personnel. Check the park website for gold-mine tour schedules.

After leaving the site of Glenora Plantation, the hike cruises the shoreline of Lake Anna through what is known as the Big Woods. The forest is not old growth but does exude a primeval scenic aura. From the Big Woods, hike out Turkey Run Trail to the old Taylor Homesite. You'll find a chimney, stone foundations, crockery, and even an old bed frame there. William Taylor bought his 100 acres for $250 back in 1879. He and his wife, Rachael, raised six children on this quiet hill. Look around for other clues to the past, then leave them for others to discover. The land stayed in his family until it was purchased as part of Lake Anna State Park. Lake Anna State Park was established in 1983. The area was formerly known as Gold Hill, then the Big Woods. The last part of the hike rolls through serene forest back to the trailhead.

Miles and Directions

0.0 Start by the rear of the main park trailhead, on a spur leading to the Sawtooth Trail. Immediately enter forest. Pass a well site used to water a steam engine for a portable sawmill that operated here in the Big Woods. Meet the Sawtooth Trail in a short distance. Head left on the Sawtooth Trail in holly, sweetgum, hickory, and oak. Note the fitness stations located along the trail.

0.8 Reach a stream. A hiker bridge crosses the unnamed creek. Ascend.

This stone chimney no longer warms residents of the Taylor Homestead.

0.9 Intersect the Glenora Trail. Go left toward the Smokehouse exhibit and Glenora Plantation Site. This road was used by those accessing the plantation. Gain obscured views of Lake Anna on both sides.

1.7 Meet the Big Woods Trail. You will return here later. For now, keep straight on the Glenora Trail toward the plantation. Pass through ever-shrinking clearings. Watch for deer here.

1.8 Reach the site of Glenora Plantation and the still-standing plantation smokehouse. Explore, then continue south toward Lake Anna.

1.9 Meet the shore of Lake Anna. Enjoy some watery vistas, then backtrack past Glenora.

2.1 Turn right on the Big Woods Trail. Soon you'll pass the site of a barn associated with Glenora Plantation, located to the left of the trail. Parts of the foundation and rusty relics remain. Continue hiking in forest, with Lake Anna in view through the trees. Shortly turn away from the main lake into an embayment.

2.4 Cross a pre-park, pre-lake road that now leads into the water. The embayment to your right continues to narrow.

2.9 Span the unnamed stream again, also using a hiker bridge. A horse ford runs parallel to the bridge. Gently climb from the stream.

3.2 Meet the Turkey Run Trail. Turn right here and quickly pass the Cedar Run Trail dropping off to your left. Stay with the Turkey Run Trail, cruising out a ridge.

3.4 Dead-end at the Taylor Homesite. Explore the area and view the still-standing chimney. Backtrack.

3.6 Pass the intersection with the Cedar Run Trail and the Big Woods Trail. Stay with the Turkey Run Trail in rich forest. If you want to extend your hike by a half mile, take the Cedar Run Trail to Lake Anna and back up to the Turkey Run Trail.

3.9 Pass the second intersection with the Cedar Run Trail. Stay on the Turkey Run Trail, gently rising in oak woods.

4.4 Come alongside the road leading to the park cabins. Pass through a field.

4.5 Arrive at the main park trailhead, completing the hike.

9 Assateague Coast Guard Station and Lighthouse

Head to Assateague Island, where you can walk along the crashing Atlantic shoreline on a protected beach. Visit a preserved Coast Guard station that's still weathering the sands of time. Your return trip leads you astride the quieter shores of Toms Cove and an old fish-processing factory. After your first hike a short drive takes you to the trailhead to reach the Assateague Island Lighthouse. Walk among wooded ancient dunes, then rise to reach the 1860s beacon, enhanced with views from its heights.

Start: Beach-access parking on Chincoteague NWR
Distance: 3.5-mile loop, plus 0.3-mile separate loop
Hiking time: 3–3.5 hours
Difficulty: Moderate; sand walking can be tiresome
Trail surface: Sand
Best season: Anytime beach access is open
Other trail users: None
Canine compatibility: Dogs not permitted

Land status: National wildlife refuge
Fees and permits: Entrance fees required
Schedule: 6 a.m. to at least 6 p.m. year-round, open later in warm season
Maps: *Chincoteague Trails; USGS Chincoteague East*
Trail contact: Chincoteague National Wildlife Refuge, PO Box 62, Chincoteague Island, VA 23336; (757) 336-6122; www.fws.gov/northeast/chinco

Finding the trailhead: From the intersection of US 13 and VA 175 on the Eastern Shore near the Maryland state line, take VA 175 east, reaching the village of Chincoteague after 12 miles. Continue east 1.3 miles past a roundabout and reach Chincoteague National Wildlife Refuge. Pay your entrance fee at either the toll booth or visitor center, then proceed toward the Toms Cove Visitor Center (passing the Lighthouse Trail). Once at the visitor center, turn right and follow the road 0.4 mile to the dead end at the beach access and the Over-Sand Vehicle entrance at the end of a turnaround. Trailhead GPS: N37 52.889' / W75 20.894'

The Hike

Assateague Island presents a cornucopia of history. This long sandy barrier on the east coast of Virginia and extending into Maryland has long attracted people to its shores. First came the Indians who named it, then early English settlers who grazed their livestock and left ponies as their legacy to the island. Ships great and small wrecked on its shores, leading to the erection of the Assateague Lighthouse in the 1830s. The national seashore and wildlife refuge were created in the mid-twentieth century, followed by the establishment in 1922 and subsequent abandonment in 1967 of a US Coast Guard Station on its southernmost tip.

This hike visits two of the aforementioned places: the old Coast Guard station and the working lighthouse. The bounty of the ocean has always attracted people to its shores. The aboriginal Virginians who lived here enjoyed the fruits of the estuaries, from crabs to fish, while simultaneously fighting mosquitoes and storms. Being on the easternmost part of the North American continent, Assateague Island was quickly utilized by the settlers who eventually became Americans. The ponies of the island are the visual reminder of that era. It is romantic to think of the four-legged beauties swimming to shore after a shipwreck, but likely they were simply set out here to graze without fences. Simple fishermen lived out here too, especially on the adjacent island of Chincoteague, as it was protected somewhat from the direct wrath of the Atlantic Ocean.

▶ During World War II the Coast Guard men stationed at Assateague Island patrolled the beaches, looking for Germans on- and offshore.

The shifting shoals of the Atlantic surely were a constant threat to early mariners. In 1833 the first Assateague Lighthouse was built. However, its lack of height and its dimness made it less than helpful. A second lighthouse, the one we see today, was begun in 1860 but not completed until 1867, as the Civil War interrupted its progress.

This lighthouse, 142 feet in height, was built on a high wooded dune. The oil-burning lamps required constant maintenance, and for a century lighthouse keepers

Assateague Village

After the Assateague Lighthouse was rebuilt in the 1860s, it allowed easier and safer access to the tidal inlet lying between Chincoteague and Assateague Islands. This attracted commercial fishermen and oyster harvesters to settle along the inlet. Many of them homesteaded in the shadow of the Assateague Lighthouse. Upwards of 200 people lived here, from cattle grazers to storekeepers to school teachers and preachers, in addition to those who made their living from the sea.

Things changed at Assateague Village in 1922. A doctor from Baltimore by the name of Samuel B. Fields bought most of the Virginia portion of Assateague Island. He fenced in and closed access to his property to the villagers. They could no longer get to Toms Cove, a rich harvesting area. One by one they began to move from Assateague Island. Interestingly, many of them simply jacked up their houses and floated the structures across the channel dividing Assateague Island from Chincoteague Island and resettled on Chincoteague. A cemetery and a few building foundations are the only relics of Assateague Village. In the 1940s Dr. Fields sold his land to the US government and it became the heart of Chincoteague National Wildlife Refuge, a place we can now all enjoy.

The Assateague Coast Guard Station still stands resolute many decades after use.

lived in the shadow of the red-and-white-striped beacon. The oil lamp was replaced by electric lights long ago, and the brick lighthouse is now fully automated, rendering the lighthouse keeper's job obsolete. Today you can hike to the lighthouse on a short trail and visit the historic circular tower. For a fee, you can climb up the tower when it's open. The light makes a double flash every 5 seconds, which is its unique characteristic that helps mariners identify it, as there are 450 East Coast lighthouses still maintained today by the US Coast Guard.

Speaking of the Coast Guard, your first hike takes you along the coastline to the old Coast Guard Station, enjoying a direct Atlantic beach experience, walking along a slender spit of land dividing the Atlantic from Toms Cove. Low dunes occupy the center of the spit and are sprinkled with sea oats. Whether the tide is up or down will affect exactly where you walk. There is no official trail.

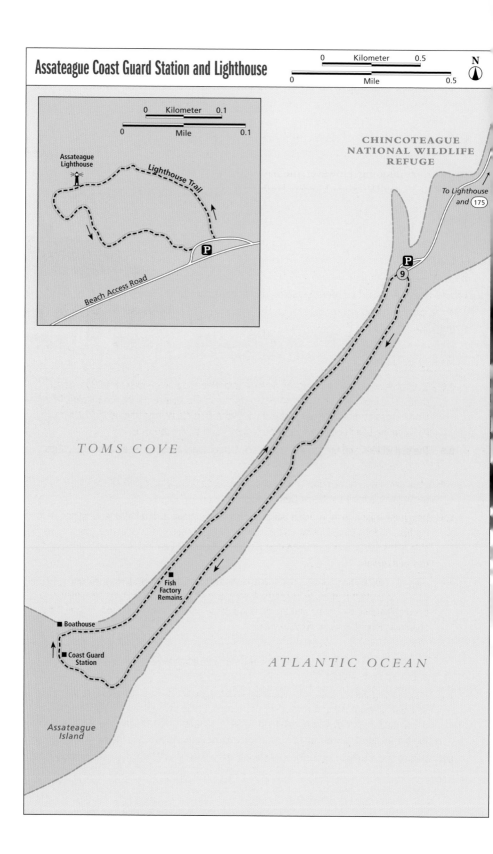

0   Kilometer   0.5

0   Mile   0.5

N

0   Kilometer   0.1

0   Mile   0.1

Assateague
Lighthouse

Lighthouse Trail

P

Beach Access Road

CHINCOTEAGUE
NATIONAL WILDLIFE
REFUGE

To Lighthouse
and 175

P

9

TOMS COVE

Fish
Factory
Remains

Boathouse

Coast Guard
Station

ATLANTIC OCEAN

Assateague
Island

At 1.8 miles you will reach the Assateague Beach Coast Guard Station. This two-story wooden building with an observation tower and adjacent outbuildings, along with a boathouse, was constructed in 1922. It was occupied for nearly fifty years by brave men who did what they could to make the waters around Assateague and Chincoteague Islands safer, rescuing imperiled boaters. In between they battled winds and mosquitoes. The shifting barrier island and the shallowness of water access was the station's undoing. However, the national seashore has worked to preserve the station, a designated Virginia historic landmark.

Several other trails can be enjoyed while here at Chincoteague National Wildlife Refuge. Though not necessarily historic, they present different faces of the island's natural beauty. The Wildlife Loop makes a 3-plus-mile circuit around a wetland and is ideal for observing waterfowl. Be apprised the track is open to vehicles after 3 p.m. The Woodland Trail is a favorite. It wanders through pine forests and passes by an overlook where wild ponies can sometimes be spotted. The Bivalve Trail spurs off the Woodland Trail and offers access to Toms Cove. Check at either of the two visitor centers on the refuge for more information.

Miles and Directions

0.0 Start by leaving the beach-access parking area. Head southwest along the Atlantic over wide, tan beach sands. Toms Cove lies to your right. The Atlantic crashes to your left. This area is open to over-sand vehicles, with a permit, from September through mid-March. Posts on the beach delineate the limit of their travel on the bay side.

0.5 The spit widens and the Assateague Beach Coast Guard Station comes into view. Dunes and vegetation increase.

1.7 Look right for a road cutting through the dunes. Take this roadbed and follow it away from the Atlantic, toward the Coast Guard station.

1.8 Reach the main two-story white building. Explore the grounds and imagine living and working here for long periods. Stay off the dock of the boathouse. After exploring, join the bay side of the spit. Your return route may change, subject to bird-nesting closures and/or tidal ups and downs.

2.4 Pass the concrete and shell foundations of an old fish factory. Commercial harvesting was an important part of life in nearby Assateague Village. The tabby ruins have nearly been obliterated by storms and the tides. Continue cruising along the shore of Toms Cove, absorbing inland views across the water.

3.5 Return to the parking area. From here, drive to the Lighthouse Trailhead. Pick up the Lighthouse Trail at a kiosk. Enter forest of sweetgum, live oak, and laurel oaks. Soon rise to a wooded ancient dune.

3.7 After walking the wooded dune, reach the Assateague Lighthouse. The 145-foot-tall brick structure, painted red and white, rises tall against a blue sky. At times the lighthouse can be climbed (fee). Views open to the northeast, toward the site of Assateague Village, from the tower base. Enjoy the interpretive information before dropping off the dune.

3.8 Return to the Lighthouse Trailhead, completing the hike.

Richmond and
Southeast Virginia

The brick path led to the Occoneechee Plantation house before it burned to the ground.

10　Belle Isle

An Indian village, a Civil War prison camp, an iron foundry, a rock quarry, and now a city park . . . Belle Isle, on the National Register of Historic Places, is a history museum unto itself, smack-dab in the middle of the James River. Today you can visit the locales where it all happened, and see relics of the past on trails that lead to and through the island, all set in natural beauty amid the rapids of the James. Interior paths extend beyond the described loop, allowing for extended rambling and additional discoveries.

Start: Near the Civil War Visitor Center at Tredegar
Distance: 2.4-mile loop with spurs
Hiking time: About 2–2.5 hours
Difficulty: Moderate
Trail surface: Concrete, gravel, dirt, pavement
Best season: Year-round
Other trail users: Bicyclers, joggers
Canine compatibility: Leashed dogs permitted

Land status: City park
Fees and permits: None
Schedule: Open daily year-round
Maps: *Exploring the James Guide; USGS Richmond*
Trail contact: James River Park, 4001 Riverside Dr., Richmond, VA 23225; (804) 646-8911; jamesriverpark.org

Finding the trailhead: From exit 74A on I-95 in Richmond, take the Downtown Expressway to the first exit, Canal Street. Follow Canal Street to South Fifth Street. Turn left on South Fifth Street and follow it to the dead end at Tredegar Street. Turn right on Tredegar Street. The trail starts just before you pass under the Lee Bridge. Parking for the Belle Isle hiking trail is located near the Lee Bridge on the north side of Tredegar Street. Hourly parking is also available at the Civil War Visitor Center on Tredegar Street. (Both lots open after 9:30 a.m. weekdays to deter commuter parking.) Trailhead GPS: N37 32.080'/W77 26.809'

The Hike

This hike is one of Virginia's most interesting for reasons historic, scenic, and logistical. Part of James River Park, Richmond's fantastic set of destinations astride the James River, Belle Isle is first reached on an innovative and exciting pedestrian suspension bridge hanging under the Robert E. Lee Bridge (US 301). It then descends to Belle Isle, where a loop hike exploring layers of Virginia history unfolds.

A rich forest overlays granite on this 65-acre teardrop-shaped island, bordered by rocky shoals. Come to a flat upon reaching the isle—the place where Powhatans farmed and were visited by none other than Virginia's first settler, Captain John Smith, in 1607. Richmond's founding family, the Byrds, owned the island until the 1770s. In the early 1800s the river's waterpower was harnessed by a nail-making factory.

During the Civil War Yankee soldiers were incarcerated on Belle Isle. The Belle Isle prisoner camp was a rough and dangerous place. The prison had no walls but was

The brick wall of an iron forge recalls early Virginia history.

encircled by a low earthen hump of land. Confederate guards picketed the main area, aided by constantly manned cannon emplacements atop an island hill, which then had hardly a tree upon it. Union soldiers were promised if they crossed the earthen hump, they would be shot dead, leading the encirclement to be called a "dead line," the precursor to the term in common use today, meaning "due date," at least for us authors.

The loop trail heads upstream along the James, passing Hollywood Rapids, named for the cemetery across the river. These Class III–IV rapids challenge whitewater kayakers and provide a sonorant background for this hike. You cannot resist heading to the rocks where whitewater flows and herons feed. Belle Isle sits amid the 7 miles of shoals that played a major role in Richmond's founding and very placement on the map. These rocks provide excellent views across the river.

Ahead, the trail curves past a quarry where granite was extracted after the Civil War. The main pit is now a fishing pond. Reach a picnic shelter and the west island tip. A spur trail leads to Civil War gun emplacements atop a hill to your left and a trail leads right to First Break Rapid.

More history waits ahead as you curve around the island's south side. Here lies a millrace and remains of an old plant, the Virginia Electric Power Company, in operation from 1904 to 1967. Be careful around the metal remnants of this plant. User-created trails wind amid the works. An official spur trail leads to the South Side Rocks, a series of massive boulders great for hopping, normally with little water between them. This access trail travels over the head of the millrace that funneled water into the hydroelectric plant.

> A significant number of prisoners incarcerated at Belle Isle were from the South. Members of East Tennessee's 2nd Volunteer Infantry decided to side with the Union, were captured, taken to Belle Isle, and shown the wrath of the Rebel guards due to their disloyalty to the Confederate cause.

An iron forge from an earlier time greets hikers as they meet the south side access to Belle Isle. Only a windowed brick wall remains, standing eerily astride the trail. You will also see a stone shed, once used as a dynamite shack. Imagine all the noise and industry and men raking over Belle Isle. What stories these relics of the past could tell!

Your adventure isn't over when you complete the loop and return to Lee Bridge. A side trip to the island's east tip presents extensive river and downtown views, as well as the preserved remains of the Old Dominion Iron and Steel Company, which operated here until 1972. Yet more trails meander among the hills of the island center if you wish to explore further. Be apprised the interior trails can be confusing, as mountain bikers have created additional paths outside of the official ones.

Belle Isle Cemetery

There is a marked cemetery on Belle Isle. However, many more people were buried on the island than are identified with gravestones. During the height of the Civil War, up to 30,000 Union prisoners of war were held here. Deaths occurred on a regular basis and it is said that graves were scattered all over the island. After the war, efforts were made to disinter the Union soldiers. The found bodies were then reinterred at Richmond National Cemetery. It is likely that still others lie unmarked beneath the soil of Belle Isle.

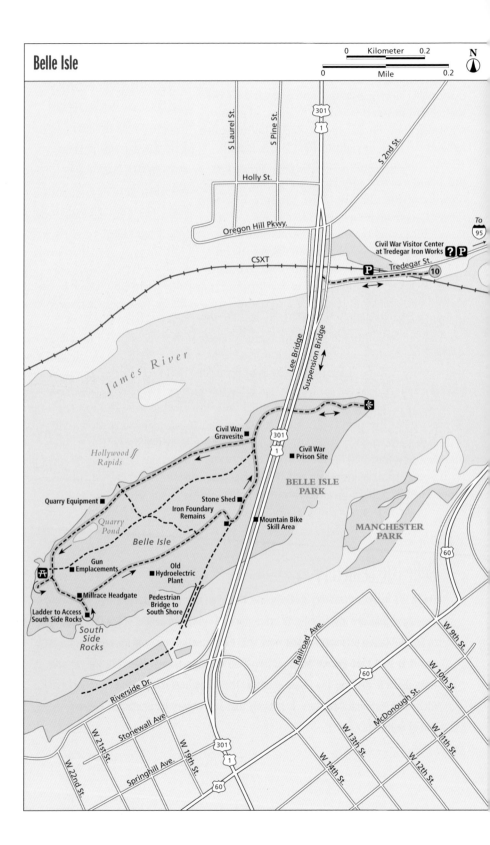

Miles and Directions

0.0   Start near the Civil War Museum at Tredegar; join the paved path westbound along Tredegar Street above the James River. Arrive under the Robert E. Lee Bridge. Turn up the path looping to the suspension bridge under the Robert E. Lee Bridge. Cross the James River, enjoying stellar views. Note the old Richmond & Petersburg Railroad pilings below that once connected Belle Isle to downtown Richmond. It was known as the "Bridge of Sighs" for the feelings of dread when Union soldiers first saw infamous Belle Isle prison camp.

0.2   Return to land and reach Belle Isle. A plethora of interpretive information and sites lies immediately in front of you. It is hard not to aimlessly wander about. For a methodical exploration of the island, head right, upstream along the James River, passing through the old Civil War prison site. Reach the loop portion of the hike. Stay right, entering woodland of sycamore, as another path heads uphill to the island interior.

0.7   Pass Hollywood Rapids. Spur trails lead to the rocks, great for sunning or accessing the water. The old granite quarry site lies ahead, in operation during the late 1800s and early 1900s.

0.8   Pass the still Quarry Pond, which features a fishing dock, on your left. This loop keeps westerly along the margin between the still pond to your left and raucous river rapids on your right.

0.9   Reach a picnic shelter and a spur trail leading right to the island head. Another trail leads left and uphill to gun emplacements, then along the high center of Belle Isle. Still another trail leads to a boat ramp at First Break Rapid. Curve around to the quiet south side of island.

1.1   A spur trail leads right across the millrace headgate to a ladder accessing the South Side Rocks. This is a fun place to boulder-hop and enjoy some of the natural features of the James River. The main loop trail runs alongside the millrace to your right.

1.3   Pass the old hydroelectric plant on your right. It is not a safe place to explore, but user-created trails wind among its vegetation-covered remnants.

1.4   Reach a trail junction. Here, a wide track leads acutely left to the island's interior.

1.5   Pass the brick wall of an iron foundry to the right of the trail, then reach an intersection. Here, a trail leads right to the James River's south shore. This loop heads left back in the flats near the Robert E. Lee Bridge. Note the mountain bike skills area within sight of the foundry.

1.6   Complete the loop portion of the hike after passing the stone dynamite shed. From here, head right, walking toward the east island tip, passing under the Old Dominion Iron and Steel Company frame.

1.8   Reach the east end of Belle Isle. Soak in excellent views of the city and the James River. Begin backtracking to the trailhead.

2.0   Start crossing back over the "bridge under a bridge," returning to the mainland.

2.4   Reach the trail's end along Tredegar Avenue near the Civil War Visitor Center at Tredegar.

11 Canal Walk at Richmond

On this hike you will explore Richmond's riverside past, showcased after years of underappreciation. This urban hike in the heart of downtown starts at Brown's Island, then goes along restored canals originally dug for boats to circumvent the rapids of the James River. It goes around, under, and over the modern infrastructure while interpreting the interaction of yesteryear's peoples and this locale. The Canal Walk consists of hard surface for its entire distance. It is fun to follow the trail and absorb the numerous informational displays, including medallions inlaid onto the pathways.

Start: Near Civil War Visitor Center at Tredegar
Distance: 2.0-mile figure-eight loop
Hiking time: About 2-2.5 hours
Difficulty: Easy
Trail surface: Concrete
Best season: Year-round
Other trail users: Commuters, history buffs, runners, diners

Canine compatibility: Leashed dogs permitted
Land status: City park
Fees and permits: None
Schedule: Open daily year-round
Maps: *Canal Walk; USGS Richmond*
Trail contact: City of Richmond, 900 E. Broad St., Richmond, VA 23219; (804) 646-7000; richmondgov.com

Finding the trailhead: From exit 74A on I-95 in Richmond, take the Downtown Expressway to the first exit, Canal Street. Follow Canal Street to South Fifth Street. Turn left on South Fifth Street and follow it to the dead end at Tredegar Street. The trail starts near the intersection of Tredegar and Fifth Street at the bridge onto Brown's Island. Parking here can be tricky. Hourly parking is available at the Civil War Visitor Center on Tredegar Street, or you can park at the Belle Isle hiking trail locale under the railroad tracks beyond the museum. (Both lots open after 9:30 a.m. weekdays.) Trailhead GPS: N37 32.080' / W7 26.809'

The Hike

In establishing the Canal Walk, the city of Richmond demonstrated real commitment to preserving its past, especially when you consider how the Canal Walk was integrated into today's infrastructure. And combined with other historic attractions downtown, from Belle Isle to the Civil War Visitor Center at Tredegar, you can spend a full day exploring the important pieces of Virginia's past, a living timeline stretching from the late 1600s to today. In addition, while strolling along the restored canals of downtown, you can learn about history through displays and enjoy the watery views as well as food, fun, and entertainment, plus get a little exercise while doing it. So, don't feel bad when you order extra cream in your latte while watching others travel the multimillion-dollar route ingeniously laid out through and under—even over—the downtown infrastructure.

The route is marked and signed, not only for directions but also with notable information. It is a must-see for history buffs. Strategically located emergency

The Canal Walk traverses old art-filled buildings.

phones are there to ease your downtown walking worries. It will be hard to get up a head of steam as you stop to learn the information on the medallions embedded into the concrete walkway, as well as other signage. Water borders the route nearly its entire way, which adds scenic value to a historic overlay that covers various eras, from when no white man roamed the shores of the James River to the heady railroad days when tracks spread like veins over the land, resulting in the famed Triple Crossing.

On your first trip you will be wondering how the Canal Walk was integrated into the downtown riverfront. First, join a walkway connecting to Brown Island and explore that piece of land. The walk then saddles alongside the Haxall Canal. Interestingly, the Haxall Canal started in 1789 as a simple millrace, designed to turn a grinder and process grain for consumption. The millrace was later extended and deepened as part of the canal system built to allow boats to head up- or downstream along the James without having to navigate the rapids astride Richmond and beyond.

Richmond's first electric trolley car ran on May 4, 1888. The initial runs attracted crowds of lookers. Newspapers reported that the trolley cars "scared old ladies and dogs."

Civil War significance is never far away in Richmond. This walk passes piers of the rail bridge that brought Jefferson Davis to his inauguration as president of the Confederate States of America. See where the world's first electric trolley transportation system began. Back in 1888 Richmond's public transit system consisted of horse-drawn carriages, but then an electric line was developed using energy generated by the outflow of the Haxall Canal. These electric-powered trolleys ran through downtown and beyond for six decades, providing an interconnected artery of electric transportation. But widespread use of cars did them in.

Of course, the canals themselves are historic, built in the late 1700s through the 1800s to allow boats to travel around the rapids of Richmond, expanding commerce. When the first part of the first canal was opened in 1790, it was the first commercial canal in the United States. Remember, these canals were hand dug. It was part of a greater canal network linking Lynchburg and Richmond. In the 1850s more than 200 boats a day were using the locks and canals, greatly enhancing trade between the western part of the Old Dominion and the capital city. It seems Richmond has been at the forefront of transportation changes! Like most canals throughout the nation, railroads were the undoing of the canals. In the 1880s rail tracks were laid over the towpath next to the canal. Floods damaged the locks and they fell into despair. The canals along the walk have been restored.

Visit the cross laid by early English explorer Christopher Newport, who interacted with the Powhatan Indians stationed along the rapids of the James River. Upon landing at what became Richmond, he found an Indian village here. The falls of the

Waterpower

Back a couple of centuries, downtown Richmond looked very different—no shiny buildings and roar of cars and trains. Back then the only roar came from the falls astride Richmond. But it was these cataracts that caused an industrial center to develop here, spurred by transportation and power. The river provided transportation from the ocean to this point. The falls were the first impediment to boats. Yet early Americans saw these falls as a source of gravity-fed waterpower. They harnessed this waterpower, producing flour and other products, then used the river to ship them. Now we see the James River from a scenic perspective, or maybe as a place to fish, swim, or ply a kayak, but it was once the most valuable asset of a growing Richmond.

Canal Walk at Richmond

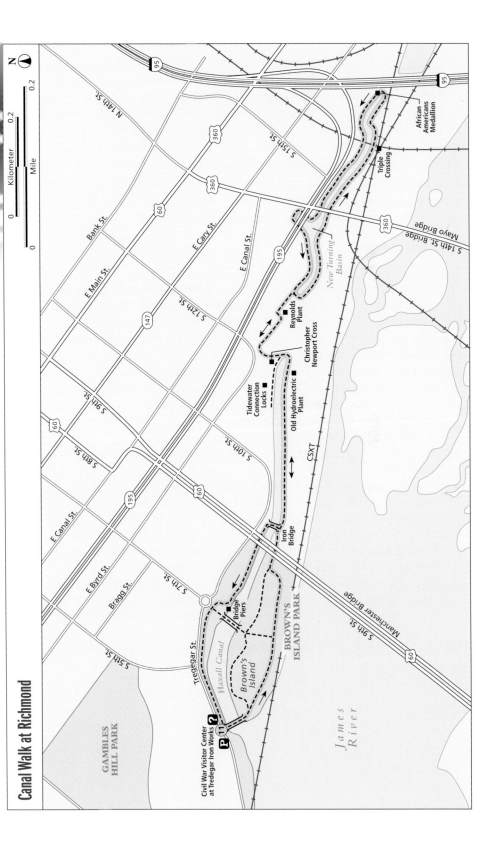

James River had been an intersection of aboriginal trade routes well before Newport considered crossing from England to what became Virginia.

The Triple Crossing represents another layer of history here on the waterfront. As its name hints, the Triple Crossing was the world's first three-way railroad intersection. Consider a break in your walk with a boat cruise on the lower Tidewater Connection Locks. You will take a 40-minute ride on the old canal. Your guide narrates the boat tour, with a heavy emphasis on history. Tickets can be purchased at the New Turning Basin. On your return trip look beyond the walk at the high-rises of downtown and the river in the distance, and ponder how the canals of Richmond were begun in 1784, advocated by none other than George Washington himself.

Miles and Directions

0.0 With your back to the Civil War Visitor Center at Tredegar, leave Tredegar Street to join Brown's Island on a dam/bridge. Once on Brown's Island, pass the Powhatan Chiefdom and Manchester & Free Bridges informational medallions inlaid into the path. Continue east along Haxall Canal. View rapids of the James River.

0.2 Pass under the Manchester Bridge. An arched iron pedestrian bridge leaves left across the canal. This will be your return route.

0.5 Pass within the roofless walls of an old hydroelectric plant.

0.6 Reach the end of the Haxall Canal near the Christopher Newport Cross. Leave left toward 12th Street, passing the Reynolds plant, then join the Tidewater Connection Locks via the steps. Shortly you'll cross over to the north side of the lock, then pass under the 14th Street Bridge, then cross back over to the south side of the canal.

0.8 Pass under the Virginia Street Bridge. Emerge at the New Turning Basin, where boat tours are available.

1.0 Reach the Triple Crossing. Head back to the north side of the canal near the African Americans and the Waterfront informational medallions. Turn back up the canal here, though the trail extends to Dock Street under I-95 and is slated for more expansion.

1.2 Curve around the north side of the New Turning Basin and the tour-boat ticket area. Continue under the 14th Street Bridge and the Tidewater Connection Locks to reach the Reynolds plant again. Backtrack up the south side of the Haxall Canal.

1.7 Reach the arched pedestrian bridge to cross the Haxall Canal and walk new terrain. Pass under the Manchester Bridge. Climb steps near the Seventh Street roundabout auto access. A larger pedestrian bridge connects Seventh Street to Brown's Island. Head west along an elevated path, paralleling Tredegar Street.

2.0 Complete the walk by returning to the Canal Walk beginning near Fifth and Tredegar.

12 Floodwall/Slave Trail

Enjoy downtown Richmond panoramas and shoals of the James River as you trace an elevated floodwall. Next, join the Slave Trail through woods along the river. End at historic Manchester Docks before retracing your steps. Bring your camera: The views of Richmond and the river are unparalleled from the floodwall.

Start: Near intersection of Semmes Avenue and Seventh Street
Distance: 4.4 miles out and back
Hiking time: About 2.5-3.5 hours
Difficulty: Moderate
Trail surface: Asphalt, gravel, concrete, mulch, natural surfaces
Best season: Sept-May
Other trail users: Exercising office workers

Canine compatibility: Leashed dogs permitted
Land status: City park
Fees and permits: None
Schedule: Open daily 7:30 a.m. to dusk
Maps: *Exploring the James Guide;* *USGS Richmond*
Trail contact: James River Park, 4001 Riverside Dr., Richmond, VA 23225; (804) 646-8911; jamesriverpark.org

Finding the trailhead: From Main and Belvidere in downtown Richmond, take Belvidere / US 1 / US 301 south across the James River on the Lee Bridge. Turn left onto Semmes Avenue (US 60) just after crossing the James River. Follow Semmes for 0.5 mile to a signed lot on the left of the road, just before the intersection of Semmes and Seventh Street. The trail leaves from the back of the parking area, away from Semmes Avenue. Trailhead GPS: N37 31.660' / W77 26.674'

The Hike

This hike presents glimpses into Richmond's past and incredible views of the capital's downtown area. Your views come from atop a floodwall across from downtown. Though the floodwall wasn't built with recreation in mind, it has become an integral link in the James River Park trail system. The top of the floodwall serves as an elevated pathway from which you can view the lowermost rapids of Richmond and downtown beyond, as well as panoramas of the city's south side.

Beyond the floodwall the hike joins a wooded corridor bordering the James River. Here you can enjoy an urban woodland walk and end up at Ancarrow's Landing, formerly known as the Manchester Docks. At this point turn around and walk both paths once more. Like other downtown trails, these routes have been ingeniously integrated into existing infrastructure. The engineering feats

▶ Even though importation of slaves was outlawed in Virginia in 1778, more than 300,000 slaves born in the United States (and probably others who were smuggled in from Africa after the practice was outlawed) were brought to the Manchester Docks and sold at the auction blocks here, then sent onward, mostly to the Deep South, before the Civil War ended slavery.

Rapids of the James River are viewed from the floodwall, backed with the Richmond skyline.

to include these trails show foresight and determination. Virginians are lucky to have this hike so close to their historic capital.

Floods have plagued Richmond throughout its existence. The worst floods in recent years have come on the heels of hurricanes. The floodwalls, which are on both sides of the James, were begun in 1988 after two decades of planning. Only the south-side wall has a walkway atop it. The south floodwall stretches some 13,000 feet in length, over 2 miles, while the north-side floodwall, bordering downtown, extends just under a mile at 4,500 feet. The walls are designed to protect the riverside areas up to 32 feet above normal river flows, especially Shockoe Bottom, on the south side of the James River, where this hike takes place.

From the trailhead parking area, it takes a little wrangling to make the floodwall, but join it shortly after passing under the Manchester Bridge. The views then come nonstop as you look out on the iconic skyscrapers of Virginia's capital city and the unruly rapids of the James. Expect to see herons, geese, and other watery wildlife in the river below, and wood debris piled up against the rocks. The old Manchester Canal, now just a quiet waterway on the backside of the floodwall, once took boats around the river rapids.

The canal is named for the town of Manchester, once distinct from the city of Richmond, before being absorbed by the capital city in 1910. Manchester and Richmond were formerly rivals, competing for trade and industry lining the rapids of James. In fact, the canal you pass on this hike was the only one built on the south side of the river, while rival Richmond extended their system eventually to Lynchburg and beyond. This sealed the fate of Manchester as its river trade withered and Richmond flourished.

The Floodwall Walk works past Mayo Bridge. Then you travel inside the floodwall. Note the graceful arches of the Mayo Bridge. The first Mayo Bridge, made of wood, was erected in 1784. The concrete one you see today replaced that one. The wooden bridge was burned during the Civil War, and for a time a pontoon bridge spanned the James. Briefly join a levee, then descend to Maury Street where it passes under I-95 and then joins the Slave Trail. The scenery changes from a sun-splashed elevated walk to a riverside riparian forest jaunt in a matter of feet. The sounds of

Hurricanes and Richmond

Throughout its history Richmond had been flooded, but never as severely as when Hurricane Agnes dropped 16 inches of rain over central Virginia in 1972. The James River soaked Richmond, and river waters reached 6.5 feet higher than the historical 200-year-old record of 36.5 feet. More than 200 street blocks were under water, Richmond's water supply was cut off, much of the south side of the river was inundated, and the National Guard was called out to protect life and property. Thirteen storm-related deaths occurred throughout the Old Dominion. Damage ran up and down the East Coast, with mud and debris leaving behind a mess to clean up. Hurricane Agnes was the impetus that got the floodwall started here, paired with incredible floods from Hurricane Camille that hit Richmond just three years earlier. City leaders decided to act on their floodwall plans, erecting the $134 million barrier to prevent the rising waters of the river from overflowing again. Some argue it has had mixed success: While preventing waters from overflowing on the James, it has also trapped waters on the outside of the wall, flooding Shockoe Bottom.

Floodwall/Slave Trail

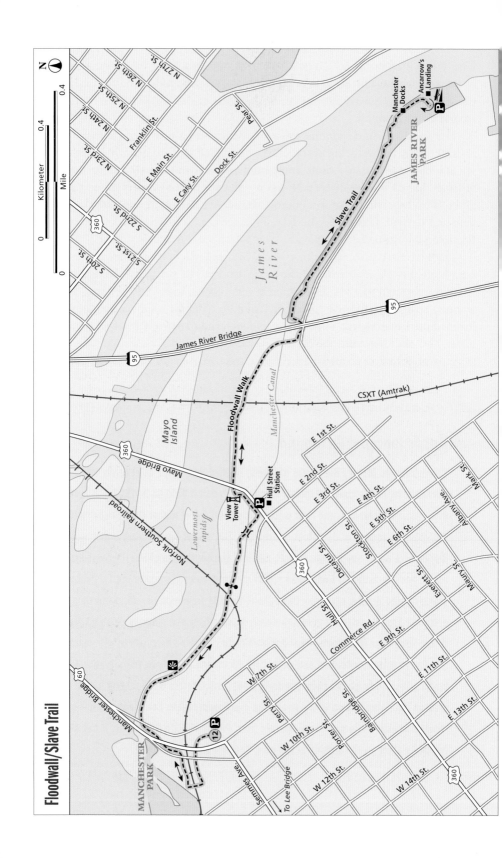

I-95 fade. Revel in the lush forest. As you merge onto the Manchester Docks, the weighty stone walls beside the James were actually put in during the late 1800s to handle heavy cargo.

The docks originally served as a colonial trading post. The docks were made of wood back in the days when slaves were unloaded here starting in the late 1700s and later shipped to the Deep South to work newer plantations. The grassy area at the dock site is now a popular fishing venue. The trail then leaves the grassy area and wanders a short bit through the woods to emerge onto the parking area and boat ramp accessible by Brander Street. The area is now known as Ancarrow's Landing, named for environmentalist and champion protector of the James River, Newton Ancarrow. He passed away in 1991. Today, the docks come alive with anglers and boaters in season.

Miles and Directions

0.0 Start with your back to Semmes Avenue; follow the concrete walkway leading toward the James River. Pass under the Manchester Bridge and travel west to shortly reach a pedestrian bridge crossing the Norfolk Southern Railroad.

0.2 After crossing the pedestrian bridge you can head right, following an old railroad grade to an elevated vista of downtown. The Manchester climbing wall is just below. However, to reach the floodwall, head left after the bridge and descend to reach a trail junction. Pass under the Manchester Bridge a second time, now heading easterly, downstream along the James River.

0.4 Join the floodwall, officially named the Floodwall Walk.

0.6 Reach a designated vista point that offers a postcard view of the heart of Richmond. Old Manchester Canal is to your right.

0.8 Cross over a gate in the floodwall through which a railroad track passes, then drop off the floodwall.

0.9 Bridge the Manchester Canal.

1.0 Reach Hull Street. Turn left here, passing an alternate trail parking area, then come to circular steps leading to an elevated vista. Stay on Hull Street toward the Mayo Bridge, passing through a floodwall gate, then veer left, descending, and pass under the Mayo Bridge, resuming easterly. A spur trail leads left to the lowermost rapids of the James.

1.4 Pass under the CSXT rail bridge.

1.5 Reach Maury Street, turn left, pass through the floodwall and under I-95, then join the Slave Trail, short for Manchester Slave Docks Trail.

2.1 Open onto a grassy area at the Manchester Docks. Keep along the waterfront.

2.2 Reach the trail's end after passing through a short strip of woodland and making the Ancarrow's Landing parking lot. Backtrack to Semmes Avenue.

4.4 Reach the Semmes Avenue parking lot near Seventh Street.

13 Cold Harbor Battlefield Loop

This hike circuits through an important conflict site during the Union's attempt to capture the Confederate capital of Richmond. The crossroads at Cold Harbor, now in the suburbs of Richmond, provide a quiet forested park with user-friendly trails that belie its violent past. Leave the battlefield visitor center, crossing an open field. Enter woodlands, passing earthworks dug during an eleven-day siege pitting the troops of Robert E. Lee against Ulysses S. Grant. Take the extended loop past Bloody Run, a stream that crosses the battlefield. Curve around the property in rolling terrain, climbing to a hill overlooking the theater of war, before returning to the visitor center.

Start: Cold Harbor Visitor Center
Distance: 2.1-mile loop
Hiking time: About 1.5-2 hours
Difficulty: Moderate
Trail surface: Gravel and natural-surface path
Best season: Year-round
Other trail users: None
Canine compatibility: Leashed dogs permitted

Land status: National park
Fees and permits: None
Schedule: Open daily year-round
Maps: *Richmond National Battlefield Park; USGS Seven Pines*
Trail contact: Richmond National Battlefield Park, 3215 E. Broad St., Richmond, VA 23223; (804) 226-1981; www.nps.gov/rish

Finding the trailhead: From exit 31A on I-295, east of downtown Richmond, take VA 156 north for 3.9 miles to a stop sign. Turn left at the stop sign, staying with VA 156 north for 0.9 mile farther, then turn right into Cold Harbor Battlefield. Immediately park on your right at the visitor center. Trailhead GPS: N37 35.121'/W77 17.220'

The Hike

Preserved battlefields in the Old Dominion not only safeguard state and national history, they also provide green space as the urban areas expand outward. Such is the case with Cold Harbor Battlefield, part of Richmond National Battlefield Park. This unit of the national park service maintains several locations important to the War Between the States. Some have short interpretive trails, others have no trails at all, but each of the sites preserves and shares a chapter—the American Civil War—that remains one of the most significant times in American history.

Landlocked Cold Harbor was a quiet crossroads east of Richmond back in late May of 1864. Things weren't going to well for the Rebels, as the superior manpower and equipment of the Union, due to its manufacturing base and other organizational reasons, was taking its toll. Ol' US Grant was maneuvering for Richmond, to take the capital and end the war. Grant and regal Robert E. Lee had been battling back and forth across central Virginia, Lee always on defense.

Grant wanted the crossroads at Cold Harbor. He sent General Phillip Sheridan to take them on May 31, 1864. Sheridan found Confederate defenders but overcame

Battlefield earthworks glow ironically in the morning light.

them and took the crossroads. The South dug in at the present battlefield. Robert E. Lee was determined to retake the crossroads at Cold Harbor, and Grant wanted to push through the Confederates and on to Richmond. The first couple of days were full of sparring as the Confederates fortified their defenses.

The Union launched a massive assault on the morning of June 3. Within an hour, thousands of Federals lay dead and wounded. Still others were pinned down, under fire but with nowhere to go. They dug trenches with anything they had while the injured lay where they fell for as long as four days, while Lee and Grant negotiated a cease fire. In the meantime soldiers on both sides enhanced their defense, ready for siege.

Over the ensuing days Grant changed his mind, abandoning the direct route for Richmond. The Battle of Cold Harbor was the last major field victory for Robert E. Lee. Grant headed south for Petersburg, to cut off supplies to Richmond and Grant, realizing he could wait out the supply-starved South.

> The main battle at Cold Harbor, that of June 3, started in the murk of dawn, at 4:30 a.m., and was over in an hour's time.

Today, the battlefield loop trails are used more by local recreationalists looking for a natural haven than Civil War buffs or historical hikers like us. However, after hiking here, no matter the season, it is hard to deny the beauty found in this valley of Bloody Run.

You will first pass through a field, then enter alluring oak-hickory woods, where earthworks can still be seen. This area saw hand-to-hand fighting seldom seen in the current era. This fighting led to an unusual occurrence in the Civil War—a turned trench. A turned trench is an earthwork dug by one side that is lost through fighting then occupied by the other side. When passing more earthworks imagine living in them for 11 days—the heat, the filth, and the fear. Even though it was dangerous to move about, companies rotated in and out of the most dangerous and potentially deadly earthworks, to spread the most dreaded assignments around.

The trail passes some once-gruesome sights, the "killing fields" where Federals died in literal piles, and Bloody Run, a stream said to have flowed red with the dead that fateful morning of June 3. In the end more than 18,000 soldiers were killed, wounded or captured. Your final climb up a hill shows what an advantageous site this was for the Confederates, especially with their well dug trenches topped with "header logs," a slightly elevated log set above the trench which allowed soldiers to shoot out from the slit between the log and the trench, literally protecting their heads, but offered for the enemy little at which to fire.

Finally, the trail emerges from the woods and you are back at the visitor center. The building is full of interpretive information that lends visual understanding to the Battle of Cold Harbor.

What Is Nearby? Garthright House and More

Just down the road from Cold Harbor Battlefield stands the Garthright House. The heart of the house was constructed in the 1700s, and added on later. It was used as a hospital not only for this battle but also during the Battle of Gaines Mill, in June of 1862 (Gaines Mill Battlefield, within a couple minutes' drive of Cold Harbor, also has trails). Though you can't enter the Garthright House it is worth a stop and has interpretive information outside. Also, Hanover County has a Cold Harbor Park that features a short interpretive trail visiting reserve Union soldier sites.

The Cold Harbor National Cemetery, also located nearby, has over 2,000 Union fallen buried within its sobering borders, and will remind you of the sacrifices of our soldiers throughout the history of our country.

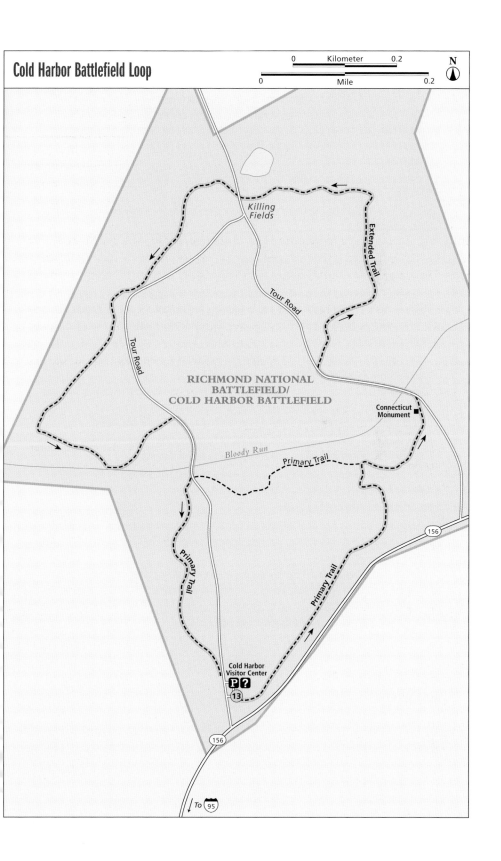

Cold Harbor Battlefield Loop

0   Kilometer   0.2

0   Mile   0.2

N

Killing
Fields

Extended Trail

Tour Road

Tour Road

RICHMOND NATIONAL
BATTLEFIELD/
COLD HARBOR BATTLEFIELD

Connecticut
Monument

Bloody Run

Primary Trail

156

Primary Trail

Primary Trail

Cold Harbor
Visitor Center

P ?

13

156

To 95

Miles and Directions

0.0 As you face the Cold Harbor Battlefield Visitor Center, look right for a sign and foot trail leaving away from the visitor center and running roughly parallel to Cold Harbor Road. Immediately pass under pines bordered by emplaced cannon. Note the monument commemorating the Battle of Cold Harbor. The trail then travels northeast on a mown path through an open field.

0.2 Reenter woods. Watch for shallow earthworks hastily dug by the Union, to help protect them from snipers.

0.3 A small land bridge takes you over an earthwork. Enjoy the interpretive information scattered along the trail.

0.4 Come to an intersection. Stay right here on the Extended Trail. The Primary Trail leaves left and stays within the heart of the battle zone, along Bloody Run. The Extended Trail is rooty and sandy.

0.5 Reach the Connecticut Monument. It honors those slain from the Constitution State. The trail joins the tour road heading left, just beyond the monument. Cross Bloody Run. Watch for more earthworks. The underbrush has been cleared to allow better viewing of the fortifications.

0.7 Leave right from the tour road on a sandy path. Holly trees are prevalent. One part of the trail takes you through a trench.

1.1 Come to the Cold Harbor "killing fields," very near a pond and the tour road. This saw fighting so deadly for the Union, men were falling on top of one another and those still living used the piled bodies as cover. Cross a road leading away from the battlefield.

1.3 Briefly join the tour road very near the battlefield boundary, then leave right away from the tour road. The terrain undulates a bit among pines and hardwoods.

1.6 Come alongside Bloody Run and some very well preserved breastworks. Note how these fortifications were laid at angles to fight against attacks from multiple sides.

1.7 Rejoin the tour road and head right.

1.8 Reach a trail junction just after bridging Bloody Run on the tour road. Here, the Primary Trail leaves left along Bloody Run. This hike, however, stays right with the Extended Trail and climbs a hill.

1.9 Level off. Here, well-preserved earthworks make for excellent vantages from which to command the battlefield. The trenches were deep and Confederates could shoot down on the attacking Union soldiers.

2.1 Emerge onto the tour road within sight of the visitor center.

14 Petersburg National Battlefield

This hike loops the Poor Creek drainage of Petersburg National Battlefield, Civil War site of the longest siege in American history. Leave the earthworks of Fort Haskell and travel through bottoms, hills, and by the old Taylor Farm, all of which played roles in the Union blockade of Petersburg. Along the way discover miles of earthworks dug by soldiers during the ten-month blockade. Other hiking trails and the auto tour road provide more exploration opportunities at this large historic and natural site in the heart of Petersburg.

Start: Tour Stop #6 on Park Tour Road
Distance: 2.7-mile loop
Hiking time: About 1.5-2 hours
Difficulty: Moderate
Trail surface: Gravel with some natural-surface path
Best season: Year-round
Other trail users: Bikers, equestrians
Canine compatibility: Leashed dogs permitted

Land status: National park
Fees and permits: Parking fee required
Schedule: Open daily year-round
Maps: Petersburg National Park Eastern Front Trail Map; USGS Prince George
Trail contact: Petersburg National Battlefield, 1539 Hickory Hill Rd., Petersburg, VA 23803; (804) 732-3531; www.nps.gov/pete

Finding the trailhead: From exit 52 on I-95 in Petersburg, take Wythe Street (VA 36) for 2.5 miles to the battlefield. Head to the visitor center, pay your entry fee, obtain a map, then join the Park Tour Road. Follow the Park Tour Road or Siege Road to Tour Stop #6, on your right. Trailhead GPS: N37 13.958' / W77 21.267'

The Hike

The ten-month siege of Petersburg was one of mostly boredom for the soldiers of the Confederacy and the North, but it was interspersed with battles. One such encounter was the Battle of Fort Stedman on March 25, 1865. General Robert E. Lee was determined to pierce Union lines and take Ulysses S. Grant's military railroad, then concentrate his troops to fight Grant more effectively. The Rebels blasted through the Yankee lines but weren't able to hold their position, and were pushed back. This hike starts at the earthworks of Fort Haskell, where tightly packed Bluecoats repulsed the Confederate charge. From this point, you head south to the site of the Taylor Farm, where but a brick foundation remains from its Civil War destruction. The loop then wanders amid earthworks still faintly visible under a lush forest.

The trails here at the Eastern Front of Petersburg National Battlefield are well marked and maintained,

▶ During the siege of Petersburg, Clara Barton, the founder of the American Red Cross, served as superintendent of nurses for the Union.

A replica of an earthworks defense as built by Civil War soldiers

with intersections marked by concrete posts with an accompanying letter. The entire loop is open to hikers, bikers, and equestrians. Much of the loop is singletrack path. The woods and fields the trail travels are favorable for deer and wild turkey.

Walk over to the earthworks at Fort Haskell, just across from Tour Stop #6. This square was the scene of intense hand-to-hand fighting. The open bucolic lawn makes it hard to imagine such happenings today. The first part of the hike uses the Poor Creek Trail, a singletrack path traveling southbound in classic pine-oak-hickory woods, roughly paralleling Park Tour Road on one side and Poor Creek on the other. A keen eye will spot manipulated land, whether it is from the siege or later as farms. Look for level spots, lines of trees, and even aged forest.

The path nears the Norfolk Southern Railroad. Petersburg was a rail hub during the Civil War and was the reason for Grant marking it for takeover. The hike then

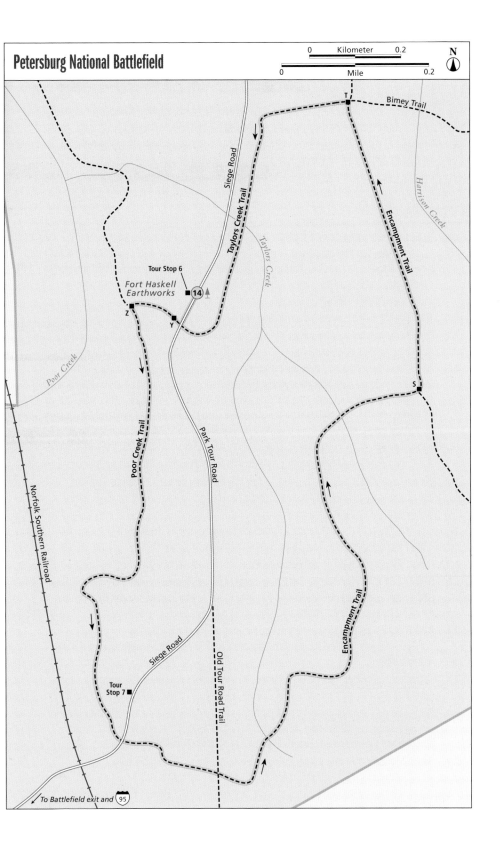

0   Kilometer   0.2

0   Mile   0.2

N

T

Bimey Trail

Siege Road

Taylors Creek Trail

Taylors Creek

Encampment Trail

Harrison Creek

Tour Stop 6

Fort Haskell
Earthworks

14

Z

Y

S

Poor Creek

Poor Creek Trail

Park Tour Road

Norfolk Southern Railroad

Encampment Trail

Siege Road

Old Tour Road Trail

Tour
Stop 7

To Battlefield exit and 95

reaches Tour Stop #7, where the Taylor family plantation, Spring Garden, was left in ruins. You can now see brick foundations of the home, lying in repose atop a quiet grassy knoll, contrasting an earlier violent time. The balance of the loop joins the mostly wooded Encampment Trail, where trenches and earthworks lace a gorgeous forest amid pretty Taylors Creek and its tributaries. Most of the terrain is revegetated, with trees and brush growing amid the trenches and pits, but they are still visible even in the lushness of summer. A final pair of turns on the Taylors Creek Trail brings you back to the trailhead.

Miles and Directions

0.0 Start by leaving Tour Stop #6. Walk across the road to visit the earthworks of Fort Haskell. Then walk south down Park Tour Road to reach a trail and post Y. Head back into the woods after passing alongside the earthworks. Walk just a short distance to reach post Z and the Poor Creek Trail. Head left on the Poor Creek Trail, joining a southbound singletrack path.

0.5 The Poor Creek Trail curves west, nearing fields.

0.7 The Poor Creek Trail comes within sight of the Norfolk Southern Railroad, then pops out onto a field, aiming for Tour Stop #7. The railroad lines were the prize for the Union.

0.8 Come near Tour Stop #7. Atop the hill to the north stands the brick foundation of the Taylor home. Their farm was destroyed during the war. Cross Park Tour Road and stay left on gravel doubletrack, beginning the Encampment Trail as it heads east. This area, true to its name, was the site of Confederate lines, stretched out in defense, camped for months during the siege. Relic linear earthworks and circular dug pits are visible in the woods and along the trail.

1.0 The Encampment Trail turns north and dips into Taylors Creek, a tributary of Poor Creek.

1.2 Hickory Trail leaves right for the park ranger station. Stay with the Encampment Trail. The rich, tranquil woods belie yesteryear's battle and today's encirclement by the urbanity of Petersburg.

1.6 Intersect the Wilcox Trail. It leads left to cross Taylors Creek then return to Tour Stop #6, officially shortcutting this loop. Stay right with the Encampment Trail.

1.7 Dip to span a tributary of Taylors Creek. Pass more earthworks.

1.8 Reach post S. Here, continue the Encampment Trail left, joining a wide old roadbed, while a spur trail leads right for a horse-trailer parking area near park headquarters. Holly trees are prevalent under a tall overstory.

2.2 Reach post T and a four-way intersection, just after passing through a gas line clearing. Turn left, westbound, now on the Taylors Creek Trail, cutting back across the gas line clearing.

2.3 Come just a few feet from Park Tour Road. Turn left here, southbound, running parallel to the road.

2.4 Bridge sandy but small Taylors Creek. Shortly pass the parking area for Tour Stop #6 and this hike. To make the full hike, keep straight on the Taylor's Creek Trail. Ahead, pass the other end of the Wilcox Trail just before curving right to meet Park Tour Road.

2.7 Reach Tour Stop #6 after backtracking up Park Tour Road, ending the hike.

Petersburg Battlefield Bonus Hike

Other trails lace the Petersburg National Battlefield. An additional enlightening hike makes a 3.4-mile moderate loop, with a few hills. The now-wooded lands present a natural respite contrasting with the dark Civil War days. Start at a replicated siege site, then walk along Harrison Creek, an important battle line during the Petersburg siege. Traverse other historic roads used back then.

Park at Tour Road stop #3. This tour stop details soldier life and siege tactics from the Civil War. Hike doubletrack paths, passing alongside Harrison's Creek. This quiet stream slips through shady woodland, giving no hint of its importance as a battle line where Union and Confederate soldiers faced one another. Beyond Harrison's Creek the trail joins old Meade Station Road, an important army provision route during the siege. Finally, the hike loops back on the historic Prince George Court House Road.

The rolling terrain is canopied with hardwoods, cedars, and pines. The park service manages the forest using prescribed fire and you may see evidence of this, especially along the Battery 7 Trail.

With your back to the Tour Stop #3 parking area, take the wide trail heading south on the Attack Road Trail. At 0.2 mile, intersect the Water Line Trail and keep forward to reach post B and a three-way intersection. Turn right here on the Harrison's Creek Trail. At 0.9 mile reach post R. Stay with the Harrison's Creek Trail past post Q, now on a singletrack path meandering through piney woods.

At 1.3 miles cross the Park Tour Road and reach Tour Stop #4. Harrison's Creek is to your left. Keep along Harrison's Creek and reach post N, then post M, and join the Friend Trail. Turn right, climbing away from Harrison's Creek. At 1.9 miles cross a tributary of Harrison's Creek. At 2.0 miles climb to make post L and the Park Tour Road. Keep straight, joining the Battery 7 Trail. Travel level lands. At 2.7 miles reach Post I. Turn right and head due south on Meade Station Trail. This path follows the supply line used by Union soldiers during the siege. At 2.9 miles reach post G. Stay with the Meade Station Trail. At 3.1 miles reach post E to meet Prince George Court House Trail, which was used by both armies to haul men and supplies. Turn right, joining the old road-turned-path. Reach post D, keep straight on the Prince George Court House Trail. At 3.4 miles return to Tour Stop #3, completing the bonus hike.

15 Chippokes Plantation

This hike explores one of the oldest continually operating farms in the United States. Begun in 1619, the 1,400-acre farm, listed on the National Register of Historic Places, contains more than twenty architecturally significant buildings. You will start at the park visitor center. Walk along the James River beach, then cross College Run. From there, the trail rises to meet the heart of the plantation, where you can explore a working farm, outbuildings, and the mansion. The Farm and Forestry Museum is a must-stop. Check out actual implements of farming days gone by that will hold your fascination.

Start: Park visitor center	**Land status:** Virginia state park
Distance: 2.4 miles out and back	**Fees and permits:** Parking permit required
Hiking time: About 2.5-3 hours, including visit to museum	**Schedule:** Open daily year-round
Difficulty: Moderate	**Maps:** *Chippokes Plantation State Park; USGS Lancaster*
Trail surface: Asphalt	**Trail contact:** Chippokes Plantation State Park,
Best season: During park festivals	695 Chippokes Park Rd., Surry, VA 23883;
Other trail users: None	(757) 294-3625; virginiastate
Canine compatibility: Leashed dogs permitted	parks.gov

Finding the trailhead: From Hopewell, take VA 10 for 35 miles to the community of Surry and the intersection with VA 31. After VA 31 and VA 10 diverge in Surry, stay east on VA 10 for 3 more miles to VA 634, Alliance Road. Turn left on Alliance Road and follow it for 3.6 miles to turn left into the state park. Follow the signs to the park visitor center. Trailhead GPS: N37 08.735' / W76 44.330'

The Hike

Chippokes Plantation stands on a hill overlooking the wide, scenic, and tidal lower James River. The dramatic setting is worthy of the noble plantation building and the surrounding gardens. The Italianate brick home we see today was built in the 1850s. The two-story mansion features a third-story windowed cupola that provides views to the river beyond. Tours are held between 1 and 5 p.m. Friday through Monday and other assorted times seasonally. The land went through multiple hands since its original establishment. Despite the title changes, the tract remained intact and is perhaps America's oldest continually worked farm.

The last owners, Mr. and Mrs. Victor Stewart, lived at Chippokes from 1917 to 1967, then deeded over the land to the commonwealth of Virginia under the stipulation that it remain a working farm and the state establish a museum of Virginia's agricultural history. That museum, located on the grounds, free with your park admission,

Trailside beach on the Potomac River ▶

▶ Over a nearly 400-year period, Chippokes Plantation was longest held by the Ludwig family, from 1684 to 1824.

and accessible during this hike, was an unexpected highlight for me. I spent an inordinate amount of time walking among the displays that included farm implements, logging tools, cotton-raising and cotton-ginning gadgets, everything from seeding to cultivating and processing that which grew from the ground. A special section is devoted to items used in the farming home life. I strongly suggest devoting time in your visit to soak in the museum. The park also has more standard offerings, from a swimming pool and campground to cabins to equestrian trails, plus a few more hiking trails that trace old farm roads.

During your hike you will see other buildings. The River House is the oldest. Its multiple chimneys rise tall against the Tidewater sky. You will see other small houses, built for those who actually farmed the land. They are still inhabited to this day by working planters, as the ongoing operations honor the stipulations of the Stewarts.

The hike starts at the visitor center, situated on a picturesque bluff overlooking the wide James River. Take note of the nearby picnic area with a fine water view. If you cannot wait to check out the riverside beach, pick up the short trail leaving from behind the visitor center. It switchbacks down to the beach. Our hike uses the College Run Trail. It descends to a freshwater cypress swamp. Look for eerie knees of the cypress rising above the swamp. Cypress trees are also identified by their wide buttressed trunks at the base. Their leaves resemble needles and are deciduous, turning an orange-brown before dropping in fall. Cypress wood is extremely rot resistant, hence its use in bridges, boats, and docks. The trees thrive in wetlands that would rot other species.

This is near the northern edge of the cypress range. Uncommon in the Old Dominion, cypress only grow in the Tidewater and Eastern Shore in Virginia, extending up the Delmarva Peninsula to Delaware. Cypress extends south to Florida and west to southeast Texas and up the Mississippi River Valley roughly to the latitude of the Delmarva Peninsula.

Soon come alongside the James River. Little shortcut paths cut to the sand-and-shell shore, a water-swept inland beach. While standing on the shore (you won't be able

Chippokes Plantation Sawmill Exhibit

In addition to the farming artifacts on display, Chippokes Plantation also features a permanent sawmill exhibit. A working operation, this is the forestry part of the farm and forestry museum. This sawmill was purchased by the plantation owners back in the 1930s. It is operated on special weekends in conjunction with other events held at the park. Check ahead of time, then time your visit if you want to see this part of the past come alive.

Farm implements from the plantation museum

to resist checking it out), contemplate the boats of Virginia's past, from the Powhatan Indians to the Jamestown settlers to Revolutionary War and Civil War ships, passing beneath Chippokes Plantation. And you can join the ranks of those who have floated the James. The park offers guided canoe trips on weekends during the warm season.

Rise to the greater Chippokes Plantation after crossing College Run. Leave the forest behind. Instead, you will see a working farm, complete with live animals, tractors, and farm workers keeping up the massive spread. Depending on the time of year, you may see a variety of tasks that keep the farm working, as well as the actual growing of crops.

Ahead, you will reach the mansion, rising in the yon. Turn into the grounds, exploring the gardens, gaining different vantages of the brick structure. If you want to tour the inside, call ahead to make sure it will be open during your visit. Walk around to the cook house and the carriage house, negotiating the uneven brick walkways. If you wish to walk more, a series of trails spoke away from the mansion area, leading to other areas of the plantation, along waterways, and to overlooks.

Miles and Directions

0.0 Start on the College Run Trail, located on the auto turnaround in front of the visitor center. Follow the asphalt track downhill away from the visitor center. Shortly pass a freshwater cypress swamp, then come along the James River. Short spur trails lead to the beach along Virginia's most notable waterway.

0.4 Cross College Run on a bridge. Take a moment to gauge the direction of the tidally influenced stream. An alluring sand spit extends into the James River. Continue beside the river before rising to a wooded bluff.

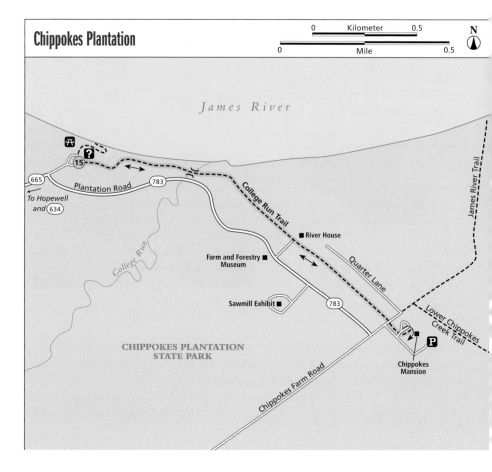

Chippokes Plantation

0   Kilometer   0.5

0   Mile   0.5

N

James River

665

To Hopewell
and 634

Plantation Road

783

College Run Trail

College Run

River House

Farm and Forestry
Museum

Quarter Lane

James River Trail

Sawmill Exhibit

783

Lower Chippokes
Creek Trail

P

**CHIPPOKES PLANTATION
STATE PARK**

Chippokes Farm Road

Chippokes
Mansion

0.6   Level out after climbing the bluff. The trail merges into an old farm road. The terrain is open now, save for planted trees. Buildings are visible to the southeast.

0.8   Come to an intersection. Here a path leads right to the Farm and Forest Museum. The River House stands to your left. Save your visit to the museum after visiting the plantation. For now, keep straight on the old farm road, passing smaller, occupied farmhouses, barns, and fenced pastures with animals. Huge cedars flank the lane, lending a sense of the past.

1.1   Come to an intersection. Chippokes Plantation is visible ahead, while Chippokes Farm Road leaves right. The James River Trail leads left, tracing another country lane. Keep straight for the mansion.

1.2   Reach Chippokes Plantation. Explore the grounds and other buildings, including the gift shop. On your return trip to the visitor center, stop by the Farm and Forestry Museum. Allow ample time to view the hundreds of fascinating artifacts.

2.4   Reach the visitor center, completing the hike.

16 Battle of Dam No. 1 at Newport News Park

This scenic hike takes place at one of Virginia's most attractive and well maintained urban preserves: Newport News Park. Within this large multipurpose getaway is the site of the Battle of Dam No. 1. Cross a wooden bridge above the site of Dam No. 1, then walk a combination nature/historic trail that explores the history of the area. Stop by a lake overlook, cross a marsh boardwalk, and travel through scenic rolling terrain along miles of earthen fortifications, some of the best preserved in the state.

Start: Parking area near the Discovery Center
Distance: 3.4-mile figure eight with spur
Hiking time: 2–2.5 hours
Difficulty: Moderate
Trail surface: Natural-surface path
Best season: Winter for viewing earthen fortifications
Other trail users: None

Canine compatibility: Leashed dogs permitted
Land status: Newport News city park
Fees and permits: None
Schedule: Open sunrise–sunset year-round
Maps: Newport News Park; *USGS Yorktown*
Trail contact: Newport News Park, 13560 Jefferson Ave., Newport News, VA 23603; (757) 886-7912; nnparks.com

Finding the trailhead: From exit 250B on I-64 east of Williamsburg and west of Norfolk, exit onto Jefferson Avenue, VA 143 west, turning left. Head northwest to immediately reach Fort Eustis Boulevard and a traffic light. Keep straight on Jefferson Avenue and follow it for 0.3 mile to turn right into the park. Follow Constitution Way 0.8 mile to the Discovery Center on your right. The hike starts on the left side of Constitution Way a little beyond the Discovery Center. Trailhead GPS: N37 10.966' / W76 32.214'

The Hike

In spring 1862 the long peninsula divided by the James River on the south and the York River on the north was the point where the Union army chose to advance on the Confederate capital of Richmond. Realizing this, the Confederates set up three strategic defense lines, using the swamps and streams of the peninsula to enhance their defensive positions and slow the Union advance. The Battle of Dam No. 1 took place along the second Confederate defense line of the peninsula. Here, the Warwick River was dammed to make crossing its marsh even more difficult for the North. The Confederates were simply trying to buy time to enhance the defenses of Richmond before the Yankees moved toward the Confederate capital.

Despite the Confederate defenses, Union General George B. McClellan decided to test the strength of this defense line by firing shells

▶ The Battle of Dam No. 1 was smaller than the most noteworthy Virginia conflicts yet the Confederates suffered 75 killed and wounded, while the Union, primarily Vermonters—now buried at nearby Yorktown National Cemetery—suffered 35 dead and 121 wounded.

Trail crossing of the dammed Warwick River

and mortars on the Southern men and their positions. After finding what he thought was a weak spot in the defense lines, McClellan decided to test their strength.

Thus set the stage for this battle that took place on the morning of April 16, 1862. It was truly the North versus the South in this clash, pitting Vermonters against North Carolina, Georgia, and Louisiana regiments. The Vermonters forded the War-wick River, what is now the Lee Hall Reservoir (the lake at Newport News Park), and attacked the Rebels. The Southerners were initially pushed back but then reorganized. The Vermont Legion, low on dry ammunition, was penned with the water to their back and snipers in front and suffered heavy casualties. The first part of the hike actually visits this area, and you can see the Confederate earthworks from which they took down the Union men. The Vermonters eventually withdrew back across the water.

A few weeks later the Confederates abandoned this defense line, having gained time to reinforce Richmond. Battles continued up the peninsula after this. Since that time, the actual dam built by the Confederates has been inundated, though the hike starts by crossing a wooden bridge over the site of Dam No. 1. As you head up along the reservoir, an incredible number of hand-dug earthworks stretch along the trails.

After visiting the main battle area on the Twin Forts Loop, the hike traces the White Oak Trail, an interpretive path with an accompanying downloadable brochure via the website provided above. Wander through hickory-oak woods, crossing occasional creeks. Views of the 360-acre lake are numerous and inspiring, especially on the last half of the loop. Another highlight is crossing Beaver Dam Creek, a moving marshy wetland, on a long boardwalk. Eventually you will make your way back to the bridge at the Dam No. 1 site and complete the hike. Displays about the battle are located inside the Discovery Center.

Miles and Directions

0.0 Start by picking up the White Oak Trail at the Dam No. 1 Bridge by the lake below the Discovery Center. Note the monuments to the Vermonters who died here. Walk across the wooden footbridge, gaining views up and down Lee Hall Reservoir, a storage facility for Newport News drinking water.

0.1 Return to land on the north side of the reservoir. Reach a trail intersection and the first of many earthworks. Turn left on the Twin Forts Loop, keeping the reservoir to your left. Interpretive information details the Battle of Dam No. 1. Leave the lake among hickories and oaks.

0.5 Reach a four-way intersection. Turn left here toward a lake overlook. A wooden deck opens onto the water and the main site where significant fighting took place. Backtrack to the four-way intersection, then keep straight, continuing the Twin Forts Loop. View extremely deep earthworks.

1.1 Return to the intersection by the wooden bridge after completing the Twin Forts Loop. Turn left here, rejoining the White Oak Trail as it begins to circle around the east end of the

Newport News Park: One of Virginia's finest

Newport News Park is deservedly a designated stop on the Virginia Civil War Trails tour. The battle site is on the National Register of Historic Places. You will find the park's hiker path system overlain on the battlefield both scenic and comprehensive. Allow time to enjoy more facilities here, including 30 miles of hiking and biking trails, an archery range, playgrounds, picnic areas with shelters, a fine campground with electric and nonelectric campsites, bike rentals, an arboretum, history exhibits, nature programs, golf courses, and even a 30-acre model airplane field. To help comprehend this profusion of opportunities, stop at park headquarters on your left upon entering the preserve. The visitor center is run by the Newport News Chamber of Commerce, who can provide you with more ideas to explore Newport News Park and beyond.

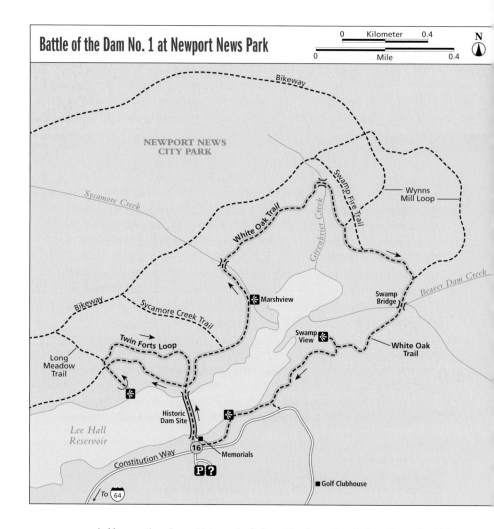

0   Kilometer   0.4

0   Mile   0.4

N

reservoir. More earthworks and interpretive information is scattered along the path, which is heavy with holly trees. Sluggish wet-weather drainages divide low hills.

1.3   Stay straight after meeting the Sycamore Creek Trail.

1.4   Come to a deck and elevated overlook of a marsh. Turn into the Sycamore Creek Valley, away from the reservoir.

1.6   Bridge Sycamore Creek on a long wooden span. These rolling woods represent the area as it likely looked back in the Civil War days.

1.9   Bridge Greenbrier Creek. It is named after the prickly green vine that will scratch hiker's legs. The White Oak Trail turns south.

2.1   Reach a trail junction. Here, the Wynns Mill trail leaves left and the Swamp Fire Trail is visible a short ways from the intersection. If you want to extend your loop by about a mile, take the Wynns Mill trail, otherwise continue straight on the White Oak Trail.

2.2   Intersect the end of the Swamp Fire Trail. Stay straight on the White Oak Trail, passing more earthworks.

The author crosses a marsh at Newport News Park.

2.4 The other end of the Wynns Mill Loop comes in on your left. Stay right with the White Oak Trail as it begins a long boardwalk crossing a wooded swamp. A resting bench on the crossing is an ideal opportunity for natural repose. Pass a second overlook atop the moving part of the Beaver Dam Creek below. Beavers are active here and you can sometimes see their dams backing up the creek. Listen for the sound of water spilling over a beaver dam.

2.5 End the long bridge and reach land. Come to more earthworks. Begin hiking southbound along the east shore of the reservoir. An abundance of pawpaw trees thicken the forest understory.

2.8 Turn right to take the spur trail to a swamp view point. Here, a resting bench overlooks a wooded wetland with open water in the distance. Resume the main loop. The open green turf of the Newport News Park golf course can be seen through the woods.

3.1 A spur trail leads left a short distance to Constitution Way. Ahead pass another overlook and a boardwalk. On the water you may see not only waterfowl but also anglers vying for bass, crappie, perch, and catfish, as well as canoers and kayakers plying the still waters.

3.4 Arrive back at the wooden bridge over the lake and the point where you started ending the hike.

17 Occoneechee Plantation

This hike at Occoneechee State Park, near big Buggs Island Lake, takes a pair of nature trails and connects to the Old Plantation Trail, where you can tour the remnants of an 1800s cotton plantation. After entering the plantation grounds, you will see remnants of their lifeways, from an old outbuilding to ice pits to the gardens that once adorned the manor. Note that this hike connects to other park trails that can add to your mileage.

Start: Upper end of state park boat ramp parking area
Distance: 1.4-mile balloon loop
Hiking time: About 1.5-2 hours
Difficulty: Easy
Trail surface: Mostly natural-surface path and gravel
Best season: Year-round
Other trail users: None

Canine compatibility: Leashed dogs permitted
Land status: Virginia state park
Fees and permits: Parking permit required
Schedule: Open daily year-round
Maps: Occoneechee State Park; USGS Clarksville North
Trail contact: Occoneechee State Park, 1192 Occoneechee Park Rd., Clarksville, VA 23927; (434) 374-2210; virginiastateparks.gov

Finding the trailhead: From downtown Clarksville, take US 58 east for 1.7 miles to the Occoneechee State Park entrance on your right. Enter the park and stay right toward the main park boat ramp. After 0.3 mile turn left and begin the boat ramp loop road. At the end of the upper parking area, on the left, look for the Warriors Path Nature Trailhead. Trailhead GPS: N36 37.908' / W78 32.028'

The Hike

As the residents of Virginia and what became the United States in general began moving westward from the East Coast, planters cleared what seemed an endless forest to plant their crops. Revolutionary War veterans were paid for their services with large land grants. Land was readily available. In those early days indigo, hemp, and some foodstuffs were produced.

Labor was, however, in short supply. Planters made up for this by using slaves to work the fields. Up until 1778, slaves could be imported from Africa. However, this practice was outlawed and became ultimately the first step in ending slavery altogether. It was patently obvious to the Virginians that fighting for their freedom from the English in Europe while simultaneously enslaving blacks from Africa were actions that contradicted one another.

▶ The Occoneechee Plantation once contained more than twenty rooms. Though the dwelling no longer stands, planted boxwoods, Osage oranges, and perennial flowers from that time period still thrive in the terraced garden.

The hike route passes by the Crudup Cemetery.

Nevertheless, the high returns for growing tobacco in the Old Dominion proved too tempting. The large plantations grew heaping harvests of tobacco, which quickly exhausted the soil. Therefore, they would have to move on to other plots to keep production up. The Occoneechee Plantation was established on roughly 3,000 acres in 1839 by William Townes. These planter farms were self-sufficient mini-communities in their own right. The rolling terrain along the Roanoke River proved productive. The Occoneechee Plantation thrived.

William Townes died after the Civil War, and the slave labor ended. The plantation house along with several surrounding acres were bought by a man named Dempsey Graves Crudup. The former Confederate captain, along with his wife and child, enjoyed life on the hilltop overlooking the valley below and tended the elaborate multiterraced garden that lay in the shadow of the house.

Unfortunately, the plantation house succumbed to fire on Christmas Eve of 1898. The family had lit candles on their Christmas tree and it caught fire, burning the

Old-Time Refrigeration

Along the way on the Occoneechee Plantation hike, you will pass two components of the plantation's "refrigeration system," representative of 1800s Virginia cold technology. Keeping things like milk and butter from quickly spoiling during the hot Southside Virginia summer months took a lot of planning and utilization of what nature provided. Here at Occoneechee Plantation they first built a dam on Mossy Creek. The low earthen structure is still visible along the Old Plantation Trail. Over time the main stream burst through the dam center, but it remains easy to find. After this small earthen dam was constructed, Mossey Creek backed up. During the winter months this small pond, around 4 feet deep, froze solid. After this freezing occurred, plantation workers, likely slaves in the early days, used saws to cut large blocks of ice and bring them to the icehouse located next to the plantation.

This icehouse was an elaborate affair. First, a deep conical pit was dug. Logs were laid in the pit to prevent the hole from caving in. A roof and small side walls were erected over the pit. After that the blocks of ice were laid into the pits, divided by alternating layers of natural material, either pine needles, which were in abundant supply in these woods, or sawdust or straw. The ice layer widened toward the top.

As the warm season wore on and the ice melted, a ladder was used to get deeper and deeper into the ice pit. With good planning and a little luck, and a not too terribly hot summer, the residents of Occoneechee Plantation could enjoy refrigerated foods until the following winter.

building to the ground. However, the foundation and outlines of the house can still be viewed, along with the Crudup Cemetery. You can also walk the terraced gardens amid plants that have lived well over a century as well as other garden enhancements. The hike also visits outlying areas of the plantation, explaining life back in the mid-1800s here in Southside Virginia.

In 1953 the Roanoke River was dammed downstream, near Castle Heights. The backup of the 48,000-acre lake extended beyond Clarksville. Much of the land that was part of the Occoneechee Plantation became submerged, lost to the waters of time. However, the plantation site and immediate lands around it were preserved and became the centerpiece of Occoneechee State Park. Facilities were developed beginning in 1968 and now include a large and busy boat ramp, the campground, cabins, and a network of trails that extends beyond this hike.

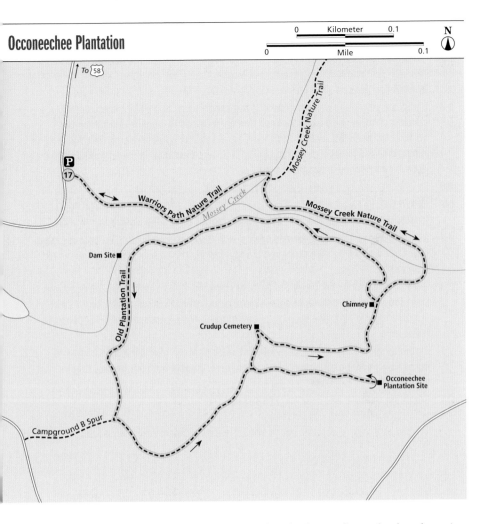

As you walk the grounds of the state park, which was formerly the plantation and the land of the Occoneechee Indians for whom the plantation was named before that, try to imagine the lives led back then and how times have changed. The hike is fairly easy and allows ample time to absorb the interpretive information as you walk. If the mileage is a little bit short, simply join the Mossey Creek Trail for some additional trekking.

Miles and Directions

0.0   Start by leaving the boat ramp parking area on the Warriors Path Trail, paying homage to the Occoneechee Indians who once called this area home. Enter pine-cedar-oak woods. Head away from the lake, briefly passing through a small clearing.

0.1   Leave left into woods. Come alongside serpentine Mossey Creek. Notice how deeply gullied the branch is. This was likely caused by erosive practices during the tobacco-growing days. Now, the banks are cloaked in moss, giving it a name, likely given by park personnel, as it is not indicated as such on official USGS maps.

0.2 Cross Mossey Creek on a little wooden bridge. Immediately meet the Mossey Creek Nature Trail. Turn right and head up a tributary of Mossey Creek, another gullied stream, bordered by ferns and pawpaw.

0.3 Bridge the gully you have been following and shortly come to a trail intersection and lone standing chimney surrounded by forest. The purpose of the structure attached to the building has been lost to time, but it likely served the main house in some form. Turn right, joining the Old Plantation Trail. Turn back down along the stream you just walked along. Note the abundance of sycamore trees.

0.5 Pass the remnants of an old dam on Mossey Creek.

0.7 Pass a spur trail leading right to state park Campground B. Continue straight on the Old Plantation Trail, in thick woods. Begin climbing the hill toward the plantation homesite.

0.8 Reach the lower end of the terraced gardens of Occoneechee Plantation. Note the large cedar trees. Turn right here on the path and head up the terraces. Walk past plants old and new.

0.9 Reach the plantation homesite. Stones outline the foundation. Interpretive information is scattered about. Stroll the auto-accessible site and ground before backtracking. Rejoin the Old Plantation Trail and soon pass the Crudup Cemetery, named for the last family to reside here.

1.1 Return to the plantation site, then turn left, away from the road access and downhill. Immediately come to the old chimney. From here, backtrack on the Mossey Creek Nature Trail.

1.4 Reach the trailhead and boat ramp parking area.

Along the Blue Ridge

View from Humpback Rocks

18 Elizabeth Furnace

This Elizabeth Furnace Recreation Area has two interconnected nature trails that present a splendid overview of charcoal production and iron making in 1800s Virginia, all in a gorgeous setting along Passage Creek, nestled between Massanutten Mountain and Green Mountain near Strasburg. The short walk is long on interpretive information and you will get to see the iron-furnace remains up close, as well as a cabin from the 1830s. Plan on adding picnicking, trout fishing, and car camping to your historic hiking agenda—it is all here at Elizabeth Furnace.

Start: Elizabeth Furnace Picnic Area
Distance: 0.9-mile loop
Hiking time: About 1-1.5 hours
Difficulty: Easy
Trail surface: Natural
Best season: Year-round
Other trail users: None
Canine compatibility: Leashed dogs permitted
Land status: National forest

Fees and permits: None
Schedule: 24/7/365
Maps: National Geographic Map #791, *Massanutten and Great North Mountain, George Washington and Jefferson National Forests; USGS Strasburg*
Trail contact: George Washington National Forest, 95 Railroad Ave., Edinburg, VA 22824; (540) 984-4101; www.fs.usda.gov/gwj

Finding the trailhead: From exit 6 on I-66 near Front Royal, take US 522 south/US 340 south for 1.5 miles, then turn right on VA 155 west. Follow VA 155 west for 5.1 miles to turn left on VA 678, Fort Valley Road. Follow VA 678 for 3.9 miles to turn left into the Elizabeth Furnace Day-Use Area and Picnic Ground. Follow the access road across Passage Creek, then dead-end in a large parking area. The hike starts in the middle of the parking area on the east side. Trailhead GPS: N38 55.736'/W78 19.617'

The Hike

Back in 1836, when this area was the back of beyond, the flats along Passage Creek were home to Elizabeth Furnace, originally known as Fort Furnace. These iron furnaces, essentially giant ovens made of stone, needed four things: stone, iron ore, rich forests, and water. The stone was needed to build the furnace. The iron ore was needed to make the final product, and the forest was needed to make charcoal to fire the iron furnace. Water was needed to power the giant bellows used to raise temperatures inside the furnace to a point where iron could be made.

The valley of Passage Creek had all four. First, the furnace was built from cut stone along Passage Creek, in a spot backed by a hill in order to access the top of the furnace. Then, a water diversion was dug from Passage Creek to power a water wheel that in turn powered the giant bellows. The forests grew rich and magnificent in the Passage Creek valley.

▶ The property around Elizabeth Furnace was acquired by the US Forest Service in 1913.

The once hot Elizabeth Furnace is now grown over with brush.

Digging out and hauling the iron ore to the furnace was no easy task. The forests were cut, the wood turned into charcoal, and the charcoal mixed with the iron ore as well as limestone. Men known as fillers dumped what was called charge (iron ore, charcoal, and limestone) into the top of the furnace. Elizabeth Furnace was 33 feet high. A landing platform stretched from the top of the furnace to the hill beside the furnace, allowing the fillers to place the material in the furnace. The uppermost part of the furnace you see today has tumbled over.

After the charge was properly heated, furnace tenders opened the base of the furnace, allowing the iron to flow into molds. These molds were known as pigs, which is how the name "pig iron" came to be.

With many people needed to operate the furnace and all the processes involved, a whole community sprang up around Elizabeth Furnace. Today, you can see a log cabin reconstructed of wood left over from that day by the Civilian Conservation

Charcoal and Iron

On this hike you will pass a leveled locale used to turn wood into charcoal. Making charcoal to fire Elizabeth Furnace was an essential part of the iron-making process. Before the first ton of iron could be forged, plenty of charcoal had to be made and on hand to heat the furnace to the proper temperature for the iron-making process to occur.

Just as with iron making, charcoal making was a long and laborious process. The person making the charcoal was known as a collier. The first order of business was chopping down trees. Woodchoppers cut in area units twenty axe handles wide, then cut the tree trunks into 4-foot lengths. Most any type of wood was usable. A level, circular plot of land was cleared, then the 4-foot lengths of wood were carefully and painstakingly stacked vertically, with a small wood chimney in the middle. Two tiers of wood were built around the chimney. The whole pile, resembling a giant cake, was covered with leaves, earth, and charcoal dust to make an airtight covering, save for the chimney. Then wood chips and kindling were dropped down the chimney and lit. Then, it too was covered.

The whole affair was allowed to smolder. Colliers used sharpened iron poles to poke air holes at the base of the pile to allow for even burning. After two weeks of burning, while being constantly attended to by a collier, the escaping smoke became a certain color, indicating the wood had turned to charcoal.

Little by little the charcoal was dug out from the pit and then placed in separate piles to keep it from catching fire. After cooling, the charcoal was then hauled to the iron furnace. It took huge amounts of wood to make enough charcoal to run Elizabeth Furnace, and nearby forest floor was quickly denuded, forcing colliers to go farther afield to get their wood.

Corps (CCC) in 1936. The cabin is accessible by a footbridge from the trailhead parking area. It is located near the Elizabeth Furnace Campground.

From Elizabeth Furnace the iron molds were hauled on wagons pulled by oxen. They were taken over Massanutten Mountain via a road that is now the Tuscarora Trail, through Shawl Gap, then down to the South Fork of the Shenandoah River. From there, it was loaded onto barges and ships to Harpers Ferry, which was then part

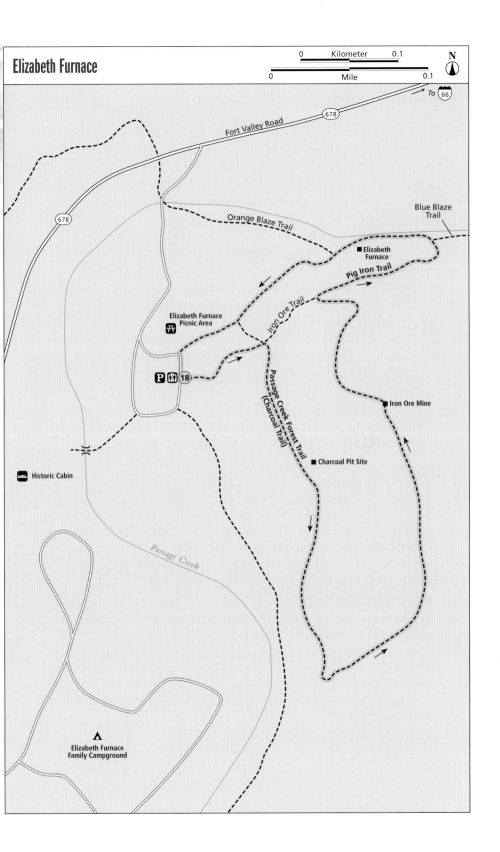

of Virginia. During the Civil War this iron was an important part of the Confederate war effort. At that time the iron was hauled to Staunton, Virginia, then taken by railroad to Lexington, and then floated down the James River to the Tredegar Foundry in Richmond.

In 1864 the Yankees destroyed Elizabeth Furnace. It was rebuilt in 1883 but was only in operation for five years before being abandoned for good due to low output and nonprofitability.

The area was in rough shape when the US Forest Service obtained Elizabeth Furnace and the surrounding valley and mountains. The hillsides had been cut over, and Passage Creek was choked with silt from mining and charcoal making. Trees were planted and Passage Creek was restored to its original channels. The CCC then constructed the picnic area and campground, though both have seen several makeovers through the decades.

The trails explaining charcoal making and iron making at Elizabeth Furnace have undergone a few changes too. You will note interpretive signage from different times. The hike as a whole is rewarding. First, you will visit the site of a charcoal pit, then a hillside where the remains of an ore mine stand. The hike then leads to the actual Elizabeth Furnace, where you can see the remnants of the furnace from the top and the bottom. I strongly recommend including a picnic, swim, and a camping trip along with your hike. I have camped here myself and give it a ringing endorsement. In addition, a well-developed trail system emanates from the greater Elizabeth Furnace area, adding plenty of hiking opportunities beyond this nature trail. Finally, be sure to visit the log cabin across the creek from the parking area.

Miles and Directions

0.0 Start by taking the trail leaving east from the middle of the parking area. It soon opens onto a small field. From here, go left and follow a wooded path to a trail intersection with two large signs, after passing a shortcut trail back to the parking lot. Here, turn right on the Passage Creek Forest Trail, also known as the Charcoal Trail.

0.2 Pass the level site of a charcoal pit. Enjoy interpretive signage about making charcoal.

0.3 Turn left (north) on the mountain slope.

0.5 Pass the iron ore mine site. Descend.

0.6 Meet the Iron Ore Trail. Turn right, shortly meeting the furnace bank where fillers accessed the top of the furnace via elevated platform.

0.7 A blue-blazed path, the Tuscarora Trail, leaves right and heads to Shawl Gap on Massanutten Mountain. Shortly reach Elizabeth Furnace. Check out the stone structure and attendant relics.

0.8 An orange-blazed trail leaves right to access the Signal Knob trail system on the north side of Fort Valley Road.

0.9 Arrive back at the large parking area, completing the walk.

19 Fox Hollow Snead Farm Loop

This Shenandoah National Park hike explores a historic farmstead and presents a good vista. The trek leaves the park visitor center, then dips to the former Fox Farm. Find signs of a pioneer past, including a cemetery. Head south on Dickey Ridge to reach the Snead Barn, part of another farm and more mountain history. The woodland walk passes an outcrop with a panorama of Shenandoah Valley and the mountains beyond. Finally, pass through Dickey Ridge Picnic Area, a fine place for a post-walk meal.

Start: Dickey Ridge Visitor Center at milepost 5.1 of Skyline Drive
Distance: 4.7-mile loop
Hiking time: About 2.5–4 hours
Difficulty: Moderate
Trail surface: Natural
Best season: When the leaves are off the trees
Other trail users: None
Canine compatibility: Pets are not permitted

Land status: National park
Fees and permits: Entrance fee required
Schedule: 24/7/365
Maps: Shenandoah National Park; USGS Chester Gap
Trail contact: Shenandoah National Park, 3655 Highway 211 E., Luray, VA 22835; (540) 999-3500; www.nps.gov/shen

Finding the trailhead: The hike starts at the Dickey Ridge Visitor Center, milepost 4.6 on Skyline Drive. From the Front Royal entrance to Shenandoah National Park, head south on Skyline Drive for 4.6 miles to the visitor center. Trailhead GPS: N38 52.306'/W78 12.222'

The Hike

This hike begins in a historic locale. The Dickey Ridge Visitor Center, worth a look itself, was originally a dining hall. Back in the 1930s visitors gathered for meals and socializing. They spent the night in rental cabins—now demolished—built when Shenandoah National Park was just coming into being. Excellent views can be had both east and west from the visitor center, as it straddles the Blue Ridge.

On the hike you will first be visiting the Fox family farm. Thomas Fox, along with his wife Martha, cleared the land in 1856. They grew corn and wheat and pastured animals. Later, Lemuel Fox and his wife Lucy operated the farm. Lemuel Fox Jr. was running the farm by the time the state of Virginia purchased the land in the 1930s. The extended family resided in several houses scattered among the fields. Today it is hard to imagine most of the land you walk through was once open, though it is now forested. The Foxes also boasted an apple orchard. Relic apple trees are scattered all over Shenandoah National Park.

▶ The term Dickey's Hill (Dickey Ridge) first appeared on a survey map in 1747.

This millstone now serves as a decorative stepping-stone at the Fox Farm.

The hardwood forest here is covered in vines. Look at the large stone walls, erected by generations of Foxes toiling the terrain, clearing the land to increase fertility and yield. These greenstone volcanic rocks were not too good for growing corn and had to be removed from the mountain soil. Interestingly, broken-down greenstone rock does make good soil.

Ahead, you will come to the Fox burial ground. Bordered in fieldstones and periwinkle, the graveyard reminds us that this land, now a national park, was once private property that settlers held dear. And before that, aboriginal Virginians claimed it as their own. The name Dickey Ridge appears in records from when Virginia was still an English colony. Ahead, you will come to a spring. This spring was likely why the Foxes chose this site for their farm. A home needs water. This spring was encased in concrete after the national park came to be. The park used it for the cabins and dining hall–turned–visitor center.

Look to the right of the trail for a decorative millstone, embedded in the ground. It was used here at the Fox farm as a decorative step and ground corn somewhere else. Step over the spring runoff and pass a rusty wire fence. The hike leaves the Fox farm homesite, passing through woods, former fields tilled by the Foxes.

The old farm road leads back toward the visitor center. Here, you rejoin the Dickey Ridge Trail, making an easy southbound track in viney woods. Look for a long rock fence to the left of the trail that runs down a sharp slope. The hike passes spur roads leading to park infrastructure facilities. The way is clearly marked with signs.

Ahead, look for an old bricked-in spring to the right of the roadbed. No telling who has drunk from there over the decades. The Snead Barn and homesite is the next highlight on this hike. Snead was a relative newcomer to what became the park. He operated a farm here and also had an apple orchard. His place became part of the park in the 1960s. The barn has been maintained by the park service. It is locked but you can peer inside and see the hayloft and animal stalls. A cellar behind the barn still stands too, and a spring trickles nearby.

The Snead Farm barn

After leaving the Snead Farm, enjoy a woodland walk, then join the Dickey Ridge Trail yet again. It takes you back north toward the visitor center on a fine, singletrack path shaded by maple, oak, hickory, basswood, and other trees.

The final part of the hike crosses Skyline Drive. Look for an asphalt path running through the center of Dickey Ridge Picnic Area. It will return you to the visitor center. Thirsty hikers will be happy to know this asphalt path passes several water fountains that serve the picnic area. After walking through the entire picnic area, you will have chosen your spot to take in a post-hike meal.

Miles and Directions

0.0 Leave the visitor center near the flagpole. Walk across Skyline Drive and come to an information kiosk with a booklet about the Fox Trail. Easterly views open beyond the grassy hill in front of you. Head left from here across grass to soon enter woods on the Dickey Ridge Trail.

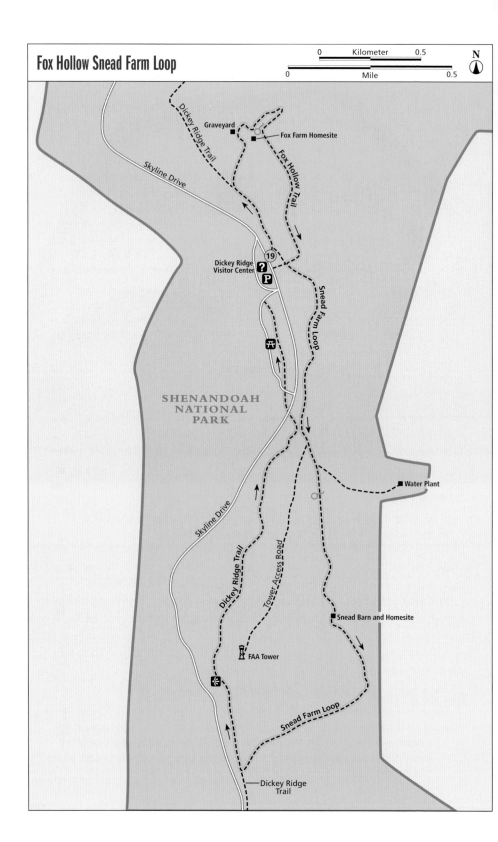

0   Kilometer   0.5

0   Mile   0.5

N

Dickey Ridge Trail

Graveyard

Fox Farm Homesite

Skyline Drive

Fox Hollow Trail

Dickey Ridge
Visitor Center

19

P

Snead Farm Loop

SHENANDOAH
NATIONAL
PARK

Water Plant

Skyline Drive

Dickey Ridge Trail

Tower Access Road

Snead Barn and Homesite

FAA Tower

Snead Farm Loop

Dickey Ridge
Trail

0.3 Turn right on the Fox Hollow Trail. As you descend into Fox Hollow, rock walls occupy the trailside, memorials of the hard work of the Fox family clearing this land, now grown over in brushy woods.

0.5 Reach the Fox family cemetery. It is bordered in stone. Continue down-trail, passing a spring.

0.7 Join up an old road that once connected Dickey Ridge to the town of Front Royal, down in the lowlands. Head south on a wide track, scrambling uphill in brushy woods.

1.3 Meet the Dickey Ridge Trail. The visitor center stands just up the hill. For a shorter, easier hike, you can return to Dickey Ridge Visitor Center. Otherwise, head left with the Dickey Ridge Trail, southbound.

1.8 Come to the junction with Snead Farm Road. Turn left here, joining a blue-blazed gravel track. Ahead, reach two road forks, each signed with the hallmark concrete trail post at all Shenandoah National Park Trail intersections. On the first fork take the road to the left—the road right leads to an FAA flight-tracking station. On the second fork take the road to the right—the left fork goes to the modern-day water plant that serves the Dickey Ridge Picnic Area and Visitor Center.

2.4 Reach a clearing. To your right is large, white Snead Barn. At the head of the clearing stands the concrete and stone foundation of a house. Look for exotic bushes still growing around the homesite. At the clearing's edge turn left, still on the Snead Farm Loop. The trail runs level before stair stepping in rocky hardwoods.

3.2 Come to the Dickey Ridge Trail. Turn right, climbing on a narrow path.

3.5 Reach a high point. A short user-created trail leads right to the FAA tower site. Stay left on the official trail, then open onto an excellent view of the Shenandoah Valley. Find the South Fork Shenandoah River below. Massanutten Mountain forms a backdrop. Make an extended downgrade.

4.3 Reach Snead Farm Road and the Dickey Ridge Trail. Turn left here on the gravel roadbed.

4.4 Cross Skyline Drive and stay with a dirt path that shortly enters the Dickey Ridge Picnic Area. Pick up an asphalt path that cuts through the heart of the picnic area, passing many tables, water fountains, and a comfort station.

4.7 Reach the north end of the picnic area, completing the hike. A narrow band of trees divides the picnic area from the visitor center parking area.

Lemuel Fox Reminisces

The last resident of the Fox Hollow farm, Lemuel Fox Jr., was interviewed by the Park Service in 1976 and thought back on his days at his home, before it was bought out by the state of Virginia. "About the best thing I like to do, I like to plow corn, up here on the hillside. We used to climb hills, plow it both ways, you know. Plow across it, keep the weeds out. Lord a 'mercy, I wish . . . I wish I could crawl back that young." Today, Lemuel Fox Jr. is gone, but vestiges of his farm remain, protected within the confines of Shenandoah National Park.

20 Thornton River Loop

Take a quiet hike through history combined with high-country trekking. Leave Skyline Drive to walk the once settled Thornton Hollow. Here, relics of settlers are scattered throughout the landscape. Wander richly forested flats between crossings of the Thornton River. The Hull School Trail leaves the lowlands and takes you through formerly settled slopes. Cross Skyline Drive, surmounting a peak, then join the Appalachian Trail back to the trailhead.

Start: Thornton River parking area at milepost 25.4 of Skyline Drive
Distance: 7.9-mile loop
Hiking time: About 2.5–4 hours
Difficulty: More difficult due to elevation change
Trail surface: Natural
Best season: When the leaves are off the trees
Other trail users: None

Canine compatibility: Pets not permitted
Land status: National park
Fees and permits: Entrance fee required
Schedule: 24/7/365
Maps: Shenandoah National Park; USGS Thornton Gap
Trail contact: Shenandoah National Park, 3655 Highway 211 E., Luray, VA 22835; (540) 999-3500; www.nps.gov/shen

Finding the trailhead: The Thornton River Trail parking area is on the east side of Skyline Drive at milepost 25.4. The Thornton River Trail starts on the left side of the parking area. From the Front Royal entrance to Shenandoah National Park, head south on Skyline Drive for 25.4 miles to the trailhead. Trailhead GPS: N38 43.439'/W78 19.198'

The Hike

I love this hike in all seasons, though winter can be a bit challenging when you factor in stream crossings on the North Fork Thornton River. Spring features wildflowers aplenty and the leafless woods make old homesites easier to find. Summer can be a good escape from the heat of the lowlands below. A few pools are deep enough for a dip. In fall low water levels make stream crossings a breeze. Late fall, when the leaves are off, will also allow easier sighting of pioneer homesites and such. Be apprised the circuit can be challenging. It has a 1,500-foot elevation gain, from the lower Thornton River to the top of the Blue Ridge. If you just walk down the Thornton River Trail to Hull School site, it is a 5.8-mile there-and-back hike with only a 1,000-foot elevation climb back to the trailhead.

▶ The Thornton River community held dances in the Hull School on occasional weekends.

Leaving Skyline Drive, follow an old pioneer road. It does not take long before you see the first rock pile, made by farmers clearing stony fields. Amazingly, one-third of Shenandoah National Park was once cleared land, parts of farms where crops were grown and animals raised. Today, nearly the entire park is wooded. The Thornton

Rock hopping the Thornton River

River Trail winds among gentle slopes. It is plausible to visualize the upper Thornton River valley as grazing land and even corn-growing land.

Ahead you will see a telltale stone pile, indicating cropland. Usually lined up as fencerows, this rock edifice is different as it is squared-off. Think of the labor entailed in building the mound, even using draft animals. The hike heads deeper into the North Fork Thornton River valley and comes near the remains of an old jalopy. The rusted car probably broke down, and whoever owned it left the rusted and stripped flivver for the national park to deal with. The park service apparently decided to leave it too. Now it is an artifact we history-seeking hikers find interesting.

Begin paralleling the North Fork Thornton River, crossing it under a mantle of sycamores, white pines, and tulip trees. Beware of stinging nettle crowding the trail in summer. Flats widen beyond the stream. Continue down Thornton Hollow. The watercourse is falling in chutes divided by pools. The North Fork Thornton River, like most Shenandoah streams, exhibits highly variable water flow. The river will split

Hull School

The old Hull School served families along the Thornton River as well as the adjacent valleys and ridges. Although you see no evidence of the school today, it was once located near the intersection of the Hull School and Thornton River Trails. Former student Bessie Woodward tells of this small, white wooden structure best: "It was a small building, but it was right lively. We had all grades, from the ABCs to American history, and anywhere from twelve to twenty students. We each had a speller, a dictionary, a reader, and geography and arithmetic books. There was no fussin' or fightin' or carryin' on at school in those days. If you didn't behave, the teacher would punish you by making you stand on one foot on a stick of wood, or you had to stand in the corner. Then the kids would tease you about that at recess. And your parents' motto was, 'If you are not going to learn, you might as well stay at home and work.'"

into braids when high but deplete to a trickle by late fall. Generally, crossings are easy, except following heavy storms. Be apprised the North Fork Thornton River is one of Shenandoah's better trout-fishing venues.

Look around for more imprints of man, visible on both sides of the river. You may see grown-over roads, directional rock walls, and rust-covered artifacts. Remember, these are cultural resources of Shenandoah. Admire them, but leave them for others to discover.

Come to the Hull School site at the intersection with the Hull School Trail. The Hull School once stood just to your right, facing downriver. After making a final crossing of the North Fork Thornton River, you will roughly follow another settler road all the way up to the Blue Ridge. Where deeply eroded or mucky, the Hull School Trail leaves the original path. Near springs, look for evidence of settlement, especially where the land is relatively flat.

The Hull School Trail ends at Skyline Drive and alternate parking. This hike crosses Skyline Drive then heads up to a knob and Byrds Nest #4. A gated fire road ends at a clearing and Byrds Nest shelter #4. This trail shelter is for day use only and was built early in the park's existence. The three-sided, open-fronted stone shelter does have a fireplace. This is one among four stone shelters given to the park by Virginia senator and big Shenandoah National Park proponent Harry F. Byrd.

Catch your breath while admiring the shelter. A narrow foot trail leads under pine and oaks and beside mountain laurel. After meeting the Appalachian Trail, the walking is easy, with only gentle hills to surmount. Before you know it, the upper end of

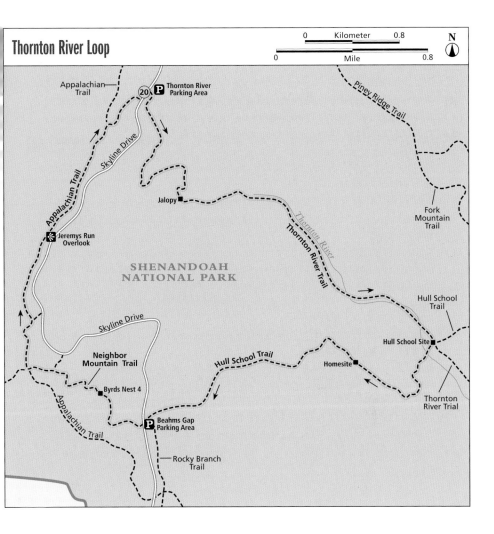

Thornton River Loop

Thornton River Trail is at hand. The hike ends at Skyline Drive just a little south of the Thornton River parking area.

Miles and Directions

0.0 Start the hike on the Thornton River Trail. Descend through rocky woods dominated by oak and pine. The wide trail is an old settler road highlighted with blue blazes. Quickly step over a spring branch flowing off the Blue Ridge.

0.4 The Thornton River Trail curves back north at 0.4 mile. Continue descending in the shade of tulip trees and oaks.

0.9 Pass near an edifice-like rock pile, site of a field partially cleared for crops.

1.0 Step over a tributary of the North Fork Thornton River. Rock walls line the settler road–turned–hiking trail.

1.4 Rock-hop the upper North Fork Thornton River. Enjoy Appalachian Mountains finery everywhere you look.

2.3 Step over a stony tributary coming in on your right just before crossing the North Fork Thornton River.

2.5 Step over the outflow of a homesite spring just before crossing the river again. You are now on the right-hand bank. The valley widens.

2.8 Cross the river again. Walk through all-but-disappeared fields.

2.9 Meet the Hull School Trail. This is the site of Hull School, though no artifacts remain. Turn right here on the Hull School Trail, shortly crossing a wide and braided North Fork Thornton River on a settler trail.

3.6 A spring flows over the trail. Look right for a homesite.

4.6 The trail tops out. Continue following an old road lined with big trees that shaded pre-park passersby.

5.1 Come to Skyline Drive and the Beahms Gap parking area. Keep straight, joining the Neighbor Mountain Trail on a doubletrack road separated from Skyline Drive by a chain gate. The Rocky Branch Trail leaves from the Beahms Gap parking area.

5.5 Top out at Byrds Nest #4. Continue the Neighbor Mountain Trail as a singletrack path weaving among mountain laurel.

6.0 A spur trail leads right to Neighbor Mountain parking area on Skyline Drive. Keep straight on the Neighbor Mountain Trail.

6.1 Turn right on the Appalachian Trail, northbound. Note how much more used the Appalachian Trail is than the Neighbor Mountain Trail. Shortly pass another spur right to Skyline Drive.

6.9 Pass just below Jeremys Run Overlook and Skyline Drive. Keep northbound on the AT.

7.6 Meet the upper Thornton River Trail. Turn right here and make a switchback, descending.

7.9 Reach Skyline Drive and the hike's end. The Thornton River parking area is to your left.

21 Corbin Cabin Loop

This hike heads into one of Shenandoah National Park's most heavily settled hollows to an authentic pioneer cabin—and you can even stay in it, with advance reservations. Back in pre-park days, Nicholson Hollow had a reputation, deserved or not, as a lawless place. You will drop steeply from Skyline Drive, then visit the George Corbin Cabin. Some say it is haunted. Your escape route takes you up the Hughes River to the Blue Ridge and the Appalachian Trail. A walk through a rocky mountain-laurel-laden ridge leads you back to the trailhead.

Start: Corbin Cabin parking area at milepost 37.9 of Skyline Drive
Distance: 4.0-mile loop
Hiking time: About 2.5–4 hours
Difficulty: Moderate, but does have 1,100-foot elevation change
Trail surface: Natural
Best season: Year-round
Other trail users: None

Canine compatibility: Leashed pets only
Land status: National park
Fees and permits: Entrance fee required
Schedule: 24/7/365
Maps: Shenandoah National Park; USGS Old Rag Mountain
Trail contact: Shenandoah National Park, 3655 Highway 211 E., Luray, VA 22835; (540) 999-3500; www.nps.gov/shen

Finding the trailhead: The Corbin Cabin Cutoff Trail is located on the east side of Skyline Drive in Shenandoah National Park at milepost 37.9. The parking area is on the west side of the scenic road and has seven spaces. The trailhead is on a hilly curve and is easily missed. Trailhead GPS: N38 36.938′ / W78 21.030′

The Hike

The Hughes River flows east off the slopes of Stony Man Mountain, cutting a deep valley known as Nicholson Hollow. This hike takes you into its upper reaches. The valley is set between two of the most noteworthy peaks in what was to become Shenandoah National Park: Stony Man and Old Rag. In the 1890s George Pollack's Skyland Lodge, standing on the shoulder of Stony Man Mountain, was drawing in mountain lovers, nature seekers, and hikers. Indefatigable Pollack blazed trails from Skyland to the geological wonderment of Old Rag Mountain. Today, Old Rag is one of the busiest hikes in Shenandoah National Park, and it is Virginia's contribution to the great mountains of America. The granite-topped peak is the park's most recognizable summit, famed for a boulder scramble and vista after vista from the rock outcrops along its shoulders.

Literally against that backdrop, back in the early 1900s, there were the families of Nicholson Hollow, pinched between Stony Man Mountain and Old Rag

▶ Approximately twenty families lived in Nicholson Hollow at the time of Shenandoah National Park's establishment in the 1930s.

Hikers gather in front of the Corbin Cabin.

Mountain, both of which brought in "outsiders," including journalists writing stories about the possibility of this new Shenandoah National Park. The families of Nicholson Hollow, minding their business for the previous 150 years, were suddenly tossed into the national limelight. And when a reporter cannot find something dramatic to report, they sometimes make it up.

The people of Nicholson Hollow were cast as mountain caricatures—lawless, shiftless, hardscrabble ne'er-do-wells. Mostly they were ordinary mountain folk, same as in the next hollow up or down the mountain chain. Fact is, in the 1930s, times were changing throughout the Potomac Highlands. Game was being hunted out, the soil was becoming depleted, and Prohibition was in effect. Some of these "tourists" that climbed Old Rag and Stony Man Mountains just might be a revenuer out to catch a man turning corn into moonshine.

Shenandoah National Park did come to be, and all the families of Nicholson Hollow were bought out. Their cabins were dismantled and possessions hauled off to where the residents would start a new life.

Except for the cabin of George Corbin. It sits right where he built it, in a flat above the Hughes River, just below the confluence with Indian Run. The cabin will lend insight into the lifeways of the people of Nicholson Hollow. The hike to the

Corbin Cabin uses a steep path created and tramped by the people of Nicholson Hollow. And here's the kicker: Corbin Cabin is available for overnight rental by the public. Even if you don't spend the night, the cabin is worth a visit and the circuit hike is rewarding, as you not only enjoy Hughes River but also gain views of Stony Man Mountain on your way out. Finally, the hike closes the loop with a trip on the Appalachian Trail (AT). *Note:* Before you start the hike, take the short, grassy connector path at the back of the Corbin Cabin parking area linking it to the AT to remember the intersection.

In 1910, when George Corbin erected his two story wood-and-chinking homestead on the banks of the upper Hughes River, deep in Virginia's Potomac Highlands, he never imagined his home would be an attraction within a national park and placed on the National Register of Historic Places. Even after Corbin and the residents of Nicholson Hollow saw the inevitability of Shenandoah National Park, Corbin believed he could live in his cabin still. But it was not to be. Corbin lived in his dwelling until 1938 when he was bought out by Shenandoah National Park and moved outside the newly established boundaries.

A legend persists that the cabin is haunted. George's wife, Nee, died there during childbirth in the winter of 1924. If you are willing to overnight it in the Corbin Cabin, obtain more cabin-rental information at patc.net.

The Corbin Cabin Cutoff Trail

The Corbin Cabin Cutoff Trail was not created by Shenandoah National Park personnel but was simply beaten down by residents living along the Hughes River in Nicholson Hollow. One such trail user was Virgil Corbin, George Corbin's son.

In the 1930s Virgil would walk up the path, then go to work, bringing water to the men working on the Blue Ridge Parkway. After distributing water all day, George would walk back down to his dad's residence and the objective of this hike.

The Corbin Cabin Cutoff Trail is steep and straight up and down. Mountain folk don't play around when it comes to climbing hills. The national park generally builds trails with a lesser gradient and takes into account factors such as minimizing erosion, stabilizing the trail bed, avoiding sensitive locations for flora and fauna, and routing toward scenic locales. In order to keep the Corbin Cabin Cutoff Trail intact, park personnel have added water bars to divert water during storms, cleared trees from the trail, and strategically placed rocks to keep the trail from washing away. Thus, the Corbin Cabin Cutoff Trail continues to be.

Corbin Cabin Loop

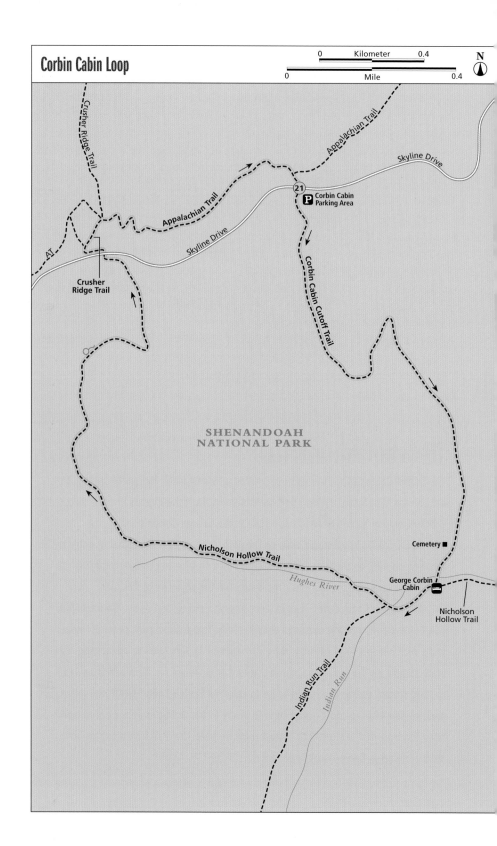

0   Kilometer   0.4

0   Mile   0.4

N

Crusher Ridge Trail

Appalachian Trail

Skyline Drive

Appalachian Trail

21   Corbin Cabin Parking Area

Skyline Drive

AT

Crusher Ridge Trail

Corbin Cabin Cutoff Trail

SHENANDOAH NATIONAL PARK

Cemetery

Nicholson Hollow Trail

Hughes River

George Corbin Cabin

Nicholson Hollow Trail

Indian Run Trail

Indian Run

Miles and Directions

0.0 Join the Corbin Cabin Cutoff Trail, descending the east side of Skyline Drive through birch, striped maple, and oak. Turn onto a narrow ridge of mountain laurel with young chestnut trees.

0.4 The path steepens.

0.5 The trail turns off the ridge and into a hollow.

0.7 Reach the head of the hollow cut by a trickling branch. Turn down the hollow. Look for rock piles scattered in the hollow, signs of former fields.

1.1 Look for a chimney through the woods to your left.

1.2 Come alongside a conspicuous rock wall. Step over a spring branch. Look right for a narrow path leading uphill to an old pioneer cemetery.

1.3 The Hughes River becomes audible. Look to your right in a flat before the stream. There you will find the remains of a forgotten structure. Its floor and roof are still intact but most of the walls have collapsed.

1.4 Rock-hop the Hughes River. To your left the Nicholson Hollow Trail has come up 4 miles from the community of Nethers. That 4-mile stretch is where most of the Nicholson Hollow residents lived. The Corbin Cabin stands in front of you. A small clearing is kept open around the cabin to reduce the possibility of forest fires burning it down. If no one is renting the building for the night, it will be shut, but you still can come up and take a seat on the porch, admiring the view. From here, head uphill on the Nicholson Hollow Trail, toward Skyline Drive.

1.5 Rock-hop Indian Run, a tributary of the Hughes River that is more rock than water. Just ahead, the Indian Run Trail leads left up to Corbin Mountain Trail. Begin circling a wide, gently sloping hollow that was surely cleared land in Corbin's day.

1.6 Step over the uppermost Hughes River.

2.1 Turn away from the Hughes River. The trail steepens.

2.7 Pass a boxed-in spring just to the left of the trail. Join a ridgeline offering views of Stony Man Mountain to the south.

3.2 Come to Skyline Drive. From here, turn and walk along Skyline Drive for 60 yards, then cross the road. Walk the last bit of the Nicholson Hollow Trail.

3.3 Meet the Crusher Ridge Trail. Turn right here and follow it uphill.

3.4 Come to the Appalachian Trail. This is the high point of the hike. Turn right here (northbound), descending by switchbacks.

3.6 Dip to a gap. The trailside vegetation becomes rocky, dry, and piney, with copious growth of mountain laurel.

4.0 Reach the trailhead after coming to a low point and trail intersection on the AT just a few yards from the Corbin Cabin parking area.

22 Skyland

This hike traverses lofty and historic terrain within Shenandoah National Park. Visit the area of Skyland Resort, where George Pollack ran his highland lodge while advocating for the establishment of Virginia's most popular national park. A trip to the vistas of Stony Man will show you why this land was protected, especially from Stony Man Mountain, where cliffs rise 3,000 feet above the Shenandoah Valley. More views await from Little Stony Man. Return via the Passamaquoddy Trail and reach Furnace Spring, once used in a copper-mining operation.

Start: Stony Man Nature Trail just off milepost 41.7 of Skyline Drive
Distance: 3.4-mile loop
Hiking time: About 2-3 hours
Difficulty: Moderate
Trail surface: Pea gravel, natural
Best season: When the skies are clearest
Other trail users: None
Canine compatibility: Pets not permitted

Land status: National park
Fees and permits: Entrance fee required
Schedule: 24/7/365
Maps: Shenandoah National Park; USGS Big Meadows, Old Rag Mountain
Trail contact: Shenandoah National Park, 3655 Highway 211 E., Luray, VA 22835; (540) 999-3500; www.nps.gov/shen

Finding the trailhead: This hike starts near the north entrance to Skyland Resort off Skyline Drive in Shenandoah National Park. At the turn you will see a sign indicating this is the highest point on Skyline Drive. This turn is at milepost 41.7 of Skyline Drive. Immediately after turning toward the Skyland Resort, turn right into the parking lot for the Stony Man Nature Trail. Trailhead GPS: N38 35.583' / W78 22.543'

The Hike

Stony Man Mountain is home to historic Skyland Resort, situated on the rooftop of Shenandoah National Park. Stony Man—at 4,011 feet, the park's second-highest point—looks like the face of a bearded man as seen from the north on milepost 38.9 of Skyline Drive at Stony Man Mountain Overlook.

On this hike you can peer from the open outcrops of Stony Man Mountain and see Skyland Resort, in business for over 120 years. Its initial proprietor, George Freeman Pollack, is the man most often credited with the formation of Shenandoah National Park.

Beyond the overlook atop Stony Man, you will drop back to the Appalachian Trail (AT), dipping through woods to emerge at a lower, yet no less impressive, open rock face—Little Stony Man.

These jagged cliffs have an especially rugged appearance as they emerge from the surrounding forest. The squared-off fields of Shenandoah Valley below contrast with the craggy mountains to your right. Hikers atop Stony Man above you resemble toy figurines on the cliffs.

Shenandoah and George Freeman Pollack

Stony Man Mountain, where this hike takes place, is the linchpin of George Freeman Pollack's 5,300 acres and where he developed Skyland Resort back in the 1890s. Then, as today, lodge guests have several opportunities to walk to outcrops such as the overlook at Stony Man and enjoy far-reaching westerly vistas extending from the base of Shenandoah Valley to the ridge dividing West Virginia from Virginia and points between.

George Pollack's involvement at Stony Man encompasses not only Skyland Lodge but also the very establishment of Shenandoah National Park and the park facilities that followed. The very first Civilian Conservation Corps (CCC) work camp in any national park was situated at Skyland. Pollack had pledged his 5,300 acres to the park should it come to be. The government answered by choosing Skyland to develop these initial national park facilities. In 1933, as Shenandoah National Park was coming to be, only the corridor of Skyline Drive had been authorized by the US Congress, so park work at that point was limited only to a strip adjacent to Skyline Drive. Later, when Shenandoah National Park was established in 1935, CCC camps and their projects spread throughout the park.

Back to George Pollack and Skyland. Mr. Pollack was a relentless promoter of his Skyland Lodge. He applied his enthusiasm for the area to the formation of Shenandoah National Park. But the story goes back further still. Back in the 1800s Pollack's father purchased the Stony Man property as part of a mining claim. Copper was being extracted from the slopes of Stony Man. Attempts were made to obtain copper on a small-time basis even before the American Revolution, but in the 1850s Miner's Lode Copper Company dug a shaft into the side of Stony Man. Copper ore was smelted down. Mules hauled the metal down the mountain via a rough trail. The mine never was profitable . . .

But young George saw more than a mine here. He saw Stony Man as a natural getaway, a highland retreat, an escape from the stifling lowland summers. So in 1894 he opened Stony Man Camp. The first guests stayed in tents. Yet the popularity of the getaway grew and Pollack expanded. He built some cabins and renamed the resort Skyland. Later, Pollack sold cabin lots and even built dining and recreation halls on the property. Every morning the tireless Pollack awoke his guests with a bugle call. He led hikes during the day, including treks on the Passamaquoddy Trail, which he built. He entertained guests in the evening and also hired area musicians.

Visitors returned year after year. Skyland grew, employing local mountaineers. He befriended his highland neighbors and even became a philanthropist of sorts. Of course, his great "good works" included helping Shenandoah National Park become a reality. Today, we can hike Pollack's trails located within Virginia's most popular natural destination, which may not have come to be without the efforts of this man.

Open crags of Stony Man Mountain present dramatic views of the adjacent terrain.

You will then join the Passamaquoddy Trail, which skirts the steep western slopes of Stony Man. This long word is Algonquin for the oceangoing fish *pollock,* also spelled *pollack.* It was George Freeman Pollack's way of naming the trail for himself. The Passamaquoddy Trail wanders under the cliffs of Little Stony Man on a stone path. Open onto a lower outcrop hat presents the Shenandoah Valley and Lake Arrowhead below. The rising slope of Stony Man Mountain shows its might.

▶ **George Freeman Pollack's ashes were cast from Bushy Head, located on the shoulder of Stony Man Mountain, in 1951.**

Walk beneath cliffs. The slope was once cloaked with hemlocks, but they have fallen prey to the hemlock woolly adelgid, a nonnative insect. Fire cherry trees are rising in their place.

Ahead you will come to Furnace Spring, now enclosed in a locked building. The copper mine purchased by Pollack's father was hereabouts. However, the shaft has long been filled and the area restored to a natural state. From Furnace Spring, climb into northern hardwoods and a few preserved hemlocks, returning to the trailhead.

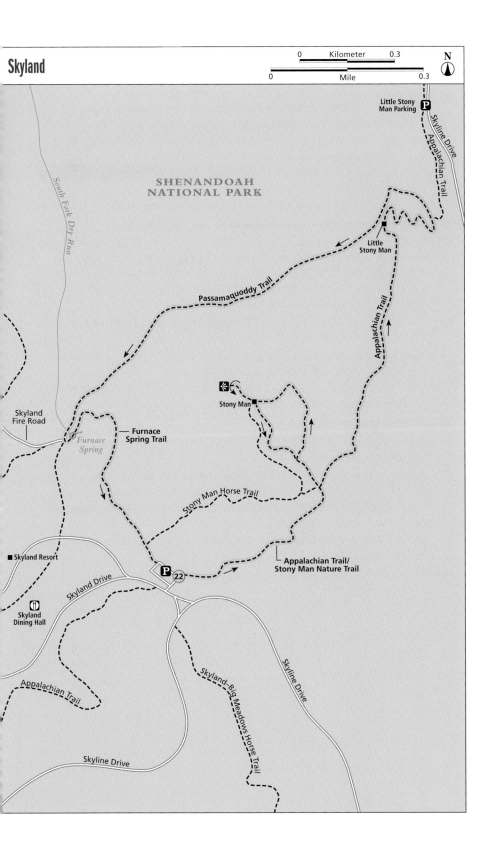

Skyland

0 Kilometer 0.3
0 Mile 0.3

N

Little Stony Man Parking P

Skyline Drive

Appalachian Trail

SHENANDOAH NATIONAL PARK

Little Stony Man

South Fork Dry Run

Passamaquoddy Trail

Appalachian Trail

Skyland Fire Road

Furnace Spring

Furnace Spring Trail

Stony Man

Stony Man Horse Trail

Skyland Resort

Skyland Drive

P 22

Appalachian Trail/ Stony Man Nature Trail

Skyland Dining Hall

Appalachian Trail

Skyland–Big Meadows Horse Trail

Skyline Drive

Skyline Drive

Miles and Directions

0.0   Start on the Stony Man Nature Trail located in the southeast corner of the parking area. This is also the Appalachian Trail, heading northbound. The two trails run in conjunction at this point. An interpretive booklet can be purchased at the trailhead. Walk a highland gravel path. Ferns carpet the woodland floor while wind-stunted hardwoods provide shade.

0.4   Reach a four-way trail intersection and the highest point on the AT in Shenandoah National Park—3,837 feet. Turn left, still ascending, heading for the top of Stony Man, staying with the nature trail. You will return to this intersection.

0.5   Stay right at an intersection and begin the interior loop atop Stony Man.

0.7   Come to a four-way intersection. Turn right for the view from Stony Man.

0.8   Soak in the westerly vista from Stony Man. Fantastic views reveal Skyland Resort, Shenandoah Valley, the town of Luray, and Massanutten Mountain running parallel to the Blue Ridge. Beyond that, North Mountain stretches as long as the Virginia–West Virginia state line. To your right, northerly, look below at the upthrust cliffs of Little Stony Man. You will be there shortly. Backtrack to the intersection with the AT.

1.1   Meet the AT again. Turn left, northbound. Drop steadily through northern hardwoods on the east slope of the Blue Ridge.

1.7   Reach the auburn cliffs of Little Stony Man. Extensive panoramas open before you. Continue northbound on the AT.

1.9   Reach a trail intersection. Leave the Appalachian Trail and head left on the Passamaquoddy Trail, built by none other than George Pollack.

2.4   Come to a rock overhang and dripping spring.

2.5   Reach the low point of the hike. You are still above 3,200 feet.

2.8   Pass under a transmission line.

2.9   Come to Furnace Spring. Water is audibly flowing behind a locked door of the springhouse. Meet the Skyland Fire Road and the Furnace Spring Trail. Make a hard left here, joining the yellow-blazed Furnace Spring Trail. Walk directly above Furnace Spring on a doubletrack, then turn into woods.

3.4   Meet the Stony Man Horse Trail and turn left, tracing it a short distance to reach the parking area and hike's end.

23 Rose River Loop

This circuit hike traces an old transmountain turnpike linking Shenandoah Valley on the west side of the Blue Ridge with Gordonsville on the east side. It first passes the Cave Cemetery, where residents who lived in this area, known as Dark Hollow, are interred. Take a side trip to Dark Hollow Falls, then descend gorgeous Hogcamp Branch to an old copper mine, with relics still visible. The hike then climbs past scenic Rose River Falls, offering more natural beauty.

Start: Parking area in Fisher Gap on Skyline Drive
Distance: 4.0-mile loop
Hiking time: About 2.5–3.5 hours
Difficulty: Moderate, but does have 900-foot elevation change
Trail surface: Gravel, natural
Best season: Spring for waterfalls and wildflowers
Other trail users: Horses on part of the route

Canine compatibility: Leashed pets only
Land status: National park
Fees and permits: Entrance fee required
Schedule: 24/7/365
Maps: *Shenandoah National Park; USGS Big Meadows*
Trail contact: Shenandoah National Park, 3655 Highway 211 E., Luray, VA 22835; (540) 999-3500; www.nps.gov/shen

Finding the trailhead: The Rose River Fire Road starts on the east side of Skyline Drive, just north of Fisher Gap Overlook, milepost 49.4, in Shenandoah National Park. The parking area is on the west side of the drive. The overlook is on a short spur loop that leaves Skyline Drive. The Rose River Fire Road starts across Skyline Drive from the overlook's north end. From the Swift Run Gap entrance to Shenandoah National Park, it is 16.1 miles to Fisher Gap Overlook. Trailhead GPS: N38 32.006' / W78 25.259'

The Hike

Getting through the Appalachian Mountains of Virginia has never been easy. The hills, the hollows, the boulders, the forests, and the general orneriness of the terrain historically made transportation difficult for those living in the shadow of the Blue Ridge. As part of the answer to this vexing problem, the Gordonsville Turnpike was built in the 1800s. It crossed the Blue Ridge in what became Shenandoah National Park at Fisher Gap. This hike follows the Gordonsville Turnpike, now known as Rose River Fire Road, for a way down to Hogcamp Branch. Built with muscle power along with horses, mules, and some blasting powder, the Gordonsville Turnpike needed a toll collector. Along came a fellow whose last name was Cave. Mr. Cave and his descendants settled all along the turnpike and even have their own cemetery, which you will pass just a short way into this hike.

Dark Hollow Falls

After Gordonsville Turnpike became established, farmers in the Shenandoah Valley used it to bring corn and apples and drive cattle and other livestock to the eastern markets. A railroad line could be accessed at Gordonsville. During the Civil War, armies from both sides traversed the road. Though it ceased to be a toll operation, the Gordonsville Turnpike stayed in use until the park's establishment. Today, the road is used by hikers, equestrians, and park personnel.

A little farther down you will follow the Rose River Fire Road / Gordonsville Turnpike into a place known as Dark Hollow. Mountain families were settled all along here as well. Upon reaching Hogcamp Branch, you are near the Dark Hollow Church site. Founded in 1920, the church operated less than two decades before closing down due to Shenandoah National Park's establishment. It is easy to see why this spot was chosen for a church. Hogcamp Branch is one of the most beautiful streams in the Old Dominion, a near religious experience. You will see evidence of that on the spur hike to Dark Hollow Falls. Hogcamp Branch puts on a scenic display while stair-stepping down to meet the Rose River, falling and crashing in every type of slide, cataract, and cascade, one spiller after another, to gather in occasional deep pools, then falling yet again. Hogcamp Branch is but one visual reason why Shenandoah National Park came to be.

▶ The bell in the Dark Hollow Church was purchased and presented by President Herbert Hoover, who had a fishing camp and retreat a few miles distant.

It is near the confluence of Hogcamp Branch and the Rose River where you can find evidence of a copper mine. Men were digging here for copper as early as the mid-1800s. However, operations grew larger when the Blue Ridge Copper Company dug its first shaft in 1902. They established several buildings—a regular mine camp—to extract the rich copper ore. Though the ore was rich, the veins were narrow and difficult to access, eventually shutting the mine. You can still see a tailings pile and a concrete base where the air compressor for the miner's pneumatic drills was placed. The shafts have all been filled.

The final point of interest on this hike is all-natural: Rose River Falls. You will follow the Rose River upstream to view the aquatic ribbons spilling over a rock face. Beyond this two-tier cataract, the trail travels along the Rose River before turning away and ascending the Blue Ridge.

Leaving the Park

Many settlers in the rocky hollows and steep hills of what became Shenandoah National Park were happy to sell their land to the government and get out. However, many others were not. Generally, these mountain people were suspicious of government in general and wanted the "Feds" out of their lives. And when it came time to leave, signing papers and official documents—brought to them by government officials—was tricky business. Some who did not want to leave stalled for time, avoiding all paperwork. Some even hired lawyers. In the late 1930s a few landowners were literally carried off their land, refusing to leave their family homesteads. The government did grant them the right to be interred at their family cemeteries. When you go by the Cave Cemetery on this hike, look at the burial dates. Many of the folks buried there were laid in the ground long after Shenandoah became a national park.

Rose River Loop

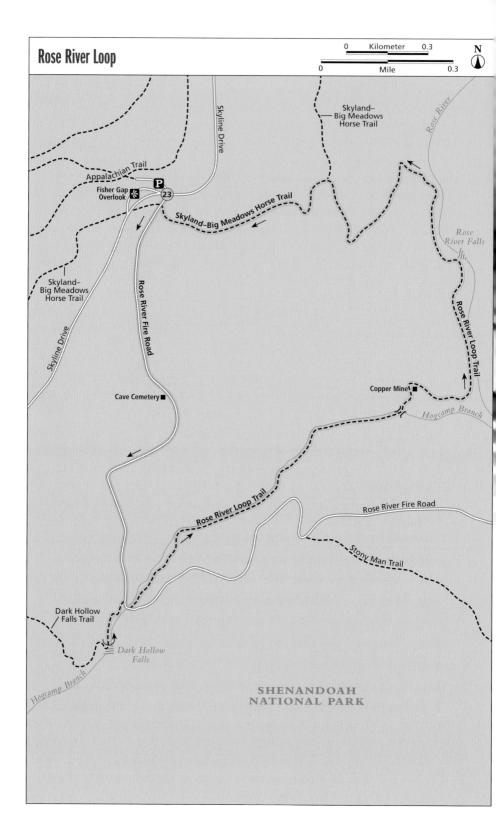

0   Kilometer   0.3

0   Mile   0.3

N

Skyland–
Big Meadows
Horse Trail

Rose River

Skyline Drive

Appalachian Trail

Fisher Gap
Overlook

P

23

Skyland–Big Meadows Horse Trail

Rose
River Falls

Skyland–
Big Meadows
Horse Trail

Skyline Drive

Rose River Fire Road

Rose River Loop Trail

Cave Cemetery ■

Copper Mine ■

Hogcamp Branch

Rose River Loop Trail

Rose River Fire Road

Stony Man Trail

Dark Hollow
Falls Trail

Dark Hollow
Falls

Hogcamp Branch

SHENANDOAH
NATIONAL PARK

Miles and Directions

0.0 Join the gated Rose River Fire Road on the east side of Skyline Drive. Hike a short distance down Rose River Fire Road to meet the Skyland–Big Meadows Horse Trail. Continue downhill on Rose River Fire Road, on a wide gravel track under maples and white oaks. This is the old Gordonsville Turnpike. The track levels out among locust trees, former farmland.

0.5 Pass the spur trail to the Cave Cemetery on your right, atop a grassy hill. Watch for gnarled apple trees hereabouts.

1.0 Meet the junction with the Dark Hollow Falls Trail at a bridge over Hogcamp Branch. Observe the 30-foot fall just above the bridge. Turn right here, heading up the Dark Hollow Falls Trail to Dark Hollow Falls.

1.2 Reach Dark Hollow Falls. It starts narrow, then makes a wide drop, falling in multiple tiers, a total of 70 feet. During the warm season, tourists will be gathered at the base of the falls. Most hikers have come the short distance from Skyline Drive via the Dark Hollow Falls Trail. Backtrack to Rose River Fire Road.

1.4 After returning to Rose River Fire Road, cross the bridge over Hogcamp Branch. Just beyond there, join the Rose River Loop Trail downhill along Hogcamp Branch.

2.1 Reach a bridge spanning Hogcamp Branch. The steel span arches well over and above Hogcamp Branch. Turn left here.

2.2 Rock-hop a small stream, then reach the copper mine site. A path leads to the top of the tailings, backed against a rock bluff. Notice the stone and iron works at the mine.

2.5 Come to a signpost near a large wooded flat. Turn left here and head upstream along the Rose River. It is also promenading national-park-level beauty. Ahead, the Rose River Loop Trail leaves the river, climbing sharply in a fern forest and around the rock bluff that forms Rose River Falls.

2.8 Reach Rose River Falls. Beside the trail the watercourse drops over a rock ledge about 25 feet, spreading out in ribbons before reaching a pool. Be sure to take the spur trail downstream to view the lower half of Rose River Falls. It drops as a narrow chute over another rock ledge and beyond the viewing spot. Be careful if you try to access the pool of the lower falls. Past the falls, continue up the perched Rose River Valley.

3.1 Come to concrete signpost. A now-closed trail once led right. Stay left here on a wide trail, leaving the Rose River. Gently climb into drier, oak-dominated woods.

3.6 Meet the Skyland–Big Meadows Horse Trail. Stay left here, as the horse trail and Rose River Loop run in conjunction. Continue climbing.

4.0 Meet the Rose River Fire Road. It is but a few steps to Skyline Drive and the hike's end.

24 Rapidan Camp

This hike takes you to the mountain camp established by President Herbert Hoover in 1929. Created as a presidential retreat, the collection of buildings at the confluence of Mill Prong and Laurel Prong has been preserved, and you can see the Brown House, where President and Mrs. Hoover stayed while here, as well as other buildings and sites where world leaders were hosted, world problems tackled, and a little trout fishin' was undertaken as well.

Start: Milam Gap on Skyline Drive
Distance: 7.2-mile loop
Hiking time: About 3.5-4.5 hours, plus 1 hour at Rapidan Camp
Difficulty: More difficult due to distance and elevation change
Trail surface: Natural
Best season: Summer for interpretive information
Other trail users: None

Canine compatibility: Leashed pets only
Land status: National park
Fees and permits: Entrance fee required
Schedule: 24/7/365
Maps: Shenandoah National Park; USGS Fletcher, Big Meadows
Trail contact: Shenandoah National Park, 3655 Highway 211 E., Luray, VA 22835; (540) 999-3500; www.nps.gov/shen

Finding the trailhead: The Milam Gap trailhead is located at milepost 52.8, on the west side of Skyline Drive in Shenandoah National Park. It can be reached by driving north on Skyline Drive for 12.7 miles from Swift Run Gap entrance. The Appalachian Trail (AT) is accessible behind the parking area. Start your hike here, southbound on the AT. Trailhead GPS: N38 30.013'/W78 26.738'

The Hike

This circuit hike first takes you over Hazeltop, the third-highest peak at Shenandoah National Park, then uses the Laurel Prong Trail to access Rapidan Camp, the highland getaway for President Herbert Hoover (1929–33). The camp has much to see; you can even embark on a self-guided interpretive tour. Return to the trailhead on the Mill Prong Trail and check out Big Rock Falls along the way.

This is best as a summertime destination. The hike will be shaded in rich forests. In addition, you will see historic Rapidan Camp at the time of year when it was most often used by President Hoover. This is also when volunteers stationed at Rapidan Camp can take you on guided tours of the buildings and grounds. If the mileage is a bit lengthy, you can simply take the Mill Prong Trail directly to Rapidan Camp for a 3.8-mile out-and-back hike.

If you think things are hot in Washington, DC, today, you should have been there when there was no air-conditioning. For over one hundred years, our nation's leaders tried to escape the swampy lands astride the Potomac. However, as the office of the

The Hoovers' cabin at Rapidan Camp

presidency grew more complex, fast-paced, and challenging, it became difficult for the leader of our country to simply "break off" for the sake of weather convenience.

Our thirty-first president, Herbert Hoover, came up with a plan: Find a place in the Appalachian Mountains within 100 miles of the Capitol and above 2,500 feet to stay cool and to keep the mosquitoes at bay. Oh, and there was that little matter of trout fishing. His getaway needed a trout stream nearby. Such a place was found in the upper Rapidan River Valley, at the confluence of Mill Prong and Laurel Prong. Hoover purchased 164 acres and the US Marines commenced building the camp and the access roads to it. The camp was initially named Five Tents for the five canvas structures initially built there. This was the original dwelling site for Herbert Hoover. Ultimately, cabins grew out of these five tents. You can still see the fireplace of one of them. The camp grew further still. Eventually, thirteen structures were built, and that is not including a smaller camp for Marines nearby to protect the president, and another camp 2 miles distant for his cabinet.

President Hoover loved his camp and loved trout fishing. It is said that he would jump out of the car upon arriving at Camp Rapidan and immediately commence trout fishing, still clad in coat and tie. Yet the getaway was more than a fishing retreat. The president conducted business here at all

▶ There were only five months between the time the Rapidan Camp site was chosen as a presidential retreat and the first time President Herbert Hoover used it.

hours of the day and night. He had a phone installed (he was the first president to have a phone installed in the Oval Office of the White House) at Camp Rapidan and conducted international as well as domestic business. He also hosted world leaders here. His detractors joked about him conducting business while tossing a fishing line or sitting in front of a campfire on a log.

Today, only three structures remain from the camp: the Creel, which today houses volunteers to conduct programs at Rapidan Camp. The Prime Minister's Cabin stands nearby. You can tour it during the warm season without a guide. This building offers loads of interpretive information about life at the camp. The Brown House, where President and Mrs. Hoover stayed, has been restored and furnished to its appearance as it was when they used it. Visitors can only get in with a guide. Check with the Shenandoah National Park website for dates on which the Brown House can be toured. It is well worth the time in your trip to see this treasure inside and out.

After Hoover's presidency ended, he donated the land for the establishment of Shenandoah National Park and worked toward making Rapidan Camp a permanent presidential retreat. Other presidents had different ideas. The last president to stay here was Jimmy Carter. Much of the camp was left to the Boy Scouts, who altered its appearance. Some of the outbuildings fell into disrepair, and in the early 1960s, ten of the original thirteen buildings were removed. However, the historical importance of Rapidan Camp has been recognized and today the site is well protected and chock full of interpretive information—well worth exploring. Please give yourself at least an hour down here.

Miles and Directions

0.0 Hike southbound on the Appalachian Trail from Milam Gap. Note the abundance of apples trees in this area. Immediately cross Skyline Drive and reach a trail junction. To your left is Mill Prong Trail, your return trail. Keep straight on the AT on a gentle uptick.

0.4 Make a sharp right turn. The AT is truly heading south toward Hazeltop. The trail grade rises slightly on a narrowing ridge. In places the AT is arrow-straight.

1.9 A spur leads right to a stone prominence and vista. Soak in an unobstructed panorama west of the South Fork Shenandoah River Valley and undulations of mountains in the yon.

2.0 Reach the crest of Hazeltop, third-highest summit in Shenandoah, at 3,812 feet. A gnarled oak stands next to a large embedded rock and is the actual peak. Note the small balsam fir to the left of the trail. It is a survivor of the forests thriving much farther north in New England. Its needles are flat, fragrant, and not sharp. Leave the summit and come to a left turn. To your right are two red spruce trees, another member of the Canadian forest.

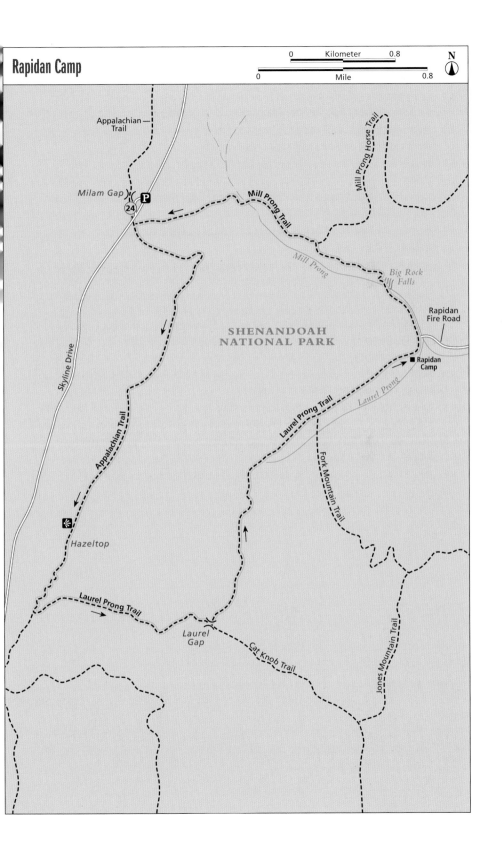

0   Kilometer   0.8

0   Mile   0.8

N

Appalachian Trail

Mill Prong Horse Trail

Milam Gap

P

24

Mill Prong Trail

Mill Prong

Big Rock Falls

Rapidan Fire Road

SHENANDOAH NATIONAL PARK

Rapidan Camp

Skyline Drive

Laurel Prong Trail

Laurel Prong

Appalachian Trail

Fork Mountain Trail

Hazeltop

Laurel Prong Trail

Laurel Gap

Cat Knob Trail

Jones Mountain Trail

Its needles are a darker green, rounded, and sharp, contrasting with the balsam fir. These trees grow only in a few locations in Shenandoah.

2.4   Come to a trail junction. Turn left on Laurel Prong Trail. Cross several springs flowing over the boulder-laden slope. The rocky path makes for slow going.

3.4   After descending sharply come to Laurel Gap and a trail intersection. Turn left, staying on the Laurel Prong Trail. The Cat Knob Trail goes straight.

3.9   Pass a spring after winding through "the Laurels," a thicket of mountain laurel. Keep descending.

4.1   Rock-hop Laurel Prong. Look for stone fences from settler farms from pre-Camp Rapidan and Shenandoah National Park times.

4.7   Intersect the Fork Mountain Trail. Keep straight on the Laurel Prong Trail, which has now widened to a fire road.

5.3   Arrive at Rapidan Camp. The camp lies in a lovely wooded setting. Walk around and check out the three buildings and interpretive information. There are short nature trails here too. Give it at least an hour. Imagine the president and his compadres strategizing on subjects of national import—and trout fishing too. Back then hemlocks shaded and cooled the flat. The evergreens were destroyed by the hemlock woolly adelgid, an exotic bug. Leave Rapidan Camp on the Mill Prong Trail, which starts near the Creel Cabin. Ascend along the steep-sided valley.

5.7   Rock-hop Mill Prong just below Big Rock Falls. The cascade slides 15 feet over a rock face into a large, deep pool. Continue an uptick.

6.1   Intersect the Mill Prong Horse Trail. Stay left, still on the Mill Prong Trail. Cross a tributary of Mill Prong.

6.6   Rock-hop a now wide, shallow, and stony Mill Prong once more. Ascend through ferny forest.

7.2   Reach the trailhead after intersecting the AT and turning right to cross Skyline Drive.

25 Pocosin Mission

This short ramble off Skyline Drive first takes you past a mountain cabin, then down to a gap and the remains of an Episcopalian mission. Here you can visit what remains of the mission's wooden living quarters and the stone church. It was from this highland pass where the folk of the mission branched out, working with the local mountaineers on eternal questions.

Start: Parking area near The Oaks Overlook on Skyline Drive
Distance: 2.0 miles out and back
Hiking time: About 1.5–2.5 hours
Difficulty: Easy
Trail surface: Natural
Best season: Year-round
Other trail users: None
Canine compatibility: Leashed pets only

Land status: National park
Fees and permits: Entrance fee required
Schedule: 24/7/365
Maps: *Shenandoah National Park; USGS Fletcher*
Trail contact: Shenandoah National Park, 3655 Highway 211 E., Luray, VA 22835; (540) 999-3500; www.nps.gov/shen

Finding the trailhead: From the intersection of US 33 and Skyline Drive at Swift Run Gap, drive north on Skyline Drive for 6 miles to milepost 59.5. Look on your right for a road and a sign that reads Do Not Block Fire Road. Turn onto this road and park in one of the gravel spots. The Pocosin Fire Road starts here. This parking area is 0.4 mile south of The Oaks Overlook and 1.6 miles north of Bald Face Mountain Overlook. Trailhead GPS: N38 24.795' / W78 29.312'

The Hike

This is a short and easy hike at Shenandoah National Park, doable by the whole family. Leave Skyline Drive on the wide and easy Pocosin Fire Road (closed to public vehicles) and explore the ruins of the Pocosin Mission, where a brave Episcopal minister attempted to save the souls of surrounding mountaineers. Explore the ruins of the mission and other nearby signs of habitation, including a cemetery. If you want to expand your hike, head down Pocosin Hollow, passing many old-growth trees on your way down to a tumbling watercourse, where you'll find a nice spot to picnic or relax. Alternatively, you can take a stroll on an adjacent parcel of the Appalachian Trail (AT) to enjoy a view from a rocky slope.

Chances are you are going to drive by the hard-to-find trailhead—most people do—but a simple turnaround at an overlook will have you back on track. The entrance to the parking area is narrow and it seems to sneak up on you.

In 1904 the mountains that became Shenandoah National Park were a backwater, a place civilization had passed by, left in the relentless pursuit of America's westward-looking manifest destiny. A young Episcopalian minister saw an opportunity among

A stone wall marks the old Pocosin Mission.

these hill folk to convert souls to Jesus. He set up shop in a highland gap just east of the Blue Ridge. He named the mission Upper Pocosin. The area was called the "Dark Pocosin" before his arrival. That oughta give you an idea of what this locale, bordered by Lewis Mountain to the north and Bald Face Mountain to the south, was like.

Now, if a survey had gone around among the people of Dark Pocosin, most would have said they were Christians, however, they weren't excited about having a preacher coming in. See, in those times, devout Christians were on the front lines of a temperance movement sweeping the country, and there were more than a few backwoodsmen making and/or drinking moonshine. The locals thought the missionary might look less than kindly on their actions, perhaps even turn them in to the law.

Some of the locals decided to scare the minister off. They made threats against his life, making sure their intentions made it to the minister's ears. The mission suffered a setback when carpenters hired to build the initial facility—a chapel that would double as a schoolhouse—were intimidated into quitting their jobs despite the scarcity of work in these Potomac Highlands.

> ▶ The Breeden family once had a cabin and small farm where the PATC Pocosin cabin now stands. Members of the Breeden family briefly stayed at Pocosin Mission after their farm was purchased by eminent domain.

However, instead of running off, the minister confronted one of the ringleaders. The minister came to the door of the mountain cabin and knocked. When the ringleader opened the door, the minister introduced himself and said, "I hear you want to kill me." The mountaineer couldn't help but admire such courage. Slowly the area residents were won over.

The minister began having Sunday sermons, and attendance grew. Later he added a barn and a smaller building where donated clothing was sold for cheap, a sort of thrift store that helped the locals purchase inexpensive clothing while the revenue helped run Pocosin Mission.

Later, a modest stone church was built. You can see the remains of it today. The mission did have an effect on the local people. Rowdiness, drinking, and fighting declined. Church attendance rose. They applied the lessons they learned. Upper Pocosin Mission became a community center of sorts, with area residents gathering for music, games, and ministry. Out-of-town volunteers would come and help at the mission, staying for a month or so at a time. The mission remained in operation until Shenandoah National Park came to be. As the reality of being evicted from their homes set in, mission workers introduced the locals to the outside world, taking them on trips to the city and mentally preparing them to leave their historic family lands.

Today, Upper Pocosin stands silent, crumbling a little more every season, covered more and more by the ceaseless growth around it. The same goes for the cabins, fields, and roads of the people who once were affected by the mission. Time waits for no one.

The hike to the mission site is an easy one. Once at the gap and trail intersection at Upper Pocosin, follow the footpath to the steps of the old church. View the walls made of native stone. The other nearby building is barely standing. I believe this is the mission workers' cabin. Parts of the structure were built with hand-hewn logs; boards, nails, and even tarpaper were later additions. At your feet there is much broken glass, parcels of clay pipe, and even crockery shards. Look around for the cemetery, where a few graves are marked with simple stones.

As you tour the area, imagine the work of these missionaries, spreading Christianity among locals who had rarely traveled more than a day's horseback ride from their places of birth.

If this hike seems too short, take a side trip down Pocosin Hollow. To get there, continue down the Pocosin Fire Road and veer left on the Pocosin Hollow Trail after a quarter mile. From this point forward, you should have the path to yourself.

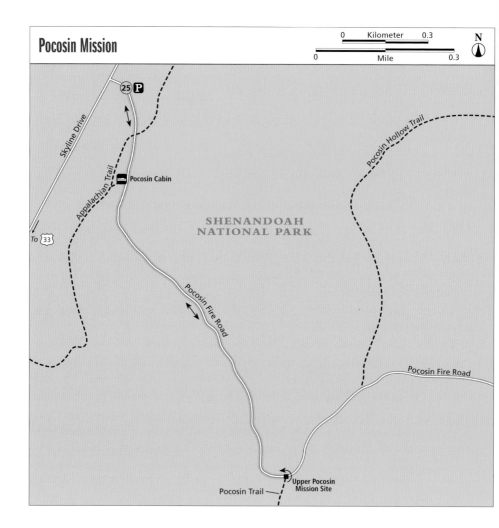

0   Kilometer   0.3

0   Mile   0.3

N

Skyline Drive

25 P

Pocosin Hollow Trail

Appalachian Trail

Pocosin Cabin

SHENANDOAH
NATIONAL PARK

To 33

Pocosin Fire Road

Pocosin Fire Road

Upper Pocosin
Mission Site

Pocosin Trail

Look for large old-growth trees scattered here and there along the path. The hike passes a boulder field before entering a wet-draw. This is a rich wildflower area in spring. Numerous old-growth yellow birch, oak, and tulip trees rise overhead. Come to the main watercourse of Pocosin Hollow, a tributary of the Conway River, 1.8 miles from the mission. A rock-hop will take you to the far side of the stream and a nice resting spot.

Another option is to take the AT from the intersection with Pocosin Fire Road southbound to a decent view. You will travel through rocky woods on a singletrack path. Pass a side trail to the Potomac Appalachian Trail Club cabin. Climb rocky steps, winding through boulders on a beautifully built trail leading to an outcrop with an easterly view. The view requires about a quarter-mile walk from the Pocosin Fire Road.

Miles and Directions

0.0 Leave the parking area on the Pocosin Fire Road, passing around a chain gate on a nearly level wide grade. A northern hardwood forest of red maple, sugar maple, basswood, and cherry rises overhead. Distinguishing between sugar maples and red maples is easy. Look at the leaf of a sugar maple. The curves between lobes of the sugar maple are U shaped, whereas the curves between lobes of the red maple are at right angles.

0.1 Intersect the AT. Keep straight on the Pocosin Fire Road.

0.2 Come to a clearing. This is the Pocosin Cabin, built in 1937 by the Civilian Conservation Corps, and the site of the Breeden cabin. The Potomac Appalachian Trail Club (PATC) rents this cabin out. However, you must be a member of the PATC to rent it. Soon pass a spring on the left. It is used by AT hikers and those staying at Pocosin Cabin.

1.0 Come to a trail junction. This spot is known as Upper Pocosin. To your right through the trees are the remains of the Pocosin Mission. Pocosin Fire Road continues to the left and links this area with the Pocosin Hollow Trail, while the Pocosin Trail leaves right. Backtrack after leaving the mission or expand your trek on one of the recommended additional trails.

2.0 Arrive back at the trailhead, completing the hike.

26 Browns Gap

This loop features both Virginia history and natural beauty. Start at Browns Gap, site of significant Civil War activity, especially by Confederate legend Stonewall Jackson. Head down a 200-year-old turnpike, passing a Rebel's grave. Leave the historic road and follow Doyles River past two significant waterfalls. Climb up Jones Run, viewing several old-growth trees, and see one more big cataract. Finally, complete the loop by passing by Dundo Picnic Area, once a Civilian Conservation Corps Camp, while Shenandoah National Park was being developed.

Start: Browns Gap on Skyline Drive
Distance: 6.9-mile loop
Hiking time: About 3.5-5 hours
Difficulty: Difficult due to elevation change of 1,250 feet
Trail surface: Natural
Best season: Year-round
Other trail users: None
Canine compatibility: Leashed pets only

Land status: National park
Fees and permits: Entrance fee required
Schedule: 24/7/365
Maps: Shenandoah National Park; USGS Browns Cove
Trail contact: Shenandoah National Park, 3655 Highway 211 E., Luray, VA 22835; (540) 999-3500; www.nps.gov/shen

Finding the trailhead: The hike starts at the Browns Gap parking area, milepost 83.0 on Skyline Drive in Shenandoah National Park. From the Rockfish Gap entrance station at the intersection with exit 99 on I-64, take Skyline Drive north for 21.6 miles to the trailhead, on your left. Trailhead GPS: N38 14.425' / W78 42.633'

The Hike

In addition to the history of Browns Gap, this loop hike visits three significant waterfalls and numerous other cascades while visiting two boulder-strewn canyons. The Appalachian Trail (AT) forms the final link to complete the circuit. Both Jones Run and Doyles River feature scattered old-growth hardwoods.

Browns Gap, where this hike begins, is significant as a mountain pass connecting the Shenandoah Valley to the west and the Piedmont to the east. Construction began on this turnpike in 1805. Two fellows, one from east of the Blue Ridge named Brightberry Brown and one from west of the Blue Ridge named William Jarman, began simultaneously working on this road. They met at the top of the Blue Ridge, here at Browns Gap. Legend has it that the two construction crews had a big brawl, each side bragging it had done a better job building the road.

Controversy continued. The folks west of the Blue Ridge called it Madison Run Turnpike, while east of the Blue Ridge it was called Browns Gap Turnpike. Even today, the park service gives this two-century-old road different names. Speaking of that, when the road was closed in the 1930s, residents of Grottoes and points

Upper Doyles Falls

west grumbled mightily as they had to take a more roundabout route to access Charlottesville.

The turnpike gained importance as a commercial connector and later had significance in the Civil War. In May of 1862 Stonewall Jackson passed through Browns Gap, then went on down to Charlottesville. But his forces' movements were a trick. Jackson loaded his men onto a railroad and headed back west across the Blue Ridge, defeating the Yankees near Staunton. Stonewall continued on his monthlong brilliant and well-studied Valley Campaign, where he defeated the North five times consecutively. Stonewall then returned to Browns Gap, resting his men for a week and building breastworks to cover the gap. Very little remains of the Confederate fortifications. Some Civil War scholars argue the breastworks were built in September of 1864 by Jubal Early, another Confederate leader.

The last part of the hike leads past Dundo Picnic Area. It was not always the grounds you see today, a mixture of trees and grass with scattered picnic tables, water spigots, and a restroom. Back in the mid-1930s, as Shenandoah National Park was being developed, the area was home to a Civilian Conservation Corps camp. Back then, the young men lived in hundred-foot-long barracks and dined at a large mess hall. Beside this, there were administration and office buildings, as well as a garage and clinic. Times sure have changed here at Browns Gap.

▶ Civilian Conservation Corps recruits, like those housed in what is now Dundo Picnic Area, were paid $30 per month, $25 of which went home to their families.

Miles and Directions

0.0 Leave the Browns Gap parking area and cross Skyline Drive. Immediately begin descending on the Browns Gap Fire Road. Madison Run Fire Road leaves west from the gap near the parking area.

0.4 Look for a small path leaving the road. Walk a few feet up this narrow path to the grave of William H. Howard, Confederate States of America soldier. The carved stone slab marks his

The Last Case

Via Gap stands just south of Jones Run. The level area, standing between Cedar Mountain and Blackrock Mountain, was home to several families, primarily the family that gave it the name Via. This clan had been settled in the area since the 1700s. One of the offspring, Robert H. Via, was reluctant to let go of his land when the state of Virginia began condemnation proceedings to acquire his land for Shenandoah National Park. The idea of taking private land for a public park struck Mr. Via wrong.

He took the state of Virginia to court. His argument in a nutshell: ". . . whether Virginia has power to condemn land with the sole purpose of making it a gift to the national government for national park purposes." It took over ten years for the case to weave its way to the US Supreme Court. By then much of the park was under development and the National Park Service waited anxiously for this case to be resolved, for if the Supreme Court found in favor of Mr. Via, then all the work in developing the park would be for naught.

Nevertheless, on November 19, 1935, the Supreme Court ruled in favor of the state of Virginia against Mr. Via. The last significant case concerning property condemnation to establish this national park was closed, and the park we see today came to be.

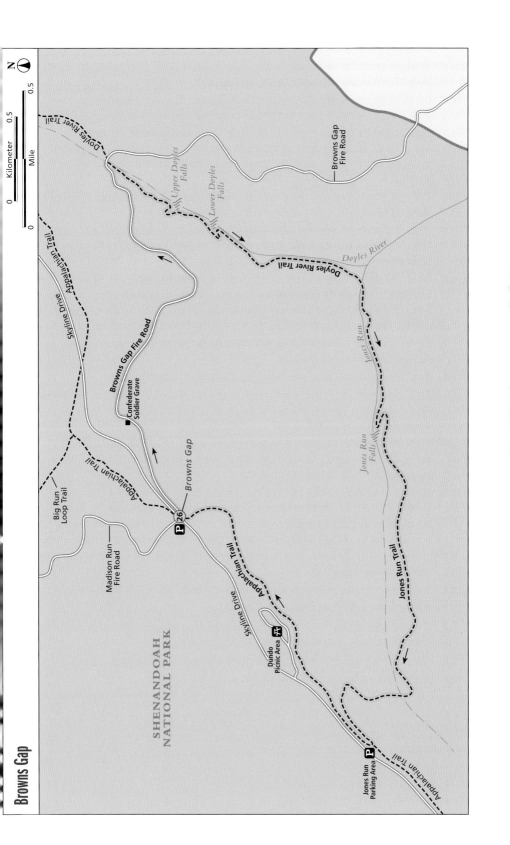

Browns Gap

SHENANDOAH
NATIONAL PARK

Skyline Drive

Appalachian Trail

Big Run
Loop Trail

Madison Run
Fire Road

P 26

Browns Gap

Browns Gap Fire Road

Confederate
Soldier Grave

Skyline Drive

Appalachian Trail

Dundo
Picnic Area

Jones Run Trail

Jones Run
Falls

Jones Run

Doyles River Trail

Doyles River

Lower Doyles
Falls

Upper Doyles
Falls

Doyles River Trail

Browns Gap
Fire Road

Jones Run
Parking Area

Appalachian Trail

N

0   Kilometer   0.5

0   Mile   0.5

interment locale. Continue down the fire road on a gentle grade. Pass through an attractive stand of pines. Views open through the trees toward the Piedmont.

0.9 On your left a brushy area contains relics indicating former human habitation, such as piled rocks. Imagine the forest as cleared and cultivated at this homesite.

1.7 Cross an iron bridge spanning the Doyles River. Reach a trail junction. Turn right onto Doyles River Trail, leaving the historic turnpike as it heads on for Browns Cove. The hike will be busier from here to the falls. Other hikers will have come from the Doyles River trailhead.

1.9 Cross the Doyles River, a normally easy rock-hop. Doyles River Trail continues along the watercourse but swings away as it approaches Upper Doyles Falls.

2.1 Come to a side trail leading to Upper Doyles Falls. Here, the three-tiered, 30-foot cascade spills into a bouldery glen where a tributary feeds the river. Doyles River repeatedly spills downcanyon in unnamed cascades.

2.4 Reach the base of Lower Doyles Falls at a sharp switchback. Lower Doyles Falls is steeper and showier, falling 63 feet. It propels over a rock lip, then pours in streamers and threads over multiple tiers to finally slow in a pool before charging on. The cataract will appear different depending on water levels. A stone face extends across the far gorge.

2.7 The trail squeezes down the narrow, very rugged gorge, and crosses a falling tributary on a wooden bridge. Continue downriver.

2.9 Meet the ideal summertime swimming hole, dark and still between rapids.

3.1 Reach a concrete trail marker and the end of the Doyles River Trail. Jones Run and Doyles River flow together below. Stay with the hikeway as it changes names from Doyles River Trail to Jones Run Trail.

3.3 Rock-hop Jones Run. Watch for old-growth tulip trees with enough diameter that several hikers would be needed to encircle them. Above, large boulders litter the canyon. Keep ascending, watching for long slide cascades.

3.8 Step over a tributary, climb a bit more, then arrive at Jones Run Falls. Here, the stream tumbles 45 feet over a solid rock face. Inviting streamside rock slabs make for ideal viewing and relaxing spots. The trail turns sharply left, circling around the rock face forming the falls. Pass the top of the falls and continue along Jones Run, viewing more tumbling water.

5.0 Join an old wagon road. The no-longer-maintained part of the wagon road once went to Via Gap (see sidebar page 142).

5.2 Step over what is left of Jones Run. Leave the wagon track, also heading for Browns Gap.

5.4 The Jones Run Trail makes a sharp left turn.

5.7 Meet the Appalachian Trail. The Jones Run trailhead and parking area are a few steps away. Turn right on the AT, northbound, toward Dundo Picnic Area.

6.3 Pass spur trails to Dundo Picnic Area. Keep straight among oaks, laurel, and pines.

6.9 Arrive at Browns Gap after descending, and complete the hike.

27 Humpback Rocks

This scenic walk starts out at the Humpback Rocks visitor center, then visits a re-created highland farmstead that includes numerous authentic buildings. From there make a loop, first heading up to the Humpback Rocks, where incredible panoramas await. Join the Appalachian Trail on an alluring woodland ramble, then trace the historic Howardsville Turnpike, which takes you back to your starting point.

Start: Humpback Rocks Visitor Center
Distance: 4.9-mile balloon loop
Hiking time: About 2.5–3.5 hours
Difficulty: Moderate, does have 800-foot ascent
Trail surface: Natural
Best seasons: Spring through fall
Other trail users: None
Canine compatibility: Leashed dogs permitted
Land status: National park, national forest

Fees and permits: None
Schedule: Mostly open but parkway will close in inclement winter weather; visitor center open May–Oct
Maps: National Geographic Map #789, *Lexington/Blue Ridge Mountains, George Washington and Jefferson National Forests*
Trail contact: Blue Ridge Parkway, 199 Hemphill Knob Rd., Asheville, NC 28803; (828) 298-0398; www.nps.gov/blri

Finding the trailhead: From exit 99 on I-64 near Waynesboro, take the Blue Ridge Parkway south for 5.9 miles to the Humpback Rocks Visitor Center on your right. The interpretive trail leading through the mountain farm and to the loop part of the hike leaves south from the visitor center. Trailhead GPS: N37 58.363' / W78 53.948'

The Hike

Take advantage of starting this hike at the Hogback Rocks Visitor Center. Inside, you can enjoy interpretive information about mountain farms as well as the area's history. You can also shop, get maps and water, use the restroom, and have a picnic here. The visitor center is the first significant stop on the Blue Ridge Parkway if you drive from its northern terminus at Rockfish Gap near Waynesboro.

This highland mountain trek starts on the appropriately named Mountain Farm Trail. It leaves the visitor center, tracing the old Howardsville Turnpike. More about that later. Here you will leave the parkway visitor center and visit the site of the William J. Carter Farm. Although no structures remain from Mr. Carter's farm, the on-site log structures are authentic. They were purchased locally, dismantled, and put back together here. Mr. Carter obtained his farm as part of a settlement land grant from the state of Virginia, which was inducing settlers to set up shop in the Blue Ridge Mountains.

The first building you will see is the log cabin. This quintessential wooden structure is permanently associated with the American frontier. And with a seemingly inexhaustible supply of trees, log cabins could be built from the woods that a pioneer cleared to create his farm. The William J. Carter Farm is designed to replicate an 1890s farmstead,

so the buildings reflect that time. A split rail fence surrounds the farm, and piled stone fences also run through the tract. The log cabin home is a simple structure with a stone chimney. And there were plenty of rocks in these mountains—just ask any subsistence farmer trying to plow through the stony soil in these Virginia highlands.

> The fields in Humpback Gap were created by a process known as "deadening." Living trees were girdled, which killed them over time. They were left standing to cure, then felled and used around the farm, ultimately leading to an open grassy pasture.

Ahead is another building, a storage shed with a base of rocks and topped with wood. It is the most architecturally scintillating of the buildings here, in my opinion. Farms back then faced the same dilemma we do today. What do we do with our stuff? Some stuff was not good enough for the house, not right for the barn but too valuable to lie outside in the elements. The barn stands in an enclosed stone-and-wood fence for livestock. Its wood shingle roof would be pricey in today's market, but back then the wood was easy to get—all it required was a little sweat equity.

The pen you see was used to hold swine just before slaughter. Here they would be fed corn to sweeten the meat. The rest of the year, the pigs were allowed to forage on their own in the woods. Almost every Virginia mountain homestead had a spring. In fact, the stream location drove the house location in most instances. The William J. Carter Farm was no different. Here you see a covered spring box to keep out the critters, as well as create a cool environment to store things like milk and butter.

Your hike follows the old Howardsville Turnpike to Humpback Gap and a parking lot on the Blue Ridge Parkway. The farmstead is left behind, but rest assured this gap was cleared as pasture during Carter's day. Now the hike changes from a leisurely interpretive stroll to a climb to the Humpback Rocks. During the days when the Howardsville Turnpike was in use, the Humpback Rocks, known back then simply as "The Rocks," were a landmark wagon drivers used to note their progress. The ascent is challenging on a wide and well-used path that used to be the Appalachian Trail (AT). Nevertheless, the view from this massive outcrop is more than worth it. From there, the William J. Carter Farm is visible but quite small. Beyond stretches the crest of the Blue Ridge, leaving north into Shenandoah National Park. To the west the mountain chain drops off to the Shenandoah Valley, which is backed by hazy mountains marking the West Virginia border. To the East falls the Piedmont. The promontory offers numerous viewing locales, and on a busy day hikers will be scattered atop it, soaking in the scene from horizon to horizon.

Our hike joins the AT, descending from the Humpback Rocks on a series of switchbacks that moderate the grade. This pleasant woodland walk gives you a chance at repose and reflection, especially since you are going downhill. Woe to hikers going

Hikers at William J. Carter Farm pass by authentic farm structures.

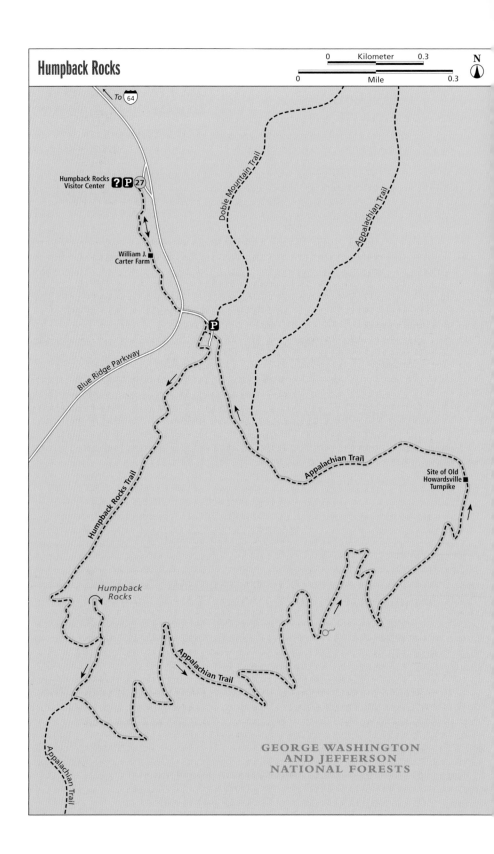

Humpback Rocks

0   Kilometer   0.3

0   Mile   0.3

N

To 64

Humpback Rocks
Visitor Center ? P 27

Dobie Mountain Trail

Appalachian Trail

William J.
Carter Farm

P

Blue Ridge Parkway

Appalachian Trail

Site of Old
Howardsville
Turnpike

Humpback Rocks Trail

Humpback
Rocks

Appalachian Trail

Appalachian Trail

GEORGE WASHINGTON
AND JEFFERSON
NATIONAL FORESTS

the opposite direction! After a while the AT joins the old Howardsville Turnpike. This road connected towns west of the Blue Ridge to those on the east side, passing through Humpback Gap. It is easy to imagine residents of the Carter Farm sitting on their front porch watching and waving at passersby on the Howardsville Turnpike.

Even though the turnpike was mostly cleared of rocks and leveled off, wagon riders still faced a bumpy ride. The walking is easy today. You will cross a few streams flowing off Humpback Mountain before returning to Humpback Gap. From there, backtrack through the William J. Carter Farm to complete the hike. Consider returning to the visitor center to learn about more outdoor opportunities on the Blue Ridge Parkway. During summer weekends farm demonstrations, gardening, and period reenactments are engaged at the farm.

Miles and Directions

0.0 Start by heading southbound from the Humpback Rocks Visitor Center on a concrete path that evolves into a gravel trail. Just ahead, reach the William J. Carter Farm. Travel through the farm, visiting the numerous buildings and enjoying interpretive information.

0.3 Pass through a fence, leaving the farm. Note the gnarled, huge oak here. Look south for a view of the Humpback Rocks, where you are headed. Follow the old Howardsville Turnpike, cross a second wooden fence, and cross the Blue Ridge Parkway. Follow the road leading to the parking area at Humpback Gap.

0.4 From the trail kiosk, pick up the Humpback Rocks Trail, leaving right and uphill toward Humpback Rocks. This is the old Appalachian Trail. Hardwoods shade the rocky forest floor.

0.8 A user-created shortcut leads to the Humpback Rocks. Please do not take this erosive path. Stay with the blue-blazed proper trail.

1.0 Begin climbing through a rugged boulder garden.

1.3 Intersect the spur trail leading to the Humpback Rocks after leveling off in a flat. Turn left, tracing the spur trail to Humpback Rocks.

1.4 Open onto the Humpback Rocks. Note all the carved initials and such in the rock. The angled outcrop offers various viewing spots that open west to the Shenandoah Valley, north to Shenandoah National Park, and east to the Virginia Piedmont. Backtrack.

1.5 Continue on the Humpback Trail, heading for the Appalachian Trail. Climb through rocky woods.

1.6 Reach the hike's high point of 3,260 feet on the north shoulder of Humpback Mountain. This is where you meet the AT. Turn left, northbound on the AT. Descend off the mountain in long, loping switchbacks on a singletrack trail. The walking is easy.

2.9 Pass a marked spring. Continue switchbacking through stony forest.

3.1 Pass through a flat and campsite. Resume the downgrade.

3.7 The AT joins the wide Howardsville Turnpike, coming in from your right. Cruise around the north slope of Humpback Mountain. Step over a few streamlets as you gently ascend.

4.2 The AT leaves right as a footpath. Stay straight with the old Howardsville Turnpike.

4.5 Return to Humpback Gap. Backtrack across the Blue Ridge Parkway, then rejoin the Mountain Farm Trail.

4.9 Arrive back at the Humpback Rocks Visitor Center, completing the hike.

28 Saint Marys Wilderness

This historic hike drops off the Blue Ridge Parkway to explore an old mine site, now reverted to nature, as part of the Saint Marys Wilderness, within the confines of the George Washington National Forest. From the highlands, you will pass along Mine Bank Creek, which boasts numerous splashing waterfalls and cascades. Open into the Saint Marys River valley, then head to a riverside ore-processing locale, where concrete remnants and grown-over slag piles reveal an industrial past that belies the splendor of the Saint Marys Wilderness.

Start: Mine Bank Creek Trailhead off milepost 23.1 of the Blue Ridge Parkway
Distance: 4.6 miles out and back
Hiking time: 2.5-3.5 hours
Difficulty: Moderate, does have 1,150-foot descent
Trail surface: Natural
Best season: Year-round
Other trail users: None
Canine compatibility: Leashed dogs permitted

Land status: Wilderness area within national forest
Fees and permits: None
Schedule: 24/7/365
Maps: National Geographic Map #789, *Lexington/Blue Ridge Mountains, George Washington and Jefferson National Forests; USGS Big Levels*
Trail contact: George Washington National Forest, 27 Ranger Ln., Natural Bridge Station, VA 24579; (540) 291-2188; www.fs.fed.us

Finding the trailhead: From exit 205 on I-81/I-64, take VA 606 east for 1.5 miles to Steeles Tavern and US 11. Turn left on US 11 north for 0.1 mile, then turn right on VA 56 east. Follow VA 56 east for 5.4 miles to the Blue Ridge Parkway. Join the Blue Ridge Parkway northbound and follow it for 4.1 miles to the Mine Bank Trailhead on your left, just before reaching the more easily identifiable Fork Mountain Overlook, which will be on your right. Trailhead GPS: N37 54.721'/W79 5.214'

The Hike

This hike combines Virginia's mountain beauty with history. The setting is the Saint Marys Wilderness, a 10,000-acre parcel of the George Washington National Forest, designated by the US Congress. Though its wilderness designation has been in place for decades and the woods have literally gone back to the deer and bears, the Saint Marys River watershed has had a long history of development. The old-growth forests that once cloaked this gorgeous mountain gorge were first harvested for fuel wood, bark for tanning hides, and for construction timber used in the Shenandoah Valley.

Other, larger logging operations followed. Later, the valley was mined for iron ore and manganese by the Pulaski Iron Company. They ran a railroad spur from the Shenandoah Valley up the Saint Marys River to its confluence with Chimney Branch. A series of mine

▶ The Saint Marys Gorge was designated a wilderness by Congress in 1984.

Remains of an old iron ore processing locale

openings as well as processing areas sprang up in the Saint Marys Gorge. The mining period started in 1910 and really ramped up during World War I, then tapered off, and finally phased out in the 1950s. Among the 20 or so miles of trails, hikers can find locales where mining, processing, and transporting the ore took place.

This particular hike heads to a processing area near the confluence of Mine Bank Branch and the Saint Marys River. It starts on the Blue Ridge Parkway, which offers the best and safest wilderness access, particularly if you are camping overnight in the gorge. The lowermost trailhead on St. Marys Road has suffered from auto break-ins in the past. I wouldn't leave my car there overnight, therefore I won't recommend it for you. Furthermore, the trail leaving from there has been washed out and compromised by floods over the years. It can be very rough in places, yet it is heavily used because it offers the quickest access to Saint Marys Falls.

Our hike leaves the Mine Bank Creek Trailhead, atop the Blue Ridge on the south side of the Saint Marys Gorge. It soon drops off the ridge crest and enters the

Water Quality and the Saint Marys River

The Saint Marys River is not only desirable for its historic value and wilderness waterfalls, it is also an important Virginia brook-trout fishery. The gorge is one of those places where anglers go not only to catch fish but also to fish in a beautiful setting. However, between its mining past and acid deposition, the water quality of the Saint Marys River was compromised. In a cooperative effort among the James Madison University, the US Forest Service, and the Virginia Department of Game and Inland Fisheries, the water quality of the Saint Marys River has been restored. This was done by a process known as liming. The goal was to reduce acidification of the water. Limestone, mined in the nearby Shenandoah Valley, was introduced into tributaries of the Saint Marys River. The limestone particles then flow into the main river, neutralizing acid in the water. Using dump trucks and helicopters, limestone was put into the watershed for the first time in 1999. The water quality has improved ever since, as has the trout fishery, as well as habitat for nongame species. The water quality of the Saint Marys River and its tributaries continues to be monitored.

Mine Bank Creek valley, a heavily wooded and scenic watershed full of waterfalls. These waterfalls are at their boldest from late winter through spring and can slow to a mere trickle in fall. In spring the valley will be rife with wildflowers, from pink-hued white trilliums to bleeding hearts and more. Massive boulders and rock ramparts are scattered throughout the valley. Along the way down you will spot a rough roadbed. The trail will follow this. Ore was transported down this route to a processing area near the Saint Marys River. It is hard to imagine moving ore through this rugged terrain.

The Mine Bank Creek Valley finally opens up, easing the almost endless falling water. The Saint Marys River Gorge seems wide open in comparison. You head up the Saint Marys River and it isn't long before reaching a mine site and processing area in a flat nestled between the Saint Marys River and a nameless tributary. You will see the timeworn concrete walls of a processing area, metal relics, and fairyland-looking slag piles, grown over with grass and trees. This is a fun place to explore. Visit the mine area, the campsites, and the river. There are no deep mine shafts to fear.

If you have some extra energy, consider heading down to Saint Marys Falls. To reach the falls, hike downriver on the Saint Marys Trail, passing other mine sites and making your way over a ridge, before descending into cascade-rich Sugartree Branch. From there, hike the spur trail to Saint Marys Falls. Saint Marys Falls tumble 10 feet over a ledge between quartzite walls deep in the gorge. The large pool at the base is

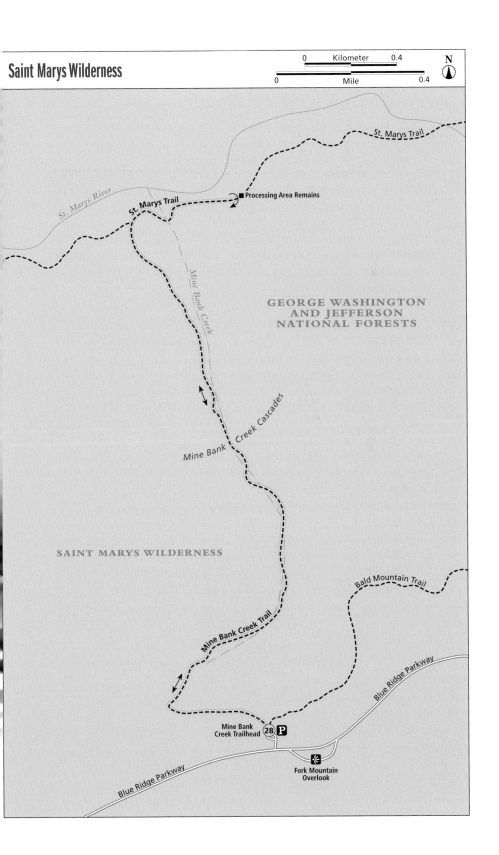

Saint Marys Wilderness

0   Kilometer   0.4

0   Mile   0.4

N

St. Marys Trail

St. Marys River

St. Marys Trail

■ Processing Area Remains

Mine Bank Creek

GEORGE WASHINGTON
AND JEFFERSON
NATIONAL FORESTS

Mine Bank Creek Cascades

Mine Bank Creek

SAINT MARYS WILDERNESS

Bald Mountain Trail

Mine Bank Creek Trail

Blue Ridge Parkway

Mine Bank
Creek Trailhead   28   P

Fork Mountain
Overlook

Blue Ridge Parkway

surrounded by jagged boulders and short cliffs. More pools and falls are upstream, but they are a challenge to access. The distance between Saint Marys Falls and the junction of Mine Bank Creek Trail with the Saint Marys Trail is about 2 miles one-way.

Miles and Directions

0.0 As you are facing the Mine Bank Creek Trailhead kiosk, you will see a gated forest road to your left and a faint woods road to your right. In between the two is a singletrack foot trail that starts near the gated forest road. This is the Mine Bank Creek Trail. Follow the Mine Bank Creek Trail north, entering the Saint Marys Wilderness and shortly intersecting the Bald Mountain Trail. Stay left with the Mine Bank Creek Trail.

0.3 After walking through pines, mountain laurel, and oaks, make a big turn to the right and descend into the Mine Bank Creek valley.

0.5 Step over Mine Bank Creek for the first time. The stream may be dry in fall at this elevation. Rhododendron, black birch, and yellow birch rise in the cooler, moister valley.

0.8 Hop Mine Bank Creek a second time, dropping deeper into the bouldery vale.

0.9 Cross Mine Bank Creek again, this time just above a waterfall that makes a series of stair-step cascades.

1.0 Cross over to the right-hand bank of Mine Bank Creek.

1.1 Cross over to the left-hand bank of Mine Bank Creek. Soon step over a tributary, adding flow. Big bluffs rise on both sides of the valley. The path becomes rockier.

1.3 Come to Mine Bank Creek Cascades. This fall spills about 60 feet over an angled slide. More waterfalls drop downstream. Begin to follow a stony but cleared tram road once used to haul ore. The creek and road separate.

1.9 Intersect the Saint Marys Trail after the Mine Bank Creek valley perceptibly widens. For this historic hike, turn right, heading up the Saint Marys River (Go the other way to access Saint Marys Falls).

2.1 Cross Mine Bank Creek for the final time. Wander through relatively level forest, passing campsites.

2.3 The trail crosses an unnamed tributary of the Saint Marys River. Just across the tributary stand concrete relics of an ore-processing area. Look around for grown-over slag piles, iron rails, and other evidence. The whole area is worth exploring. Backtrack when finished.

4.6 Arrive back at the Blue Ridge Parkway and the Mine Bank Creek Trailhead.

29 Brown Mountain Creek

Take a hike into Appalachian Mountain history by visiting a formerly inhabited hollow. The Appalachian Trail (AT) is your conduit for exploring the valley of Brown Mountain Creek. Here, a gorgeous wooded valley is centered by a raucous creek, once populated with scores of sharecroppers. While hiking, look for evidence of these former residents, from old stone fences to stone spring boxes to even a chimney, all fading into the past as the forest grows ever taller and lush.

Start: Long Mountain Wayside on US 60
Distance: 4.6 miles out and back
Hiking time: About 2.5–3.5 hours
Difficulty: Moderate, does have 850-foot descent
Trail surface: Natural
Best season: Late fall through spring
Other trail users: None
Canine compatibility: Leashed dogs permitted

Land status: National forest
Fees and permits: None
Schedule: 24/7/365
Map: National Geographic Map #789, *Lexington/Blue Ridge Mountains, George Washington and Jefferson National Forests*
Trail contact: George Washington National Forest, 27 Ranger Ln., Natural Bridge Station, VA 24579; (540) 291-2188; www.fs.fed.us

Finding the trailhead: From exit 188 on I-81, take US 60 east to and through Buena Vista for a total of 13.1 miles to reach the Long Mountain Wayside (you will cross the Blue Ridge Parkway after 8 miles). Parking is available at the wayside, but the southbound part of the AT leaves from the gravel pull-off on the south side of US 60, just before you reach the wayside. Trailhead GPS: N37 43.418'/W79 15.064'

The Hike

The Appalachian Trail (AT) presents memorable views from many mountain peaks while coursing through Virginia. Think about McAfee Knob, Stony Man Mountain, and Humpback Rocks, just to name a few. The AT's aquatic adventures are less celebrated. However, near Buena Vista the AT drops off the Blue Ridge and does a little waterside traveling. Here, along Brown Mountain Creek, hikers can take America's most famous footpath—of which there are more miles in Virginia than any other state—and walk through the remains of a settlement stretched along the stream. Moreover, you will see remnants of a world left behind. Most easily seen are the stone fences, built by hand with perhaps the help of a solitary mule, from rocks embedded into the mountain soil, where residents tried their hand at raising corn, tobacco, and wheat. The hardscrabble land did not produce the best yields. However, the Brown Mountain Creek valley was home to these agrarians, who once lived as slaves until freedom came their way after the Civil War. Some owned their own land though. Names like Mose Richardson, Grandma Ann, and Camden Sandridge stretched down the valley, living their lives in relative seclusion.

A rock wall graces the trail.

To quote an interpretive sign in Brown Mountain Valley: "Observe as you walk. Be aware that history surrounds you. Keep your eyes and mind open to explore the secrets held by the land." Heed that advice. Sharp-eyed trail trekkers will spot nonnative bushes and flowers blooming in spring. Someone else might see a broken pottery shard, or maybe the metal from an old potbellied stove. Whatever discoveries you find, leave them for others to find for themselves.

When the USDA Forest Service purchased this valley in the Blue Ridge, they thought to interview residents who called it home. And from these interviews, they preserved a piece of Virginia's past. It is a past less grand than creating a new nation from a howling wilderness or fighting battles of the American Revolution or cataloging the dynamics of economic change brought about by the railroads. However, the lifeways of the people along Brown Mountain Creek are an essential thread in the tapestry that fashions Virginia's history.

Mr. Taft Hughes, born in 1909 and one of a family of ten children raised along Brown Mountain Creek, recalls his and his sibling's day-to-day life. "There wasn't nobody around us much. We just mostly stayed at home. We would go out and find a persimmon tree and get persimmons or apples or shake a chestnut tree. That's what we looked forward to the most, picking up chestnuts and grapes and what have you."

His mother cooked on an iron stove and at the fireplace in winter. For breakfast, mother would whip up hoecakes, made from flour. The children sweetened it with sorghum molasses or fruit preserves, homemade of course. His family had a small apple orchard along Brown Mountain Creek. Then there was the family garden. Almost every resident strewn along the valley had their own garden, fenced to keep the livestock and other critters out. There would be bacon after a pig had been slaughtered, then smoked for preservation. They kept a cow for milk.

Their house, barn, and outbuilding were made from local chestnut logs, some of the stoutest, longest-lasting wood around. Taft's house had an upstairs and that was where the kids slept. The beds were store-bought but the mattresses were large muslin bags filled with "tick." Ideally, tick would be made from feathers, but the kids' mattresses were filled with straw. When first filled, the straw mattresses would be comfortable, but over time the straw fell flat. The tick would then be replaced.

▶ The land along Brown Mountain Creek was purchased by the USDA Forest Service during the 1920s. Residents of Brown Mountain Creek moved on, some to big cities up north, others just outside the national forest boundaries.

Brown Mountain Creek was their world. Taft never left the valley until he was 11 years old, when he rode a wagon to Buena Vista, maybe 12 miles distant. As a teen, he would walk to Buena Vista, roughly following the route US 60 uses today.

Of course, all that walking would wear out a pair of shoes. The Taft family did buy their shoes, but the footwear had to last, one pair for maybe a year or more. His mother did make clothes for her ten offspring. She would order the cloth from catalogs such as Sears Roebuck, then sew the shirts. Kids then only had a few outfits and generally wore clothes until they wore out.

And farm work wore clothes—and kids—out. They performed daily chores, which varied with the time of year. But there were always animals to take care of and barns to clean, plus cutting and curing tobacco, laying in wheat, sowing and stripping corn too. However, tobacco was the primary cash crop.

In the evenings the family would recount their day. Mom would read the Bible to her children, as well as the newspaper, which they got on a weekly basis via the US Mail.

Although that slower, simpler life is in the past, you can still walk back into that time, and take your time exploring beyond the trail. It is a drop from the gap on Long Mountain where the AT slips down to Brown Mountain Creek, near the confluence with another stream. Rock piles are all that is left of a gristmill that once ground

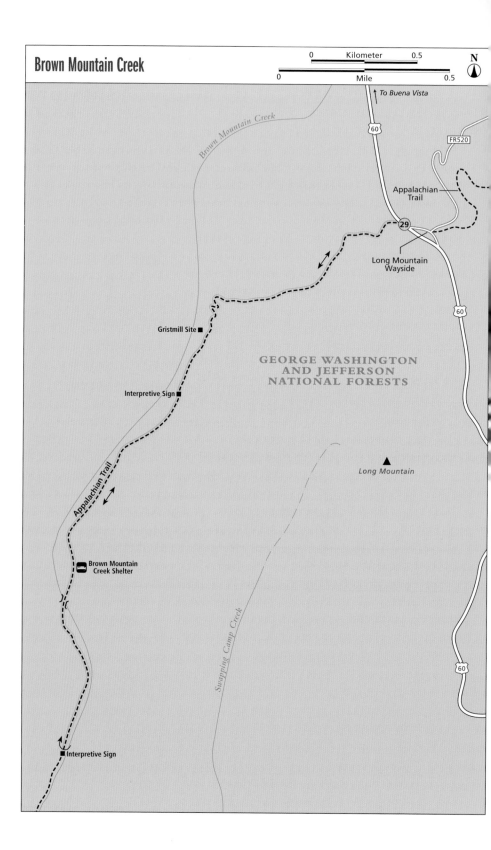

Brown Mountain Creek

0 Kilometer 0.5

0 Mile 0.5

N

To Buena Vista

Brown Mountain Creek

60

FR520

Appalachian Trail

29

Long Mountain Wayside

60

Gristmill Site ■

GEORGE WASHINGTON AND JEFFERSON NATIONAL FORESTS

Interpretive Sign ■

Appalachian Trail

Long Mountain

Brown Mountain Creek Shelter

Swapping Camp Creek

60

■ Interpretive Sign

corn and wheat into flour for the locals. The footpath then travels among narrow flats, along slopes hemmed in by the creek, and back to flats where rock walls still stand. And then the AT passes a shelter used by modern-day backpackers, with their lightweight camping gear and processed, dried foods that would baffle the former residents of Brown Mountain Creek.

History buffs will then cross the stream on a bridge, passing more homesites and a forgotten past until they reach an interpretive sign a short way before the AT leaves Brown Mountain Creek for good. On your return journey you will likely see more relics that paint a portrait of the Old Dominion's past.

Miles and Directions

0.0 Start by heading southbound on the Appalachian Trail, leaving US 60. Head downhill in scrubby woods. Immediately descend under a power line. Soon cross an obvious old roadbed.

0.4 Come along a tributary of Brown Mountain Creek in a steep-sided valley too small for a tent, much less a homesite. Rocks and boulders pock the pine, maple, and oak woods.

0.6 Pull away from the creek and descend via switchbacks.

0.8 Cross the unnamed creek near its confluence with Brown Mountain Creek. You are immediately in settled country. A gristmill was located near this meeting of the waters. Homesites were located up and down Brown Creek from this point. Keep downstream, as Brown Mountain Creek flows to your left on an old doubletrack wagon road.

1.0 Pass an interpretive sign detailing life on Brown Mountain Creek. The trail then pushes through a narrow portion of the stream valley.

1.4 Come to a homesite with a crumbled chimney to your left. A short spur trail leads left to a rocked-in spring at this campsite. Pass more rock walls. Look for nonnative vegetation such as privet.

1.7 Come to the Brown Mountain Creek trail shelter. Just ahead, the AT crosses Brown Mountain Creek on a footbridge. The valley widens.

2.3 Come to a second interpretive sign detailing life on the creek. This is a good place to turn around, though you can go a little farther before the AT leaves Brown Mountain Creek for good.

4.6 Arrive back at US 60 and the trailhead.

30 Bluff Mountain

This hike uses the famed Appalachian Trail (AT) to escort you up to Bluff Mountain, a somber yet scintillating place. Here lies a memorial to Ottie Powell, an area lad lost in the woods. His body was found here, astride the very peak of Bluff Mountain. The story of his disappearance and subsequent discovery has become legend. Hikers who overnight at the nearby Punchbowl Mountain trail shelter swear the ghost of young Ottie has come to visit them. Today, you can leave the Blue Ridge Parkway, hike the AT, pass the Punchbowl shelter, and walk on up to Bluff Mountain to see the wonderful panoramas and the memorial to Ottie. After that, decide for yourself if the ghost of Ottie Powell haunts these heights.

Start: Blue Ridge Parkway near milepost 51.5
Distance: 3.8 miles out and back
Hiking time: About 2.5–3.5 hours
Difficulty: Moderate, does have 1,200-foot climb
Trail surface: Natural
Best season: Year-round when skies are clear
Other trail users: None
Canine compatibility: Leashed dogs permitted

Land status: National park, national forest
Fees and permits: None
Schedule: 24/7/365
Map: National Geographic Map #789, *Lexington/Blue Ridge Mountains, George Washington and Jefferson National Forests*
Trail contact: George Washington National Forest, 27 Ranger Ln., Natural Bridge Station, VA 24579; (540) 291-2188; www.fs.fed.us

Finding the trailhead: From exit 188 on I-81, take US 60 east to and through Buena Vista for a total of 8 miles to reach the Blue Ridge Parkway. Take the Blue Ridge Parkway southbound for 6.1 miles to the Punchbowl Mountain Overlook, milepost 51.5, on your left. The "overlook" is actually a parking area for the Appalachian Trail and offers no views. From there, take the AT southbound, joining it across the parkway from the overlook. Do not follow the AT northbound directly from the overlook. Trailhead GPS: N37 40.446'/W79 20.065'

The Hike

There are several reasons why a mountain becomes iconic. Sometimes it is for the views, sometimes it is for what has happened there, and sometimes for the trails that course atop it. Bluff Mountain has become a Virginia Blue Ridge icon for all of the above reasons. You should visit it.

First, soak in the story of Ottie Powell. The last day of his life was what really puts Bluff Mountain on the map. Back in 1891, November it was, Ottie Powell, a little shy of 5 years old, walked to school in Amherst County, east of the Blue Ridge. It was not the only walking he was to do that day. Shortly after arriving, Ottie, along

The memorial to Ottie Powell sits atop Bluff Mountain. ▶

with the other children in the one-room Dancing Creek School, were sent into the adjacent forest to hunt up wood for the iron stove sitting in the middle of the wooden building. The teacher, Nanny Gilbert, had burned through the wood supply the previous week, as a surprise snowstorm had swept upon the Blue Ridge and adjacent communities.

The children returned to the school, wood in hand, except for Ottie. The search for him commenced immediately. It was not long before the whole community was searching for Ottie in the fields and forests east of the Blue Ridge. The cloudy afternoon darkened into dusk, and still no Ottie.

Then the rain fell. The temperature dropped. The rain turned to ice. The foul weather raised worries and dimmed hopes, especially among his parents. Where was Ottie Cline Powell? His story was passed house to house, town to town, by word of mouth and through the newspapers. The search grid expanded. At its height more than 1,000 people looked for Ottie, but as November does, it became colder, the days shorter. Hopes dimmed with the weather. Some began to wonder if he was kidnapped. Even Ottie's dad, a part-time preacher, felt almost hopeless, especially after bringing in a big-city detective from Richmond.

The winter of 1891 became the spring of 1892. Still no Ottie Powell. His disappearance was a true mystery. Then bear hunters were tracking the high country when a hunting dog stopped tracking and started howling near the crest of Bluff Mountain, over 2,400 feet above the adjacent lowlands.

The dog had not cornered a bear but had found the remains of little blue-eyed, sandy-haired Ottie Cline Powell. By the contents of his stomach doctors determined he had passed away that first night away from the school, the night the rain turned to ice. Ottie Powell died of hypothermia. Nevertheless, how did he get 7 miles from home and a half mile higher than the old schoolhouse? Why did he end up on top of Bluff Mountain? To get a lay of the land? That seems a stretch for a lost not-yet-5-year-old, especially when you consider impending darkness followed by rain and ice.

However, die he did, and his mother followed him to the grave, stricken with grief. Ottie was buried in a field near his home. The tale of Ottie Powell grew to legend when a local resident wrote a book about the lost boy and even built a cement cross atop Bluff Mountain, honoring Ottie at the spot where he perished. By then the USDA Forest Service had bought the land, and Benton MacKaye's idea of an Appalachian Trail took hold. A steel fire tower—a fire lookout—rose atop Bluff Mountain. The AT ran under it.

Visitors to the mountain, whose name was changed to Tower Hill because of the fire tower, grew curious about the cross and the story of Ottie Powell. Later, the bronze memorial we see today was erected. The fire tower, in existence since 1917, was dismantled. There was no more reason to call it Tower Hill, so the peak reverted to Bluff Mountain. That leaves today's hikers with four concrete tower supports and a set of concrete stairs going nowhere, except a few feet higher atop Bluff Mountain, seemingly to improve the cleared vistas on the small grassy crown.

The author—not afraid of ghosts—stands right in front of the haunted Punchbowl Mountain shelter.

Now, we can peer down to the west on the Maury River Valley, where it flows by Buena Vista, and west beyond that to Lexington and Mill Mountain and all the way to West Virginia. To the east the James River Valley, with all its tributaries aiming for the Piedmont, can be seen coursing through knobby hills. Somewhere down there is Lynchburg. But perhaps the best vista of all is to the north, where the gentle and sometimes steep mountains—seemingly endless—of the Blue Ridge roll on, eventually becoming part of Shenandoah National Park.

Ottie Powell, the day he died, never beheld such a view. The wooded mountain was not cleared for aesthetic purposes. Ottie enjoyed no cleared trails. Ottie had no relatively easy marked path to follow, as we do today. The mystery remains: How did he end up on Bluff Mountain?

Some say his spirit can be felt on the peak. Hikers often leave trinkets for Ottie at the memorial. Others swear they hear a little boy crying for help at the Punchbowl

Bluff Mountain

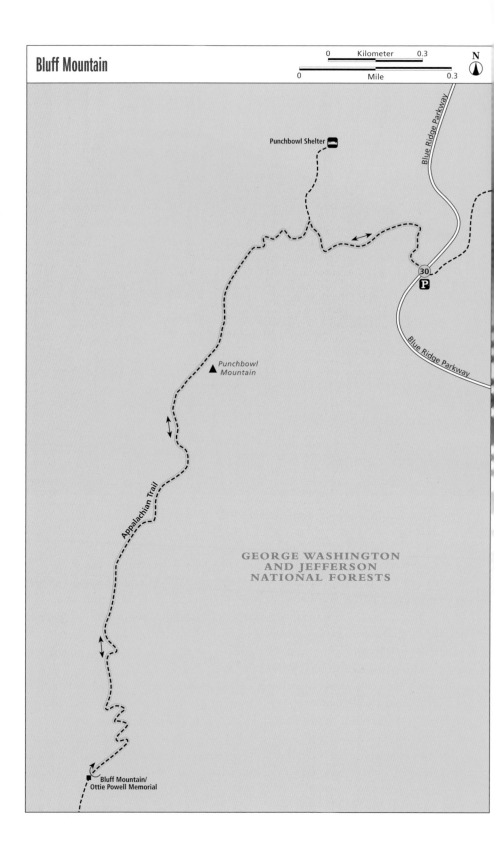

Punchbowl Shelter

Blue Ridge Parkway

30
P

Blue Ridge Parkway

Punchbowl
Mountain

Appalachian Trail

GEORGE WASHINGTON
AND JEFFERSON
NATIONAL FORESTS

Bluff Mountain/
Ottie Powell Memorial

Mountain trail shelter, which you pass on the way. I made a point to camp at the shelter but neither heard nor felt the vibes of Ottie during a long, dark night. Maybe I was not listening, but they say you can hear Ottie's voice pealing through the wind-whipped trees, after the leaves have fallen, during the dark days of November—and beyond.

> ▶ Ottie Cline Powell was the fifth of eight children.

Miles and Directions

0.0 Start by heading southbound on the Appalachian Trail, across the parkway from the parking area. Climb up a little hollow. The ascent steepens underneath oak, maple, and hickory woods.

0.4 Reach a trail intersection. A spur trail leads right a quarter mile to the Punchbowl Mountain trail shelter. Here you will find a three-sided wooden shelter, a pond and a small stone-encased spring, and a privy too. Perhaps you may hear the ghost of Ottie Powell. For now, stay left, still on the AT, ascending through mountain laurel and chestnut oaks growing amid scattered lichen-covered boulders.

0.6 Level off on the crest of the Blue Ridge. Congratulations, you have just climbed 600 feet. Continue southbound on the AT. Begin working your way over gentle Punchbowl Mountain.

0.8 The rocky path tops out on Punchbowl Mountain. An easy descent leads through hardwoods with scattered rhododendron and mountain laurel.

1.1 Reach a gap between Punchbowl Mountain and Bluff Mountain. Ascend.

1.5 Make the first of several switchbacks working up the north side of Bluff Mountain. Stunted pines bronze the trail bed with their needles. More switchbacks rise ahead.

1.8 Come to the shoulder of Bluff Mountain. Winter views open to the east. Even if the view isn't clear, fake it. It is a good way to catch your breath after those switchbacks.

1.9 Open onto Bluff Mountain. Here, a grassy crown is marked with concrete foundations of the fire tower that stood for over five decades and steps leading nowhere. Cleared views open to the west and east of the Blue Ridge. Note the rectangular Ottie Cline Powell memorial. Backtrack.

3.8 Arrive back at the Blue Ridge Parkway.

31 Johnson Farm

Situated in the scenic Peaks of Otter area along the Blue Ridge Parkway, this hike visits a long-lived homestead and then circles around a lake built as part of the Blue Ridge Parkway. Start your hike at the Peaks of Otter Visitor Center, 2,500 feet high, then cruise rich woods. Join the Johnson Farm Loop, where you skirt a mountainside then reach the farm, located in a high mountain flat. See the preserved homestead as well as outbuildings, and perhaps the furnished inside when open for interpretation. The hike then circles Abbott Lake, rimmed by the Peaks of Otter and a park lodge. Before finishing, stop by a preserved log structure from the 1830s.

Start: Peaks of Otter Visitor Center
Distance: 3.2-mile balloon double loop
Hiking time: About 2–3 hours
Difficulty: Moderate, does have a few steep hills
Trail surface: Natural-surface path, asphalt
Best seasons: Spring for wildflowers, fall for colors
Other trail users: Peaks of Otter Lodge guests, anglers

Canine compatibility: Leashed dogs permitted
Land status: National park
Fees and permits: None
Schedule: Open daily year-round
Maps: *Blue Ridge Parkway: Peaks of Otter;*
USGS Peaks of Otter
Trail contact: Blue Ridge Parkway, 199 Hemphill Knob Rd., Asheville, NC 28803; (828) 298-0398; www.nps.gov/blri

Finding the trailhead: From exit 167 on I-81, northeast of Roanoke, take US 11 south for 1.2 miles to the town of Buchanan. Turn left on VA 43 east. Follow it to reach the Blue Ridge Parkway after 4.7 miles. Turn left and follow the BRP northeast 5 miles to the Peaks of Otter Visitor Center, at milepost 85.9, on your left. Alternate directions: From downtown Bedford, take VA 43 west for 10 miles to reach the Blue Ridge Parkway and the Peaks of Otter Visitor Center (do not turn right into the picnic area just before reaching the Blue Ridge Parkway). Trailhead GPS: N37 26.730' / W79 36.560'

The Hike

The historic Johnson Farm is situated almost 2,800 feet high on the shoulder of Harkening Hill, looking out on the Peaks of Otter. The bucolic site recalls a time when things moved slower. However, a lot has happened here in this mountain-rimmed bowl rising above Bedford, Virginia. Aboriginal Virginians have been coming here for 5,000 years, probably for similar reasons as we do today, to enjoy the cool mountains in summer, as well as hunt, fish, and camp. Signs of their occupation here at the Peaks of Otter have been continuous.

European settlers were entering these mountains around 1700. By the time the United States came to be, settlers had trickled in and the area was connected to the lands below by wagon track. Over the decades the Peaks of Otter rose in prominence as a tourist retreat to escape the sultry Virginia summers, enjoy the cool springs, and

The Johnson Farm stands in a high gap.

hike to the mountaintops and vistas respectively known as Sharp Top, Flat Top, Buzzards Roost, and Needles Eye. A century later the Peaks of Otter was at the top of the list for recreational development when the Blue Ridge Parkway came to be.

In the meantime the Johnson family was settling in on Harkening Hill. It had been homesteaded for nearly a century before the Johnsons got ahold of it in 1852. It would remain in the Johnson family for ninety years. The house we see today began in typical Appalachian style, starting out as a log cabin, expanded upon, and finally covered with siding. The house today replicates its look in the 1930s, including the furniture inside and the barn, implements, and garden of that time.

Interestingly, when the Peaks of Otter area was expanded for recreation by the park service in the 1960s, the Johnson Farm got a second look as an interpretive resource. Despite it being acquired by

▶ As the Old Dominion settled westward, early Scotchmen by the name of Ewing settled in this high vale and named the area after their homeland peaks of Otterburn.

The Hotel Mons

On this hike you will pass the site of the Hotel Mons. It was a highland getaway designed for mountain recreation as well as escaping the hot summers of the lowlands below the Blue Ridge. This tourist destination was preceded by the Otter Peaks Hotel, established in the 1850s and which lasted until 1916. But visitation to the Peaks of Otter was perfected by the Hotel Mons, built in 1920, where visitors truly relaxed in style between trips to the mountaintops above. Guests returned year after year to the hotel. They were served vegetables grown at the Johnson Farm. Members of the Johnson clan worked there through the years and were also employed guiding the tourists, running errands for them, and even taking in overflow guests. The hotel was once an important economic engine of the Peaks of Otter community. Unfortunately, the Great Depression hurt business at the hotel and it was shuttered in 1936. Many local residents left shortly thereafter. The property of the Hotel Mons was bought by the National Park Service. Today, a simple marker in front of a grassy meadow marks the site of this former getaway.

the National Park Service in 1942, the main house and outbuildings fell into disrepair. When restored in the 1960s, the house was stripped to its most primitive state, with no regard for researching the actual lives that had been lived there. Later, members of the community balked at this representation of the Johnson Farm. It has since been completely restored to its 1930s appearance and presents another side of Appalachian life, not simply that of the most primitive backwoods folk but those who had evolved with the times, capturing their life in a particular documentable state and time.

This hike leaves the visitor center and takes the Johnson Farm Trail to reach the Johnson Farm. Hopefully on your visit the farmhouse will be open and staffed by interpreters, usually on warm-season weekends and holidays. Walk inside the house and see evidence of the lifestyles of the Johnsons up close through the period furnishings, implements, and photos. The barn is stocked with tools that were used in that time.

You will then descend past the site of the Hotel Mons, before passing under the Blue Ridge Parkway via a tunnel. The hike opens onto the east side of the parkway and the hustle and bustle of the Peaks of Otter Lodge. Circle Abbott Lake, with mountains reflecting off its surface. Stop by the Polly Woods Ordinary, an early way stop for those passing through the Peaks of Otter, before returning to the visitor center and completing the hike.

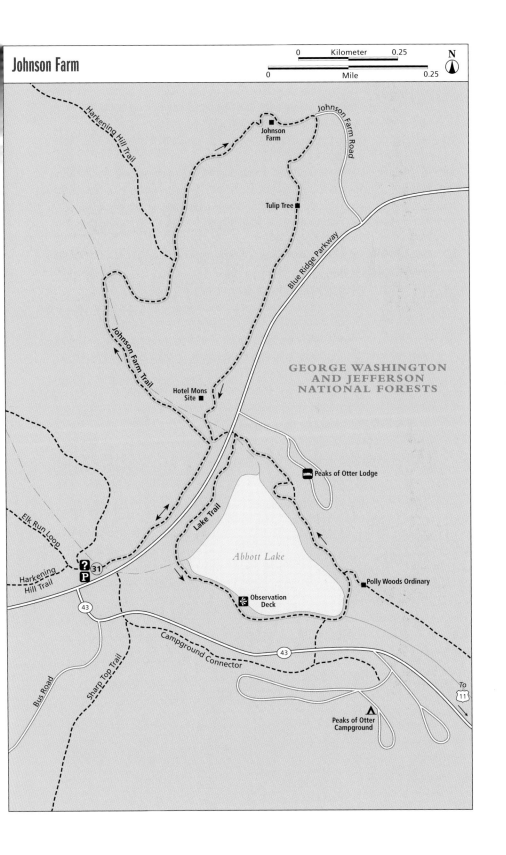

0   Kilometer   0.25

0   Mile   0.25

N

Harkening Hill Trail

Johnson Farm Road

Johnson
Farm

Tulip Tree

Blue Ridge Parkway

Johnson Farm Trail

GEORGE WASHINGTON
AND JEFFERSON
NATIONAL FORESTS

Hotel Mons
Site

Peaks of Otter Lodge

Elk Run Loop

Lake Trail

Abbott Lake

Harkening
Hill Trail

31

43

Polly Woods Ordinary

Observation
Deck

Campground Connector

43

Bus Road

Sharp Top Trail

Peaks of Otter
Campground

To

11

Miles and Directions

0.0   Start by leaving from the lower end of the Peaks of Otter Visitor Center parking lot, walking over a wooden bridge, and joining a foot trail. The Blue Ridge Parkway is just off to your right. Enter oak, maple, and dogwood forest.

0.3   Leave left on the Johnson Farm Trail, ascending a hollow. Begin a clockwise loop. Climb a ferny hollow on a singletrack path.

0.8   Intersect the Harkening Hill Trail after leaving the hollow. Stay straight with the Johnson Farm Trail.

1.1   Drop to the clearing of Johnson Farm. Take time to explore the outside and inside—if it is open. Interpreters will be on-site on warm-weather weekends and holidays. Leave the home on the old Johnson Farm Road.

1.2   Split right from the old farm road, back on narrow foot trail. Descend into a hollow, partly wooded and partly open.

1.4   Pass a huge tulip tree on your left. Enjoy views of Sharp Top ahead.

1.7   Pass the Hotel Mons site on your right. Ahead, cross a branch, then split left to pass under the Blue Ridge Parkway via tunnel.

1.8   Emerge near the Peaks of Otter Lodge. Turn right here on the Lake Trail, now circling Abbott Lake, named for the Blue Ridge Parkway's chief architect. Incredible views open on the boardwalk and gravel trail.

2.2   Pass an observation deck looking north toward the lodge and Flat Top.

2.3   A spur trail leads right to the campground. Continue your counterclockwise loop around the south side of the lake, now on an asphalt path. Cross Abbott Lake Dam.

2.4   Take the spur trail leading right to the Polly Woods Ordinary. A widow, Polly Woods, ran a way station near here (the actual spot was submerged under Abbott Lake) in the 1830s. The term "ordinary" was used for private boarding quarters in a rural setting. Backtrack and resume circling the lake.

2.7   Stay left as an asphalt path passes directly in front of the Peaks of Otter Lodge. It continues the lodging tradition in these Virginia mountains.

2.8   Complete the Lake Trail. Begin backtracking toward the visitor center.

3.2   Reach the visitor center, finishing the hike.

32 Stuarts Knob at Fairy Stone State Park

This hike at Fairy Stone State Park explores the historic and natural features of Stuarts Knob, rich with iron ore. Starting in the 1700s, this backwater experienced mining boom and bust, becoming a moonshiner's paradise. Later, the Civilian Conservation Corps (CCC) developed a state park here. Today you can see vestiges of mining operations and an attendant community on CCC-built trails, all encapsulated in hilly wooded terrain enhanced with natural beauty, including a cleared view from the shoulder of Stuarts Knob.

Start: Stuarts Knob Trailhead on Union Bridge Road, VA 623
Distance: 3.2-mile balloon loop
Hiking time: About 2–2.5 hours
Difficulty: Moderate, does have steep hills
Trail surface: Natural-surface path
Best season: Spring for wildflowers
Other trail users: None
Canine compatibility: Leashed dogs permitted

Land status: Virginia state park
Fees and permits: Parking fee required
Schedule: Open daily year-round
Maps: *Fairy Stone State Park;* USGS *Philpott Lake, Charity*
Trail contact: Fairy Stone State Park, 967 Fairy Stone Lake Dr., Stuart, VA 24171-9588; (276) 930-2424; virginiastateparks.gov

Finding the trailhead: From the town of Bassett, take VA 57 (Fairy Stone Park Highway) west for 10 miles to VA 346. Turn right on VA 346 (Fairy Stone Lake Road) north and follow it 0.4 mile to VA 623 (Union Bridge Road). Turn left on Union Bridge Road and follow it 0.8 mile to the Stuarts Knob trailhead, on your left just after a boat ramp. Trailhead GPS: N36 47.906' / W80 7.019'

The Hike

How does a state park get a name like Fairy Stone? Within its boundaries lie some unusual crystals, made of iron aluminum and silicate. Due to their six-sided shape, these crystals connect at right angles, often forming crosses. Legend has it that fairies once roamed this land in the shadow of the Blue Ridge. When the fairies learned of Jesus's death, their tears crystallized when they hit the ground. The fairies have since moved on, but the fairy stones mark the sorrowful spot where they were when Jesus died. These fairy stones were one attraction that led to this locale becoming one of Virginia's first state parks.

▶ The defunct mining town of Fayerdale was named using parts of two mine owners' names, the "F" and "A" for Frank A. Hill and "Dale" for Herbert Dale Lafferty.

Stuarts Knob is yet another attraction. This mount was found to be rich in iron ore. Starting in the late 1700s, men were mining the mountainsides using simple pick and shovel. The backbreaking work was slow and challenging. Despite the difficulty

Looking down on the state park beach

of moving the product to market, Stuarts Knob was mined this way for over one hundred years until technology made extraction more efficient.

The Virginia Ore and Lumber Company updated operations in the early 1900s. The mining town of Fayerdale sprang up, but the company and the town collapsed upon the arrival of cheaper ore from Germany. Today we can roam the trails of Stuarts Knob and see the mine sites while walking the roads used to access those mines, all contained on the slopes of a scenic wooded hillside that allows views of adjacent mountains and displays the amazing recuperative powers of nature. You will also get a chance to see the works of the Civilian Conservation Corps (CCC). Their marks are everywhere, from the lake you see below Stuarts Knob to the quarry from which they extracted stone to build the facilities still in use today.

The hike is not only historic but scenic too. You will soon rise to view the first of three mine openings, all barred for safety reasons. The hike then scales the slope of Stuarts Knob, where tulip trees regally rise. Reach a view of Bull Run Mountain and

The Civilian Conservation Corps

The Great Depression hit the United States in 1929, following a devastating stock market crash. At the time no one knew how long the economic hard times would go on. In 1933, still in the throes of economic malaise, President Franklin Delano Roosevelt initiated a government work program, the Civilian Conservation Corps, commonly known as the CCC. In it, men were hired on various projects throughout the country, including transforming Fairy Stone into the park we see today.

The first CCC boys arrived at Fairy Stone in October of 1933. They lived in tents not far from the trailhead for this hike, until finally moving into barracks built on-site. To qualify for the CCC, recruits had to be between the ages of 17 and 25, out of school, and unemployed. Eligible enrollees were often shipped far from their homes to prevent desertion. They earned $30 per month through their efforts, of which $25 went back home. At Fairy Stone they razed the town of Fayerdale, timbered the land inundated by Fairy Stone Lake and built the dam, park roads, even the cabins, bathhouses, and a restaurant. The young men also constructed the campground, swim beach, and hiking trails.

The CCC was organized into camps, generally consisting of 100 to 300 men, using a military structure with an emphasis on discipline. Each camp had its specialists, from cooks to officers. More than 2,600 camps containing a half-million men were spread across all forty-eight states. Camp life was routine. The men generally rose around 6 a.m., ate a filling breakfast, then worked until 4:30 in the afternoon, with a lunch break in the middle. Back at camp the men could do as they pleased, often writing letters home. These descriptive letters to loved ones helped build a historical record of life in the CCC camps.

Whether the CCC helped or hurt the nation's economy remains up for debate. The CCC program continued until 1942, when potential enrollees instead entered the military to fight World War II. The CCC was never abolished, only defunded to extinction. Most of the CCC boys have passed away, but their legacy lives on, in the lake, the roads, the cabins—and the trails of Fairy Stone State Park.

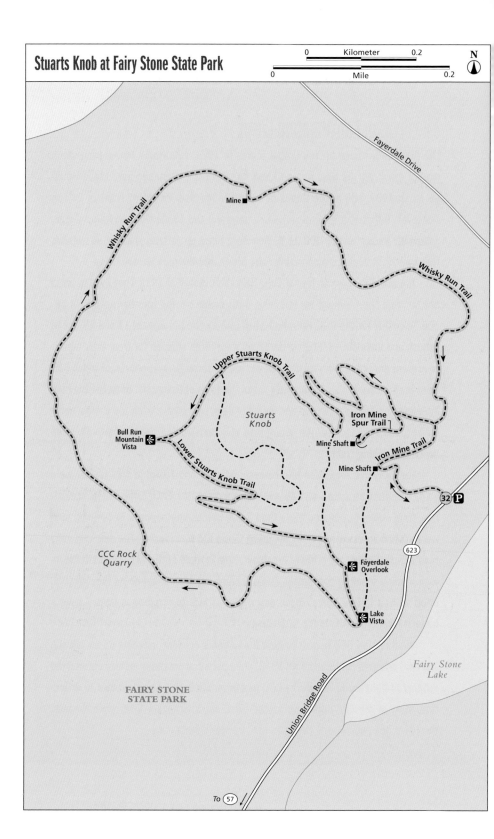

Stuarts Knob at Fairy Stone State Park

Fayerdale Drive

Whisky Run Trail

Whisky Run Trail

Mine

Upper Stuarts Knob Trail

Iron Mine
Spur Trail

Stuarts
Knob

Bull Run
Mountain
Vista

Mine Shaft

Iron Mine Trail

Lower Stuarts Knob Trail

Mine Shaft

32 P

623

CCC Rock
Quarry

Fayerdale
Overlook

Lake
Vista

Fairy Stone
Lake

FAIRY STONE
STATE PARK

Union Bridge Road

To 57

other hills of the Blue Ridge in the distance. Next, the CCC-built trails lead to a view of Fairy Stone Lake and the heart of the park facilities. The final part circles the lowermost reaches of the knob, crossing streamlets and even an old moonshine still site. The mining and lumbering had all but ended in the area, leaving the production of "corn likker" a viable and very profitable, though illegal, endeavor, as this was after Prohibition was enacted. Ironically, the CCC boys provided a new market for the moonshine. Later, the railroad and mining equipment was sold off, leaving only an altered landscape and a few relics here and there, protected within an Old Dominion state park.

Miles and Directions

0.0 Start by leaving the Stuarts Knob Trailhead on the Iron Mine Trail, heading uphill among tulip trees, white pine, and red bud.

0.1 Reach an intersection. Here, the Iron Mine Trail goes right and left. Walk a few feet left to see the first mine opening, then go right, working on a steep side slope.

0.2 Meet the north end of the Whisky Run Trail. You will return here later. For now, stay left on the Iron Mine Trail, working up Stuarts Knob.

0.3 Reach the Iron Mine Spur Trail. Take this steep path left up to another mine opening. Note the grown-over tailings near the mine site. Backtrack, then continue the Iron Mine Trail in gorgeous tulip-tree-dominated woods. Ascend the slope of Stuarts Knob by switchback.

0.7 Come to another trail junction. Here, the Iron Mine Trail leaves left. Turn right, joining the Upper Stuarts Knob Trail. Curve around the north side of Stuarts Knob, looking for unnatural diggings into the hillsides.

0.9 Veer right, picking up the Lower Stuarts Knob Trail.

1.0 Take the short spur leading right to the Bull Mountain Overlook. Gain views of Bull Mountain along with hills and valleys between. Continue on Lower Stuarts Knob Trail.

1.1 Stay right after rejoining the Upper Stuarts Knob Trail. Switchback downhill on the south side of Stuarts Knob.

1.4 Stay right at the intersection with the Iron Mine Trail. Shortly pass the spur left to the Fayerdale Overlook. A diagram shows the town's layout below.

1.5 The Iron Mine Trail takes you to an overlook of Fairy Stone Lake, the swim beach, and facilities beyond. Turn right here, joining the Whisky Run Trail. Curve past pines and mountain laurel on the south-facing slope.

1.8 Come to a steep drop-off on your left. You are atop the rock quarry worked by the CCC, which used the stone to develop the park in the 1930s. Don't try to explore it from here. Keep walking around to the west side of the knob in rocky woods.

2.1 Step over a drainage. Curve around to the north side of the knob. The terrain flattens a bit. Begin bisecting small drainages.

2.4 The Whisky Run Trail passes the final barred mine site to the right of the trail.

2.6 Look for the rocky remains of an old moonshine still just after crossing a branch. An interpretive sign details whisky making in these parts.

3.0 The Whisky Run Trail finishes its loop around Stuarts Knob. Turn left here and backtrack to the trailhead.

3.2 Reach the trailhead, ending the hike.

Southwest Virginia

Massive boulders clog the Guest River.

33 Shot Tower via New River Trail

This hike traces a historic converted rail line that leads to a shot tower—used in making lead rifle shot, one of only three such towers in the United States. Start at Foster Falls, a former milling community on the banks of the New River. Tour the assortment of old structures before walking the level New River Trail astride the powerful river of the same name. The old rail line takes you past a river ford used for hundreds of years. Reach the shot tower and take a stroll around it, appreciating the 200-plus-year-old structure before backtracking on the New River Trail to Foster Falls.

Start: Foster Falls
Distance: 3.0 miles out and back, plus touring grounds of Foster Falls
Hiking time: About 1.5–2 hours
Difficulty: Easy
Trail surface: Pea gravel
Best season: Year-round
Other trail users: Bicyclists and equestrians
Canine compatibility: Leashed dogs permitted

Land status: Virginia state park
Fees and permits: Parking permit required
Schedule: Open daily year-round
Maps: *National Geographic Mount Rogers; USGS Foster Falls, Sylvatus*
Trail contact: New River Trail State Park, 176 Orphanage Dr., Foster Falls, VA 24360; (276) 699-6778; virginiastateparks.gov

Finding the trailhead: From exit 24 on I-77 south of Wytheville, take VA 69 (Lead Mine Road) for 0.2 mile east to US 52. Turn left on US 52 (Fort Chiswell Road) and head north for 1.5 miles to VA 608 (Foster Falls Road). Turn right on 608 and follow it for 1.8 miles to VA 623, Orphanage Drive (do not take the road access to Foster Falls). Turn left on Orphanage Drive and shortly enter Foster Falls, part of New River Trail State Park. Park on the right at the restored railroad station. Trailhead GPS: N36 53.057' / W80 51.365'

The Hike

Foster Falls makes an ideal place to start a hike to Shot Tower, for it contains a history of its own. Foster Falls was a community centered on the large rapids of the New River here. In the early 1880s a millrace was built on the right-hand riverbank. The power of falling water was harnessed to help power an iron furnace, and later a sawmill to cut lumber and a gristmill to grind corn. With the advent of the railroad running along the river, the village of Foster Falls grew to add a store/community center, post office, and hotel! Time passed, the furnace cooled, and the hotel became a school, then an orphanage. By 1962 Foster Falls was a collection of unused buildings and the orphanage had moved to Wytheville.

Since becoming part of New River Trail State Park, the area has undergone a makeover. The historic buildings have been stabilized and restored, including the old train depot, now a gift/information shop. Recreation facilities have been added. Though no one lives here anymore, you can camp at Foster Falls. Read below for more about park activities.

The Shot Tower: Interesting Construction

Begun by Thomas Jackson, the shot tower took seven years to complete. Its construction is fascinating. Designed to create round lead "bullets" of differing sizes, the tower was constructed 75 feet high on a hill above the New River. To make shot, lead was liquidized in a large kettle, then poured through sieves to create the appropriate-size shot, falling 150 feet to a kettle filled with water. But wait, the tower is only 75 feet high! The second 75 feet was a narrow shaft dug into the hill. An access tunnel, at river level, was used to retrieve the cooled and hardened shot from the lower shaft as well as provide water for the cooling kettle. The long fall rounded the shot. The tower's 2.5-foot-thick walls helped keep the tower from getting too cold, allowing the shot to form. The lead and coal/wood used to heat the lead kettle was either brought up by pulleys or by hand—no one can say for sure.

Like many historic buildings and places, the shot tower fell into disuse but was renovated and reopened in 1968 by the Lions Club. The tower is generally closed for entry but is open during naturalist programs originating at Foster Falls. A barred door on the lower end allows a view into the staircase leading up to the tower top.

Your hike to Foster Falls follows the old railroad bed of the Norfolk and Western Railroad. New River Trail State Park is Virginia's longest park, extending over 57 miles along a former railroad bed. Thanks to Norfolk Southern Corporation, the state of Virginia received this railroad right-of-way. Since the tracks were removed by Norfolk Southern, the remaining trail bed was already in usable shape, and it wasn't long before the New River Trail was being used by recreationalists.

The rail trail is the primary attraction of Foster Falls, as it courses along a cinder bed and over trestles that span the New River and its tributaries. There's even a tunnel. Occasional rapids and riverside bluffs satiate the visual palate. This trail demonstrates how, in our modern era, we can preserve scenic and historic areas in the midst of human habitation.

The building of the Shot Tower was preceded by the discovery of lead, the primary ingredient in shot. Interestingly, at one time Moses Austin, father of Stephen F. Austin of Texas fame, ran the lead mines at nearby Austinville, and lent his name to the town. During the Civil War these lead mines were the chief source of shot for the Confederacy.

◀ *The Shot Tower*

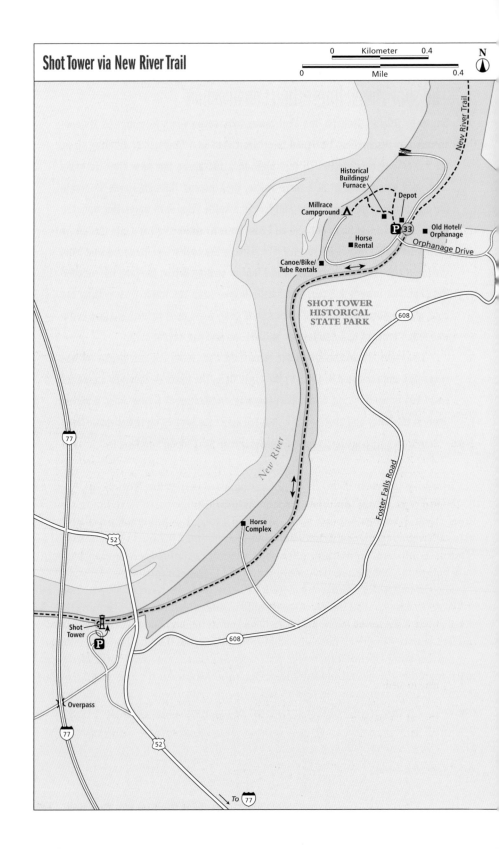

0   Kilometer   0.4

0   Mile   0.4

N

New River Trail

Historical
Buildings/
Furnace

Depot

Millrace
Campground

P 33

Old Hotel/
Orphanage

Horse
Rental

Orphanage Drive

Canoe/Bike/
Tube Rentals

SHOT TOWER
HISTORICAL
STATE PARK

608

77

New River

Foster Falls Road

52

Horse
Complex

608

Shot
Tower

P

Overpass

77

52

To 77

Millrace Campground, at Foster Falls, is in excellent condition. Nestled beneath a grove of sycamore and tulip trees, the well-groomed camping area beckons hikers and other park visitors to come back one day and spend the night. As its name implies, the campground is on the banks of the New River, on a carved-out side stream, or millrace, of the New River. The rapids of Foster Falls provide wonderful background music for campers who wish to pitch their tents here. **Note:** This is a tent-only campground. Furthermore, it is a walk-in tent campground. Campers must transfer their gear from their vehicle to little wagons used to haul gear to their chosen sites. Each camping area has a picnic table, fire grate, and lantern post. Camping is by reservation only. Sites are available most weekdays and on off-season weekends. Call well ahead to reserve a site on summer weekends, since there are only twelve campsites.

▶ In 1981 the American Society of Mechanical Engineers designated the Shot Tower a National Historic Mechanical Engineering Landmark.

There is much to do here including fishing for walleye, bass, and bream and swimming, tubing, or canoeing. A livery offers tubes and canoes for rent, as well as bicycles and shuttle service for heading out on the rail trail. Popular bike runs are from Galax to Foster Falls, or Pulaski to Foster Falls. On summer weekends the equestrian livery is open for business, enabling you to ride the rail trail atop a horse.

Miles and Directions

0.0 Start by leaving from the Foster Falls Depot southbound on the New River Trail. Immediately cross Orphanage Drive. The main facilities of Foster Falls are to your right. Soon pass an old railroad mile-marker post beside the trail. Pass above the bike/tube/canoe livery, gaining excellent river views of the rapids that comprise Foster Falls. Also, note the upper end of the millrace, dug to power industry of Foster Falls.

0.4 Travel in sometimes wooded, sometimes open areas. Pass under a large power line. Saddle alongside a quiet stretch of the river.

0.8 Pass a cedar-clad high bluff on your left after walking beneath ash, walnut, redbud, and dogwood. The river and trail separate. The flat below is occupied by the Mark E. Hufeisen Horse Complex. The I-77 Bridge crossing the New River is visible in the distance.

1.2 The entrance to the horse complex crosses the New River Trail.

1.4 Come to the curved trestle over Shorts Creek and US 52. This is the site of Jackson's Ferry, where a hand-drawn ferry was in operation from 1758 until 1930, when the US 52 bridge was built here. It is only natural that US 52 and I-77 cross the New at this location, as new road systems often follow historic pathways that make the most sense in getting from here to there.

1.5 Reach the spur trail leading left and uphill to the Shot Tower. The New River continues straight, ultimately to end at Galax, Virginia, after 26 miles. Head up the spur to explore the Shot Tower and environs, but the inner tower will be closed unless interpretive tours are going on. Backtrack toward Foster Falls.

3.0 Arrive at Foster Falls and the old depot, completing the rail trail trek.

34 Raven Cliff Furnace

This two-part walk combines the natural beauty of Virginia's highlands with its primitive industrial past. The setting is majestic Raven Cliff, rising high in the clear Cripple Creek valley of the Jefferson National Forest. Enjoy two short trails from a nice picnic area and campground. Walk up pretty Cripple Creek on the Raven Cliff Furnace Trail, then reach a still-intact iron ore smelter. Backtrack to the trailhead, and join the Raven Cliff Trail. Walk an old railroad grade, gaining more stream views and passing through a blasted bluff. Finally, descend to Cripple Creek and a ford. You'll find the area appealing. Consider incorporating other activities into the hike, such as picnicking, fishing, swimming, or camping.

Start: Raven Cliff Recreation Area
Distance: 2.0 miles for 2 out-and-backs
Hiking time: About 1.5-2 hours
Difficulty: Easy
Trail surface: Natural-surface path
Best season: Spring for wildflowers
Other trail users: Equestrians on Raven Cliff Trail
Canine compatibility: Leashed dogs permitted

Land status: Jefferson National Forest
Fees and permits: None
Schedule: Open daily year-round
Maps: *National Geographic Mount Rogers; USGS Cripple Creek*
Trail contact: Mount Rogers National Recreation Area, Route 1, Box 303, Marion, VA 24354; (276) 783-5196; www.fs.usda .gov/gwj

Finding the trailhead: From exit 70 on I-81 in Wytheville, drive 13.6 miles south on US 21 to Speedwell. In Speedwell turn left on VA 619 (Saint Peters Road). Stay with 619 for 6.5 miles. (The actual name of 619 changes from Saint Peters to Cripple Creek to Gleaves Road.) Turn right on Raven Cliff Lane, where there is a sign for Raven Cliff Recreation Area. Follow Raven Cliff Lane for 0.9 mile and dead-end at an auto turnaround. Trailhead GPS: N36 50.194' / W81 3.795'

The Hike

Early Virginia was searching for ways to utilize the natural features and resources within its bounds. Iron ore was one resource, found here in the backwaters of Wythe County near Cripple Creek. A suitable furnace location was found 4 miles distant from an iron ore mine, in the shadows of Raven Cliff, a sheer iron-stained bluff. The pyramid-shaped 30-foot-high limestone block structure we see today was the centerpiece of a greater facility that included not only buildings and land alterations to run the furnace but also homes and barns to house the men and animals that worked the remote furnace 12 miles southwest of Wytheville.

▶ Raven Cliff Furnace was constructed with local limestone and sandstone and completed with a brick chimney. It was reconstructed and improved twice after its original form, incorporating new iron-blasting technologies with each rebuilding.

Hiker bridge crosses Cripple Creek en route to Raven Cliff Furnace.

The furnace operated until 1837. Northern iron production underpriced and undercut the furnace. It was cooled for a quarter of a century, then rebuilt and refired to produce iron for the Confederate war effort. This second stage lasted until 1893, with another reconstruction and modernization of the furnace in 1875. The difficulty of moving the finished iron was ultimately its undoing, despite a spur of the Norfolk & Western Railroad being laid to the furnace site after the Civil War.

Today you can hike to the furnace and also walk along the old railroad grade, recapturing a piece of this industrial past. Raven Cliff Furnace Trail heads along Cripple Creek down to the still-standing trapezoidal iron ore furnace. Once the center of activity, a literal hotspot, the furnace lies cool and nearly forgotten. Oh, what stories it could tell!

Pick up the Raven Cliff Trail after backtracking to the trailhead. This path connects Raven Cliff Recreation Area with Collins Cove Horse Camp. Yes, it can be a little sloppy after rains, due to equestrian traffic. However, the former rail line is easy and pretty as it winds through the Cripple Creek gorge near Raven Cliff. Impressive rock-blasting work keeps the path level and creates intriguing rock bluffs. Views open the field across Cripple Creek. Look for the iron furnace below. It is most easily seen in leafless winter. The only elevation change occurs when the trail descends to ford Cripple Creek. There was once a trestle here, when the railroad was active. The foundations of the trestle still stand today.

Raven Cliff Recreation Area is a fun place to spend a day—and night. The forest service did well in purchasing this slice of the Cripple Creek Valley. Here, bluffs border one side of the large watercourse, while on the other side a partly forested hill rises to overlook the bluffs across the way. Visitors can picnic or camp, then fish, swim, hike, mountain-bike, or ride horses. And the combination of woods and meadow makes for favorable deer habitat.

A grassy picnic area runs alongside the water; it also has a shady shelter. The campground, near the trailhead, is laid out along a gravel lane with an auto turnaround at the end. Level campsites are built into the side of Gleaves Knob under a forest of white pine, maple, and oak. Campsites are higher on the right, up the hill, and lower on the left, down the hill. The campsites are well dispersed from one another, resulting in excellent campsite privacy. Gravel tent pads drain water from the twenty sites, generally available on all but summer holiday weekends.

Though the campground is not directly on the creek, it does offer winter views and quick access to the water. Anglers and swimmers both enjoy Cripple Creek.

The Centerpiece of a Forgotten Community

The actual stone Raven Cliff Furnace stands 29 feet high, 30 feet across at the base, and 9 feet wide at its peak. Note the retaining wall behind the furnace. The arches at its base are still intact. The furnace interior is full of dirt. At one time a water race ran nearby, with a wheel pit that powered massive bellows to heat charcoal in the furnace. An elevated charging bridge once poured ore, charcoal, and limestone into the furnace for smelting. A casting house, where iron molds known as pigs and sows were stored, was located east of the furnace. As hard as it is to picture today in this serene and scenic river valley, work your mind harder and visualize an entire community hereabouts, with houses, cabins, blacksmith shop, company store, horse stables, and storage sheds. Smell the burning charcoal, the cooling pig iron. Listen to the sounds of the rail line shipping the iron away, the clopping of horse hooves pulling wagons loaded with supplies for the iron workers, the ingredients being dropped into the furnace, the clanging at the blacksmith shop. Today we are left with the hushed furnace, gurgling Cripple Creek, and the cry of nearby nesting ravens—and your imagination.

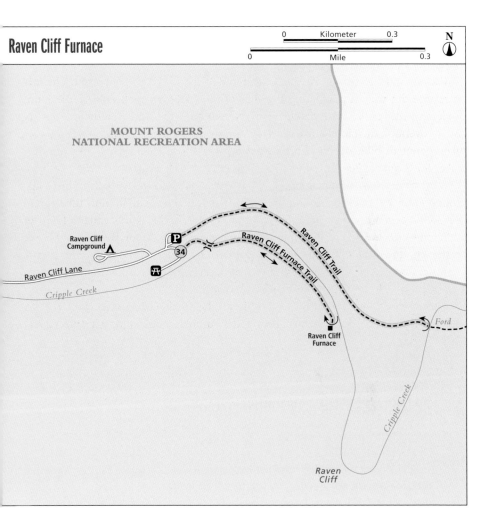

MOUNT ROGERS
NATIONAL RECREATION AREA

Raven Cliff
Campground

Raven Cliff Lane

Cripple Creek

Raven Cliff Furnace Trail

Raven Cliff Trail

Raven Cliff
Furnace

Ford

Cripple Creek

Raven
Cliff

There is smallmouth-bass fishing year-round and trout fishing during winter and spring. Swimmers can enjoy some of the slower, quiet areas near the picnic area. Sunbathers will also like the spot. What a change in activities from the days when Raven Cliff Furnace belched iron and smoke!

Miles and Directions

0.0 Start by leaving the upper parking area and walking a short distance down the road to the picnic area. Look left for a metal gate and the official beginning of the Raven Cliff Furnace Trail (save the Raven Cliff Trail for the second part of the hike). Walk upstream with Cripple Creek to your right. An unofficial connector leaves left uphill.

0.1 Span a long steel-and-wood structure over Cripple Creek. Look for smallmouth bass and other fish below. Veer left, paralleling the watercourse downstream on a level track. Grasses and brush border the mown path. Walnut trees thrive along the stream, flowing

The well-preserved Raven Cliff Furnace

clear to your left. An unofficial horse trail crosses the Raven Cliff Furnace Trail then leaves right. Stay straight with the hiker-only path toward the furnace.

0.4 Reach Raven Cliff Furnace. The combination of Cripple Creek, the furnace, a fenced field, and Raven Cliff in the background makes this a scenic spot. The hiker trail ends a short distance beyond the furnace. Backtrack to the trailhead.

0.8 Leave the trailhead, now on the Raven Cliff Trail. You are now on the post–Civil War–built Norfolk & Western Railroad grade. Begin paralleling Cripple Creek down to the right. Gleaves Knob rises to your left.

1.1 Note the small cave created to the left of the trail, from railroad blasting work. It remains dry in rains—I've waited out a storm here.

1.2 Just before entering a section of blasted rock on both sides of the trail, look right, by Cripple Creek, for the Raven Cliff Furnace below, where you were earlier.

1.3 Come to a junction after bisecting the blasted rock. An unmaintained trail leaves right, back toward the furnace, while the Raven Cliff Trail drops left.

1.4 Reach the ford of Cripple Creek. While at the ford, look for the stone trestles of the former railroad bridge. From here, it is 0.6 mile to Collins Cove Horse Camp. This is a good place to turn around to keep your feet dry.

2.0 Arrive back at the trailhead, completing the second out-and-back walk.

35 Burkes Garden from Chestnut Knob

This hike utilizes a remote portion of the Appalachian Trail (AT), rising past open meadows with stupendous mountain views. Reach an old stone cabin where a fire warden lived, manning a fire tower site at a place called Chestnut Knob, rising well above 4,000 feet in elevation. Here, you can peer down into Burkes Garden, one of Virginia's most beautiful valleys, as well as the Beartown Wilderness.

Start: FR 222 near Ceres
Distance: 9.2 miles out and back
Hiking time: About 5-6 hours
Difficulty: More difficult due to distance
Trail surface: Natural
Best season: Whenever the skies are clear
Other trail users: None
Canine compatibility: Dogs permitted

Land status: National forest
Fees and permits: None
Schedule: 24/7/365
Map: *Jefferson National Forest*
Trail contact: Jefferson National Forest, 110 S. Park Ave., Blacksburg, VA 24060; (540) 552-4641; www.fs.fed.us

Finding the trailhead: From exit 52 on I-77 near Bland, take VA 42 west / US 52 west for 4.2 miles, then stay right with VA 42 west as it diverges from US 52. Follow VA 42 for 10.2 more miles to reach the hamlet of Ceres. Here, turn right on VA 625, Poor Valley Road. At 0.4 mile it turns to gravel. At 6.7 miles Poor Valley Road becomes FR 222. It is a total of 8.0 miles from Ceres to the Appalachian Trail parking area on your left, where the AT crosses FR 222. Trailhead GPS: N37 1.362' / W81 25.498'

The Hike

Burkes Garden is one of the Old Dominion's most beautiful agricultural valleys. There is only one natural entrance to the flat cove encircled by high ridges: Burkes Garden Creek flows from the ridge-rimmed valley, creating an access portal. Burkes Garden is pocked with dairy farms and other operations that recall a way of life far removed from today's electronic universe. Having only two ways in or out of the valley, one the aforementioned natural portal of Burkes Garden Creek and the other being a torturous mountain road, the state of the local transportation system creates isolation, and the residents of Burkes Garden—numbering less than 500—like it that way.

Hikers can soak in a great view of Burkes Garden via the Appalachian Trail. The AT runs along the southeast ridges above Burkes Garden, which forms the largest historic rural district in Virginia, stretching 5 miles by 10 miles in size. Additionally, Burkes Garden is Virginia's highest valley, perched at 3,087 feet above sea level.

▶ The population of Burkes Garden peaked at 1,500 during the 1890s. Today, fewer than 500 residents occupy the isolated mountain cove.

A fire warden's cabin is now a trail shelter.

In 1748 one James Burke was working on a surveying crew, gaining the lay of the land as Virginia's colonial residents pushed westward into the Appalachians from the coast. Of course, the resident Shawnee, having Burkes Garden to themselves, did not care for these men coming into their rich hunting grounds, especially in this flat cove encircled by mountains that reliably drew in deer, elk, and bear, to be taken by their arrows. The surveying party camped in the valley that was to bear his name. James Burke had cook duties and peeled some potatoes while preparing supper. When the survey crew returned next year, a potato patch had sprung up from his peelings. His fellow surveyors jokingly named the spot Burkes Garden and the name stuck.

As often happens with surveyors, Burke remembered this rich valley and brought his family here to settle. They had a few run-ins with the Indians in the 1750s, but the locale eventually came under Old Dominion control. The westward migration passed Burkes Garden, leaving the bucolic valley to thrive in seclusion. And it remains that way to this very day. However, it almost was not to be. George Vanderbilt, owner

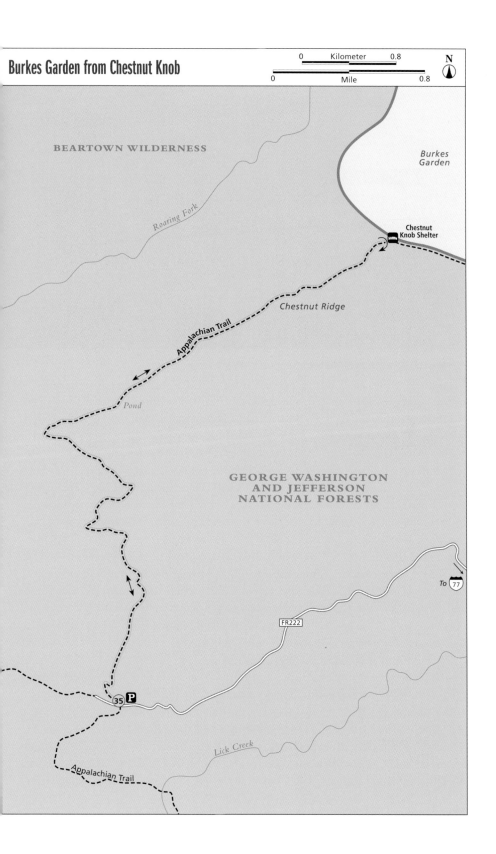

Burkes Garden from Chestnut Knob

BEARTOWN WILDERNESS

Burkes Garden

Roaring Fork

Chestnut Knob Shelter

Chestnut Ridge

Appalachian Trail

Pond

GEORGE WASHINGTON AND JEFFERSON NATIONAL FORESTS

To 77

FR222

35 P

Lick Creek

Appalachian Trail

The trail crosses open meadows en route to Chestnut Knob.

of the famed Biltmore House near Asheville, North Carolina, first tried to buy out the residents of Burkes Garden for his palatial country estate, but they would not part with their beloved land, so Vanderbilt settled for the current location of his often-toured estate. That says a lot about the splendor of Burkes Garden and the dearness to which those who own it have. Burkes Garden is still referred to as "Vanderbilt's First Choice," as well as other names such as "God's Thumbprint" and the "Tranquility Bowl." If you are interested in visiting Burkes Garden, they hold a fall festival focusing on farm life and agricultural heritage on the last Saturday in September.

It is a lovely climb from the Lick Creek Valley to the crest of Chestnut Ridge. Once atop this ridge crest, you will pass through a series of meadows, kept open by the USDA Forest Service. The clearings sport views of the surrounding ridges and the Beartown Wilderness. The final reward comes when you reach Chestnut Knob and a cleared view of Burkes Garden. Here at 4,400 feet you will not only enjoy the vista but also find the enclosed stone cabin of a former fire warden who maintained a now dismantled tower. The stone cabin now functions as an Appalachian Trail shelter, harboring hikers heading through Virginia's high country.

The Forest Service got out of using fire towers and the stationary wardens manning them back in the 1970s. After this, many of the towers were dismantled, such as this one on Chestnut Knob. However, the value of the stone warden's cabin was apparent. In 1994 the cabin was rehabilitated and then altered to become an AT shelter. Unlike most trail shelters, it is completely enclosed with a wooden door and windows. Inside stand several bunks and a table. As lonely as it was for the fire warden, the Chestnut Knob shelter is a welcome sight for AT thru-hikers seeking refuge from the elements. A cleared view of Burkes Garden opens from the northeast side of the knob. The AT continues along the east side of Burkes Garden, along Garden Mountain, for 6 miles before dropping to Hunting Camp Creek.

To get the most enjoyment from this hike, try to do it during clear weather. The views are breathtaking from multiple points along the way. The mountain meadows, being open, are subject to wind and rain. Hikers certainly would not want to be caught out there during a thunderstorm. Also, allow for plenty of time to make the hike and enjoy the views along the way. Be apprised, it is a 2,100-foot climb from the trailhead to the Chestnut Knob shelter at the hike's end.

Miles and Directions

0.0 Start by leaving FR 222 northbound on the Appalachian Trail. Begin climbing into south-facing mesic forest on lower Chestnut Ridge. Switchback uphill to join a ridge, then level off.

0.9 The trail begins climbing in earnest. Drift into a narrow valley, still working uphill. The mountainside becomes rockier underneath mountain laurel and chestnut oaks.

1.2 Step across the small stream of the narrow valley. Join an old logging road.

1.5 Cross the stream a second time.

1.8 Make a major switchback to the left. Angle northwest for the nose of Chestnut Ridge.

2.0 Come to a small level area and pass an alluring sitting rock on the right.

2.4 Reach the nose of Chestnut Ridge. Turn right, heading northeast through your first cleared meadow. Views open to the south, clear to Mount Rogers, Virginia's highest point. Dip to a gap, bisect a stand of trees, then come to a second meadow. These meadows create wildlife clearings, attracting wild turkey, deer, and birds. Note the apple trees in some of the clearings. The apple trees draw in bears in the fall.

2.7 Pass a highland pond. A spur trail leads left to a spring feeding the pond. Climb farther as grand vistas open to the southeast, behind you as you climb.

2.9 Cut through an old pasturage fence. Haw trees and fire cherry trees are reclaiming this former field.

3.2 Open onto another meadow. Break the 4,100-foot barrier. This meadow opens wide, offering views to the northwest of Beartown Ridge, topped in evergreens. Brushy Ridge stands tall to the southeast.

3.9 The AT leaves the upper end of the biggest meadow, reentering woods on a doubletrack path, bordered by extremely rocky terrain shaded by oaks and maples. Pass over open rock slabs.

4.4 Drop into a gap. Here a doubletrack trail leads right to a spring. A small pond stands to the left in the gap. Keep straight on the AT as it rises through forest. Soon open onto the last meadow.

4.6 Reach the Chestnut Ridge trail shelter. The stone structure, once a fire warden's cabin, is now an Appalachian Trail shelter. Note the concrete pillars of the former fire tower from which the fire warden scanned for conflagrations. A camper privy is off in the distance, as is a sign indicating the Beartown Wilderness. Enjoy the view into Burkes Garden, and then backtrack.

9.2 Arrive back at the trailhead on FR 222.

36 Virginia Highlands Circuit

This hike explores Virginia's highest terrain, traversing incredibly beautiful and historic topography. Start at Massie Gap, once a highland homestead and now part of Grayson Highlands State Park. Follow the Appalachian Trail (AT) through a mix of meadow and woodlands. Come to Scales, a gap where livestock grazers weighed and sold their cattle in days gone by. The AT takes you on to Pine Mountain. Here, enjoy excellent views opened by timber operations from yesteryear and see some of the wild ponies that help keep the mountain lands open. Rejoin the AT and cross over the open rocky terrain of Wilburn Ridge, named for an 1800s hunter, before completing the loop. Be apprised this high-country hike is subject to inclement weather, especially in winter.

Start: Massie Gap at Grayson Highlands State Park

Distance: 10.8-mile balloon loop

Hiking time: About 6-7 hours

Difficulty: Difficult

Trail surface: Natural-surface path, very rocky in places

Best seasons: Late spring through early fall

Other trail users: Equestrians in places

Canine compatibility: Leashed dogs permitted

Land status: Grayson Highlands State Park, Jefferson National Forest

Fees and permits: Parking permit required

Schedule: Open daily year-round, except for inclement weather

Maps: *National Geographic Mount Rogers; USGS Whitetop Mountain, Trout Dale*

Trail contact: Mount Rogers National Recreation Area, Route 1, Box 303, Marion, VA 24354; (276) 783-5196; www.fs.usda.gov/gwj

Finding the trailhead: From exit 14 on I-77 near Hillsville, take US 58 west for 48 miles to Grayson Highlands State Park. Alternate directions: From Damascus, take US 58 east for 26 miles. Enter the park on VA 362 and follow it 2.5 miles to reach Massie Gap on your right. Parking is along the road on the right. Trailhead GPS: N36 38.007'/W81 30.505'

The Hike

The hike begins at Massie Gap, a level swath of land 4,500 feet high in the Mount Rogers High Country. Mount Rogers is Virginia's highest point at 5,729 feet, is part of an elevated massif with multiple mile-high peaks, and is home to wild ponies. This mountainous terrain was once cloaked in a contiguous spruce-fir forest, an evergreen mantle coveted by commercial timber operators. Logging began in the 1880s, and rare spruce-fir forest, which covers only 70,000 acres in the entire Southern Appalachians, was cleared out. After the Virginia highlands were stripped, treeless terrain was left. Farmers saw an opportunity to grow crops where the evergreens had once stood, including Lee Massie, who settled in the mists with his family. Farmers like Massie found out the very short growing season, inclement weather, and long distance to markets made farming nearly untenable and certainly unprofitable. But the open, well-watered ridges and

View Whitetop Mountain from the Virginia Highlands.

valleys proved hospitable for cattle, and local farmers in the valleys began the practice of taking their herds to the highlands to graze and fatten during the warm season, simultaneously producing crops and hay in the lowland fields. Up top, the cool breezes kept insects at bay for the cattle, and their continuous feeding prevented the highlands from reforesting with the spruce and fir that once grew "thick as briers." At the end of summer, the cattle would be taken off the mountain. Farmers learned their herds would bring better prices if weighed and sold before trundling down the mountain back to their farms, and thus cattle were weighed for sale at a place that came to be known as Scales.

Massie Gap is part of Grayson Highlands State Park, originally known as Mount Rogers State Park. It was established in 1965, around the same

▶ The Wilburn Ridge Pony Association, founded in 1975, manages the pony herd in the Mount Rogers High Country, aiming for an annual herd of 120 animals, auctioning off excess for vet care and winter hay for the others.

Wilburn Waters: Virginia Huntin' Legend

Wilburn Waters left his imprint on the highlands of Grayson County. Born of an Indian mother and a white father, Wilburn was destined for a lifetime of hunting and trapping in Southwest Virginia. He came around in 1832 at about 20 years old, from North Carolina. Pitching a rough camp on nearby Whitetop Mountain, Wilburn roamed this high country, tussling with wolves, bears, and deer. Stories abound of Wilburn's wild exploits. While bear hunting in winter, he came upon a hunting dog and bear in a fight on the edge of a rocky knob such as you see in the high country. Wilburn jumped in the fray and tomahawked the bruin just before tumbling from the cliff. Now, that may or may not be true. The only thing we know for sure today is that Wilburn Waters was a real-life hunter and he ended up having a rocky ridge named for him.

time the USDA Forest Service acquired the adjacent high country and rerouted the Appalachian Trail through it. Today, the open country is slowly growing in, despite the resident year-round wild ponies and seasonal cattle grazing. On your hike you will leave the state park and follow the AT, gaining incredible views of and from Virginia's rooftop. Descend into historic Scales. Follow the AT from Scales, finally meeting the Pine Mountain Trail. This path walks among forests, rock outcrops, and meadows, finally rejoining the AT, which makes a three-quarter circle through the high country. Finally, follow Wilburn Ridge, named for bear-and-wolf hunter extraordinaire Wilburn Waters. Eye-popping vistas combined with rocky trail will make the final leg of your hike memorable.

Miles and Directions

0.0 Leave Massie Gap parking area on the Rhododendron Trail north toward a fence line. Pass through a gate, climbing through open slopes of Wilburn Ridge on a grassy trail. Gaze back at the Pinnacles on the far side of Massie Gap.

0.3 Merge with the Virginia Highlands Connector Trail, which has also come from Massie Gap. The two paths share the same wide, rocky treadway.

0.4 Meet the AT. Turn right here, northbound. Climb open terrain with views down to the Wise Trail shelter, where you will be.

0.9 The blue-blazed Appalachian Spur Trail leads right to the state park overnight backpacker parking area. Keep with the AT, curving toward Quebec Branch.

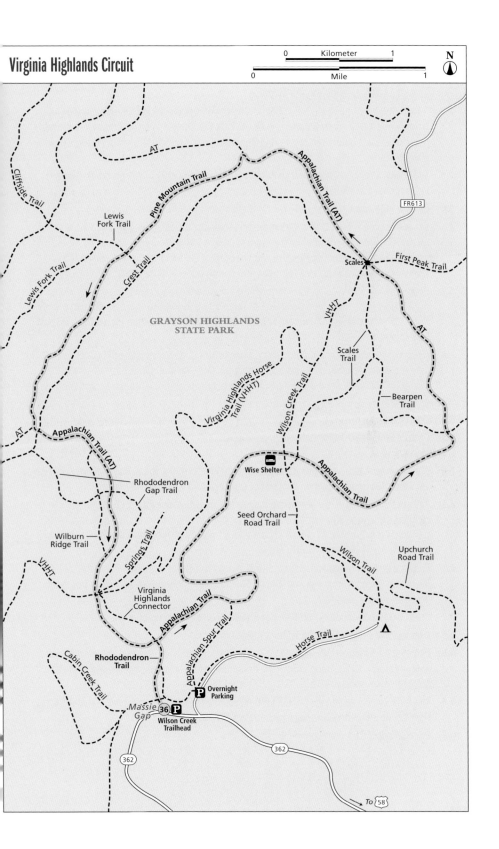

1.7 Cross Quebec Branch on a foot log. Soon, cross a walk-over-type stile and head east (downstream) along a fence line that parallels Quebec Branch. Watch for a sudden right turn off a railroad grade you are following.

2.6 Reach the Wise Trail shelter. This open-fronted wood structure stands in a meadow of grass, woods, and many blueberry bushes. Past the shelter, keep with the white blazes down to cross a stile, then span rhododendron-lined, boulder-laden Big Wilson Creek on a footbridge.

2.9 The Wilson Creek Trail leads left just before bridging a tributary of Wilson Creek. Shortly intersect the Scales Trail.

3.0 Cross a stile and enter the Little Wilson Creek Wilderness.

4.1 Leave the Little Wilson Creek Wilderness and intersect the Bearpen Trail. Keep straight on the AT, clear a stile and enter the open slopes of Stone Mountain. Follow the blazed wooden posts to incredible views of Wilburn Ridge, Pine Mountain, and forested Mount Rogers. Occasional wind-sculpted trees add a scenic touch to the meadow.

5.2 Reach the corral of Scales. Pass through the corral and several trail intersections. Here, the AT veers right, away from the corral, to enter a field broken by trees. Mostly climb away from Scales in a forest of northern hardwoods mixed with spruce that cloaks the slopes of Pine Mountain.

6.5 Come to a stile and enter a field. Skirt the meadow's edge for a couple of hundred yards before clearing another stile and intersecting the Pine Mountain Trail. Turn left on the Pine Mountain Trail. Walk amid a woodland of spruce, beech, and yellow birch accentuated by gray boulders.

6.9 Open to a large meadow with great views of Wilburn Ridge and Mount Rogers, dead ahead.

7.2 Cross a tiny stream before intersecting the Lewis Fork Trail. Stay straight with the Pine Mountain Trail.

7.5 The trail twists and turns through rhododendron and rock. The brush canopy lowers, revealing views. More views open in occasional clearings and outcrops. Keep climbing.

8.2 Intersect the AT. There is a very large outcrop to the right of this intersection that begs to be climbed. Otherwise, turn left here and resume northbound on the AT. Just past this, cross the wide Crest Trail. The AT climbs southeasterly up Wilburn Ridge. Climb a rocky knob for expansive views from over 5,500 feet.

8.7 Pass the Wilburn Ridge Trail. Shortly, the AT comes to Fatman Squeeze, where the trail pinches between a rock wall and a huge boulder. The trail becomes very rocky beyond the squeeze, slowing progress.

9.2 Cross the Rhododendron Gap Trail. Keep straight on the AT in open country.

9.5 Intersect the south end of the Wilburn Ridge Trail.

9.8 Intersect the Virginia Highlands Horse Trail just before crossing a step-over-type stile and entering Grayson Highlands State Park. Keep forward in the state park, following an old railroad grade through a field.

10.4 Meet the Virginia Highlands Connector Trail, completing the loop through the Mount Rogers High Country. Turn right and backtrack toward Massie Gap.

10.8 Reach Massie Gap, completing the hike.

37 Virginia Creeper Trail

The Virginia Creeper is the Old Dominion's most celebrated rail trail. Today, you can walk this former railroad line through one of the most scenic watersheds in the state—Whitetop Laurel Creek. Traverse several trestles as the trail intertwines with the creek, deep in mountain fastness. Your return route uses America's most famous footpath, the Appalachian Trail (AT). It offers a different perspective of this highland valley as it cruises upslope through a rocky gorge.

Start: Straight Branch parking area
Distance: 4.9-mile loop
Hiking time: About 3–3.5 hours
Difficulty: Moderate
Trail surface: Pea gravel on rail trail, natural surface on AT
Best season: Year-round
Other trail users: Bicyclists, equestrians on Virginia Creeper Trail

Canine compatibility: Leashed dogs permitted
Land status: National forest
Fees and permits: None
Schedule: Open daily year-round
Maps: *National Geographic Mount Rogers; USGS Konnarock*
Trail contact: Mount Rogers National Recreation Area, Route 1, Box 303, Marion, VA 24354; (276) 783-5196; www.fs.usda.gov/gwj

Finding the trailhead: From exit 19 on I-81 north of Bristol, take US 58 east to Damascus, Virginia. From the Little Red Caboose in Damascus, continue east on US 58 for 4.5 miles to the Straight Branch parking area, off US 58 to the right. Trailhead GPS: N36 38.645'/W81 44.407'

The Hike

Mention the Virginia Creeper Trail and folks will shortly be mentioning Damascus, Virginia. Damascus is the consummate trail town, located at the confluence of the Virginia Creeper Trail, the Appalachian Trail, and a few hundred other miles of paths within Virginia's Mount Rogers National Recreation Area, as well as the adjacent Cherokee National Forest in Tennessee. Damascus is one of those places where hikers and mountain bikers are often seen and the outdoor life is popular with many residents. This historic hike starts just a few miles out of Damascus, at the Straight Branch trailhead.

▶ The V-C Railroad once ran into Wilkesboro, North Carolina. When the railroad was abandoned, the right-of-way went back to the landowners in the Tar Heel State, thus the Virginia Creeper Trail ends at the Virginia–North Carolina state line.

The hiking starts easy on the gentle railroad grade that is the Virginia Creeper Trail. The crushed-gravel track has a blackish tint, relics of cinders from days gone by. On your way up, watch for old concrete numbered posts, leftovers from the days when trains whistled their way

along Whitetop Laurel Creek. This noisy mountain waterway provides moving visual beauty throughout the hike. The stream is stocked by the state of Virginia, and anglers use the Creeper to access promising waters for feisty trout. You will also see campsites nestled in the trailside woods. This area is popular with campers who enjoy hiking, bicycling, and fishing in a scenic setting. Bicycle-rental companies provide two-wheelers and trail shuttles on the Creeper, so expect bike traffic on warm weekends.

Originally, the Creeper brought logs from the collection of peaks, ridges, and hollows, then added passenger stops from Alvarado to Creek Junction to Green Cove to Whitetop. The rail link became vital to these rural citizens, allowing them access to urban markets and to trade their commodities in town. Some of the train stations have been preserved, adding landmarks of the past, and also currently serve as interpretive stops along the way.

Leave the Virginia Creeper Trail near the community of Taylors Valley. A single-track connector trail leads up the side of Whitetop Laurel gorge and meets the AT. Join the world's most famous footpath (and one of the oldest marked trails in America) and work your way on a rugged rock-riddled slope. The character of the hike changes dramatically. You can look down on Whitetop Laurel Creek and the Creeper Trail below, especially during leafless times. While hiking, consider the Appalachian Trail, a collaborative work of volunteers over several decades. It is a true outdoor success story and a beacon for all other trails throughout the land. Think about it: Almost everyone has heard of the Appalachian Trail, whereas most people haven't heard of most other paths.

The AT slips in and out of intermittent drainages. In summer the AT will be a leafy green tunnel. In winter you will be admiring the cliffs, boulders, and bluffs in this valley. At times the AT and Virginia Creeper come very close to one another, but the AT is most often well above the Creeper. After staying on a slope, the AT dips into a flat along Straight Branch. Here, the AT crosses US 58 and briefly enters the Feathercamp Branch valley. There are lots of streams and hills in this part of Southwest Virginia! Finally, the AT wanders west and comes to the Beech Grove Trail. This spur path leads you back to the Straight Branch parking area and the trail's end.

Miles and Directions

0.0 Leave the Straight Branch parking area, heading left on the Creeper Trail. Whitetop Laurel Creek flows to your right. Just ahead, bridge Straight Branch shortly before it flows into Whitetop Laurel Creek.

0.3 Cross your first railroad trestle over Whitetop Laurel Creek. Continue up the right bank in woods.

0.5 Cross the next trestle. Streamside views are nearly continuous.

◁ *Looping back on the Appalachian Trail*

The Creeper: How It Came to Be

The Virginia Creeper Trail was nearly a century in the making. Of course, the originators of the idea for a railroad through this slice of southwest Virginia had no vision whatsoever of backpack-toting hikers, plastic-clad peddlers, and equestrians plying their rail bed for pleasure and exercise. This part would come later, after the fundraising to build a rail by entrepreneurs vying for iron and timber resources in the nearby mountains, after the sweat produced by many men building trestles and blasting through hillsides. It came after a period of economic prosperity borne of untold millions of timber feet cut from the Virginia Highlands, followed by a period of slow decline in business for the Virginia-Carolina Railroad, or V-C, until it was nothing but fodder for railroad nostalgia buffs.

Then, in 1977 the train whistles stopped. After that the reality of a rail trail was still uncertain and a lot of effort by local groups led to the complete rail trail, which now extends from Whitetop Station to Abingdon, Virginia, a distance of over 34 miles.

Along the way, the railroad was nicknamed the Virginia Creeper, maybe for the vine of the same name that thrives locally, or maybe because of the slow nature of the railroad as it climbed through the mountains. Today, the Virginia Creeper is the most popular rail trail in the Old Dominion. The fame of this rail trail is well deserved. From Whitetop Station at 3,525 feet, the Creeper courses down through the mountains, passing vistas near and far, deep woods, small farms, and by clear, fast streams. It passes Green Cove, where an original train station still stands. In addition, the Creeper crosses numerous trestles that present treetop views looking down and all around the Whitetop Laurel gorge to finally open up at Damascus, one of the friendliest towns in a friendly state. The second section of the Creeper, from Damascus to Abingdon, heads through farmlands, meadow, and woods, and is absolutely worth the time it takes to travel it.

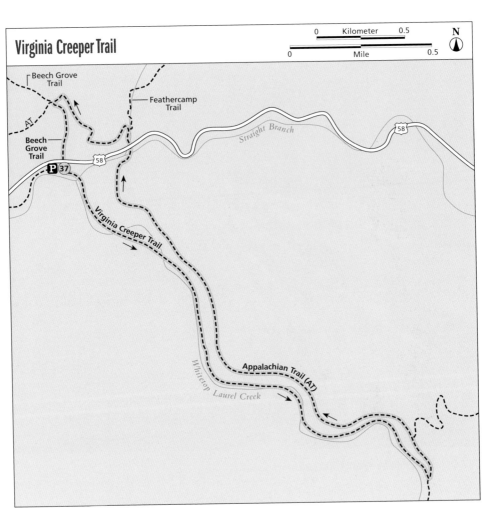

0   Kilometer   0.5

0   Mile   0.5

N

Beech Grove
Trail

Feathercamp
Trail

AT

Straight Branch

58

Beech
Grove
Trail

P 37   58

Virginia Creeper Trail

Appalachian Trail (AT)

Whitetop

Laurel Creek

1.1   Cross the next trestle. Note the cables linking the trestle to the land—they're there to recover the trestle in times of flood.

1.3   Cross another trestle. Here, a steep cliff rises high on the far bank of Whitetop Laurel Creek.

1.7   Round a curve. Here, Whitetop Laurel Creek has become very wide and rocky. Note debris piles from high-water events.

2.0   Come to the Appalachian Trail connector. Houses of the Taylors Valley community are just ahead near the Virginia Creeper Trail. This hike, however, leaves the Creeper Trail and ascends left on a singletrack, hiker-only footpath, working steeply among rocks on a slope.

2.1   Meet the Appalachian Trail as it makes a switchback. Stay left (southbound), heading back toward Damascus. Work along a hardwood-filled slope.

2.6   Traverse a tricky section of the AT. Here, the trail clambers the edge of a low cliff line.

2.7   Bridge a trickling branch on a foot log. From here, the AT bisects a boulder garden. It eventually forces you down near Whitetop Laurel Creek.

Several railroad trestles span Whitetop Laurel Creek.

3.5 Climb along a southwest-facing slope and split away from the Virginia Creeper Trail. Descend into a rhododendron-heavy flat of Straight Branch.

4.1 Bridge Straight Branch, then rise to US 58. Cross the highway and ascend along Feathercamp Branch.

4.2 Rock-hop Feathercamp Branch. You are now on the left bank, ascending the creek.

4.3 Reach a trail intersection. Here, the Feathercamp Trail heads straight but you turn left, heading up stone stairs, staying with the Appalachian Trail as it first climbs, then dips toward a drainage.

4.7 Intersect the Beech Grove Trail. Here, the AT continues straight, but you curve left on a mucky path. The Beech Grove Trail remains mucky for a short distance, then continues down a hollow.

4.9 Come to US 58 and the hike's end. From here, the Straight Branch parking area is down to your right.

38 Guest River Gorge

This hike combines history and natural beauty in the rugged mountains of southwest Virginia. Here in the Jefferson National Forest, you will hike a trail that was once a railroad grade. First pass through the Swede Tunnel, then cross the Guest River—a Virginia State Scenic River—on a high bridge. Continue down the cliff- and bluff-rimmed canyon, viewing giant streamside boulders. Pass your first waterfall, then come to a stair-step cascade set in a rock-rimmed glen before turning around.

Start: Guest River Gorge trailhead
Distance: 5.6 miles out and back
Hiking time: About 3 hours
Difficulty: Moderate
Trail surface: Pea gravel
Best season: Year-round
Other trail users: Bicyclers, occasional equestrians

Canine compatibility: Leashed dogs permitted
Land status: National forest
Fees and permits: None
Schedule: Open daily year-round
Maps: *Guest River Gorge; USGS Coeburn*
Trail contact: Jefferson National Forest, 9416 Coeburn Mountain Rd., Wise, VA 24293; (276) 328-2931; www.fs.fed.us

Finding the trailhead: From the junction of US 58 Alternate and VA 72, just south of downtown Coeburn, take VA 72 south for 2.3 miles to the signed left turn for the Guest River Gorge Trail. Turn left and follow the road 1.3 miles to the dead end at the trailhead. Trailhead GPS: N36 55.388' / W82 27.080'

The Hike

The Guest River Gorge Trail, like many rail trails, took a while to come into being. Fortunately, the Jefferson National Forest saw an opportunity when this leg of the Interstate Line was abandoned. After hiking this rail-turned-trail, you will see why the term "gorge" is used when describing the valley of the Guest River. This waterway crashes toward its mother stream—the Clinch River—cutting a deep swath through Stone Mountain. Sheer cliffs rise. Big boulders are scattered throughout the gorge and in the Guest River. The historic element of this hike traces back a century, when a railroad line was forced through this rugged

▶ In 1988 Norfolk Southern Railroad abandoned the Interstate Railroad through the gorge, then ceded the right-of-way in 1994, when the Guest River Gorge Trail was opened.

valley. The line was put through to transport coal and timber from the Coeburn area down to an already-existing rail line running down the Clinch River Valley.

The Guest River is born high in the western part of Wise County, springing forth below Fox Gap near the Kentucky state line. It cuts south through Dixiana and Lipps (great Appalachian names) before nearing Norton. Then the Guest River digs a mean

More Waterfalls Nearby

The Guest River Gorge Trail passes several waterfalls on its trip to the Clinch River. Here in the Jefferson National Forest, there's another scenic valley nearby with extensive beauty and waterfalls too: Little Stony Creek. The Little Stony Creek National Recreation Trail heads up a gorgeous valley with waterslides, cascades, and pools in a deep gorge with stone bluffs, rock overhangs, and boulder fields. Wooden footbridges keep your feet dry en route to two significant waterfalls, each dropping over stone precipices.

Little Stony Creek National Recreation Trail leaves the Hanging Rock parking area in deep woods. Rock houses and boulder gardens are strewn about the watershed. Little Stony Creek tumbles, slides, gurgles, and shoots its way toward the Clinch River, much like the Guest River. Overhead, sycamore, birch, Fraser magnolia, and maple canopy the trail. Wildflowers, from dwarf crested iris to trillium, thrive in this moist vale. Reach a wooden footbridge at 0.4 mile. The bridges you cross on this hike were brought in by helicopter.

At 1.2 miles pass a rock house on your left. Bridge over to the right bank at 1.3 miles. Cross Star Branch at 1.5 miles and look upstream at a delicate veil pourover. Ahead, open onto a streamside bedrock slab with 10-foot cascade stairs stepping over rock layers just above it. This is Lower Falls. At 2.1 miles the trail bridges Corder Branch. Note the flat bedrock where Corder Branch meets Little Stony Creek. The path steepens a bit ahead. Watch for a sheer bluff on the far side of Little Stony Creek. At 2.4 miles come to Middle Stony Falls. A viewing platform allows for a straight-on look at the curtain-type fall. It cascades about 20 feet over a vertical rock face, splashing into mist.

Continuing beyond Middle Falls, the path turns south, and it isn't long before it reaches Upper Falls at 2.5 miles. Here, the stream splits as it drops, mostly fanning out, with the left side of the fall making a slender white spill. Many visitors will have come the shorter way, upstream, from FR 701, accessible via VA 72 between the Guest River Gorge trailhead and Coeburn.

I prefer the lower access. To reach the lower trailhead of Little Stony Creek from the Guest River Gorge access, head south for 6.5 miles on VA 72 to Hanging Rock Recreation Area, near Dungannon. The trail starts at the end of the access road.

A trailside bluff is bathed in the winter sun.

valley eastward but does not reach its prime until turning south, below Coeburn, where it slices betwixt 400-foot-high sandstone cliffs, creating the gorge where the hike travels. Finally, the Guest River delivers its highland elixir to the Clinch River. Intrepid kayakers ply the Class IV–V rapids of the Guest River Gorge in spring, adding a thrill for hikers traveling the gorge during that time. Anglers cast lines for trout and smallmouth bass, using the trail for angling access.

It isn't long before your hike reveals the engineering marvels of this railroad line. The Guest River leg was once part of a greater network, much of what still exists today. The Interstate Railroad Line passes through the Clinch and Powell River watersheds, hauling coal from these hills to plants that light cities of the Southeast such as Charlotte, North Carolina.

You first pass through the Swede Tunnel, a dark and cool experience that shortcuts a sharp bend in the Guest River. Next, the Guest River Gorge Trail heads over

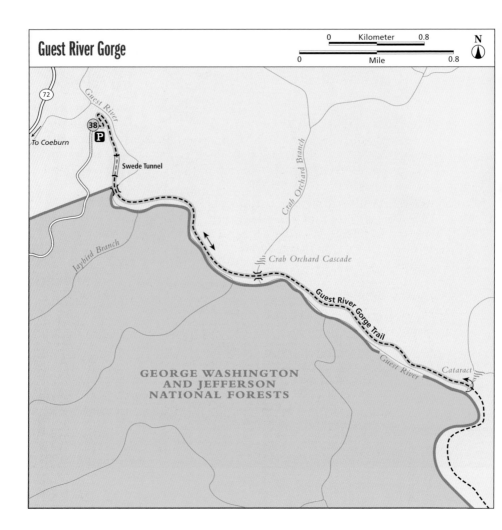

0   Kilometer   0.8
0   Mile   0.8
N

72

Guest River

38
P

To Coeburn

Swede Tunnel

Crab Orchard Branch

Jaybird Branch

Crab Orchard Cascade

Guest River Gorge Trail

Guest River

Cataract

GEORGE WASHINGTON
AND JEFFERSON
NATIONAL FORESTS

a high span that bridges its namesake stream. This trestle allows excellent views of the Guest River. Heading downstream, the trail is bordered with beauty, whether it is a rock-choked rapid, bronzed cliffs (especially visible in winter) or cascades flowing from the surrounding hillsides into the Guest River. Alluring forest grows wherever rock and trail aren't. Huge boulders, fallen from the surrounding cliffs, stand firm in the waterway. Moreover, where the gorge walls were a little too close, the railroad makers blasted it back, creating a passage for the trains.

Contemplation benches have been placed at the most scenic locales and are cues for stopping. Railroad-line mile markers keep you apprised of your whereabouts on the path. This particular hike ends at a cascade that cuts through the gorge 2.8 miles from the trailhead. Avid hikers can continue an additional 3 miles one-way to the trail's end near its confluence with the Clinch River, though most hikers are found on the first half of the trail. The path is also popular with bicyclists who regularly pedal from the trailhead all the way to its endpoint. Although the trail ends at an active railroad line, a spur path—the Heart of Appalachia Trail—connects to the town of St. Paul.

Miles and Directions

0.0 Start by leaving the lower east corner of the parking area on an asphalt track. Immediately pass an informative national forest kiosk, then curve down to meet the actual railroad grade that comprises the Guest River Gorge Trail. There is a restroom down here. Proceed right (southeasterly) on the wide, gravel former railroad grade. The Guest River flows downstream to your left and is visible through the trees.

0.3 Pass a small waterfall on your right just before reaching the Swede Tunnel. The railroad line blasted through a bend in the Guest River. Note the date atop the tower: 1922. The tunnel is only a couple of hundred feet long, and light coming from both ends allows passage without worries of stumbling through the dark.

0.4 Reach a wooden trestle that spans the Guest River a short distance after emerging from the Swede Tunnel. Enjoy views upstream at the boulder-strewn river as well as its downstream curve. The river is now flowing to your right amid rhododendron thickets, rocks, and mosses shaded by hardwoods.

1.1 Come directly alongside the Guest. Here, cabin-size boulders seemingly block the stream below.

1.5 Reach a short wooden bridge spanning Crab Orchard Creek. Look upstream for Crab Orchard Cascade, flowing about 12 feet over a bluff. There is no direct trail, but the cascade is easily visible from the trail when the leaves are off the trees. It is worth a short scramble through the woods to view this pour-over. Beyond here, the trail continues ever deeper into the gorge on a gentle grade.

2.8 Come to a stream entering from the left. Here, an unnamed creek has broken through the cliff line and created a multitiered cascade. As you face the cascade, there is also a small rock house to the left of the trail. This locale makes for a good picnic and turnaround spot. The Guest River Gorge Trail continues for 3 more miles of "gorge-ous" beauty before ending near the confluence with the Clinch River.

5.6 Arrive back at the trailhead, completing the out-and-back hike.

39 Hensley Settlement

This hike at Cumberland Gap National Historical Park climbs Cumberland Mountain on the old Chadwell Gap Trail to reach a preserved mountaintop community. Once the home of Sherman Hensley and his descendants, the remote inhabitation existed in isolation for five decades. Today, a strenuous 2,000-foot climb leads to the secluded and gorgeous locale where two dozen buildings, from homes to the schoolhouse to outbuildings, await your visit. It is truly a fascinating trip back in time.

Start: Chadwell Gap Trailhead
Distance: 9.6-mile balloon loop
Hiking time: About 6–8 hours
Difficulty: Difficult
Trail surface: Natural surfaces, very rocky in places
Best seasons: Mid-Sept through May
Other trail users: Equestrians
Canine compatibility: Leashed dogs permitted

Land status: National park
Fees and permits: None
Schedule: Open daily year-round
Maps: Cumberland Gap National Historical Park; USGS Ewing, Varilla
Trail contact: Cumberland Gap National Historical Park, 91 Bartlett Park Rd., Middlesboro, KY 40965; (606) 248-2817; www.nps .gov/cuga

Finding the trailhead: From the town square in Jonesville, take US 58 west for 24.1 miles to turn right on Caylor Road, VA 690 (The left turn will be Doc Hurst Road). Turn right and follow Caylor Road for 1.7 miles to veer right onto VA 688. Stay with VA 688 for 0.7 mile to reach the Chadwell Gap Trailhead on your left. Trailhead GPS: N36 39.233'/W83 29.772'

The Hike

The Hensley Settlement protects and preserves lifeways long abandoned in the Southern Appalachian Mountains. This former community is set 3,300 feet high in a perched mountaintop valley, where the headwaters of Shillalah Creek flow between Brushy Mountain to the north and Cumberland Mountain to the south. It remains a remote and scenic spot, the place where Sherman Hensley, back in 1904, decided to retreat from the lower reaches of Harlan County Kentucky and make his home in the back of beyond here along the Kentucky-Virginia state line. Sherman brought his wife and built on the former pasturage and woodland, set apart from the rest of the world.

▶ Sherman Hensley, the settlement's founder, lived to be 98 years of age, spending the last twenty-eight years of his life off the mountain, away from the community that bore his name.

Relatives of Hensley and his wife joined the settlement and a bona fide community was established. Despite the inroads of such things as indoor plumbing, electric lighting, and the like had made in the Southern Appalachians, the Hensley Settlement remained

Preserved home at the Hensley Settlement

cast in the nineteenth century, inadvertently preserving a self-sufficient, simple subsistence life that—despite its primitive conditions—seems romantic and unpretentious compared to today's hectic digital world.

By 1908 enough children were in the settlement to establish a simple school. The place of learning went through several incarnations, yet you can see the final wooden clapboard schoolhouse, with its wooden desks and cast-iron stove for heat. The settlement continued to expand, ultimately reaching a population exceeding one hundred residents in the mid-1920s. Residents grew their own food, raised their own animals, and used horses, wagons, or foot power for transportation. The residents did leave regularly to trade their products such as corn—and corn juice (read: moonshine)—down in Caylor, Virginia, using the Chadwell Gap Trail to make their runs.

Ultimately, the lure of civilization and money that could be made down there drew its residents from the settlement. By 1949 only its founder, Sherman Hensley,

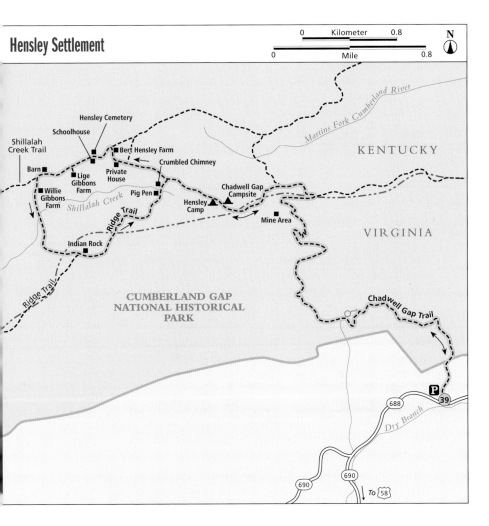

0   Kilometer   0.8   **N**

0   Mile   0.8

Hensley Cemetery

Schoolhouse

Shillalah
Creek Trail

Bert Hensley Farm

Crumbled Chimney

Barn

Lige
Gibbons
Farm

Private
House

Willie
Gibbons
Farm

Pig Pen

Shillalah Creek

Chadwell Gap
Campsite

Hensley
Camp

Mine Area

Ridge Trail

Indian Rock

KENTUCKY

Martins Fork Cumberland River

VIRGINIA

Ridge Trail

CUMBERLAND GAP
NATIONAL HISTORICAL
PARK

Chadwell Gap Trail

688

39

690

690

To 58

Dry Branch

remained. Two years later, at age 71, Hensley left the mountain himself. The buildings fell into disrepair, the forest began reclaiming once productive fields, and the Hensley Settlement was no more.

After the establishment of Cumberland Gap National Historical Park in 1959, plans were made to restore the Hensley Settlement as a historical window to the past. In the 1960s the Jobs Corp restored many structures. They continue to be maintained to this day.

The hike itself traces portions of the historic Chadwell Gap Trail. For several years the trail crossed private land, but then it was closed. The park service bought additional acreage, established a trailhead, then rerouted the trail, linking to the old path inside park boundaries. The Chadwell Gap Trail takes you through attractive

The Hensley Settlement

woodland ever higher, steeply making its way astride foreboding rock ramparts, making the crest of Cumberland Mountain. Here, join the Ridge Trail, then reach the Hensley Settlement.

The hike then leaves the settlement, crosses Shillalah Creek, and visits Indian Rock, an impressive rock shelter. Rejoin the Ridge Trail and view some old outbuildings before completing a loop, then backtracking to the trailhead. Allow plenty of time for the long hike that sometimes travels very rocky sections of path. You will also want to allow ample time for touring the settlement.

Note: The trail passes a pair of backcountry campsites and comes near yet another camp that also offers a cabin for overnighting, making a backcountry camping adventure possible.

Miles and Directions

0.0 Start at the Chadwell Gap Trailhead. Join a rocky track heading uphill through woods. Pass near private property before turning westerly in rich deciduous woods. Cross old wagon tracks and rocky trails in this former open terrain.

0.5 The trail curves left into a tulip-tree-filled hollow. Keep westerly, undulating in hills and hollows.

1.1 Reach the old Chadwell Gap Trail. Turn right here on the wide track. Briefly descend, then cross a hollow. Look right for a spur trail leading to a rocked-in spring. Sherman Hensley and other travelers on the Chadwell Gap Trail surely used this water source while heading up and down the mountain.

1.5 Curve close to a rocky drainage on your left, then quickly turn away from it.

1.6 Pass a concrete building foundation on your right. It could've been part of a coal-mining operation that once sent coal down from the mountain via tram. Continue climbing as the slope steepens. Note the rock bluffs atop the ridge.

1.9 Make a hard switchback to the left. The trail steepens.

2.1 Make a series of short switchbacks in extremely rocky, bouldery, bluff-filled torturous terrain. The slope steepens, rhododendron appears, and views open south of the mountain. The former coal mines were at 2,800-foot elevation, to the west of the actual Chadwell Gap.

2.6 Come just below the actual Chadwell Gap, but veer right, walking beneath a huge rock bluff. Keep up a lung-busting climb. Note the seemingly out-of-place concrete steps made to ease the ascent.

2.7 Reach the crest of Cumberland Mountain and the Ridge Trail. The mountain crest delineates the Kentucky-Virginia state line. Turn left on the Ridge Trail. Pass the actual Chadwell Gap, then descend past a tall rock rampart to your left.

3.0 Intersect the Martins Fork Trail. It leaves right to its namesake stream and a small rustic cabin and campsite. Keep straight on the Ridge Trail, walking the state line. Skirt around massive rock pillars.

3.4 Meet the spur trail to the Chadwell Gap campsite just after leveling off. Keep straight on the Ridge Trail. The trail remains mostly level as you enter what is described on USGS topo maps as Hensley Flats.

3.5 Pass the Hensley Camp on your right. Keep straight on the wide Ridge Trail.

3.7 Reach a signed trail junction. The Ridge Trail splits left and will be your return route. For now, keep straight on the unnamed trail leading to the Hensley Settlement.

3.9 Come to the Hensley Settlement, which opens dead ahead. A sand road/trail leads to your right past a maintenance area. Keep straight, entering open meadows while staying along a fence line. Pass a private home on your left, used by rangers and park personnel. Ahead, curve right.

4.1 Pass the Bert Hensley Farm on your right. Here, a road spurs right. Stay left and work through a mix of field and woods.

4.2 Pass the Hensley Cemetery on your right, then the schoolhouse on your left. Look in the window at the desks and heat stove. Walk astride bucolic meadows, where deer are often seen.

4.4 A road leads left down to the Lige Gibbons Farm, a beautifully intact wooden structure. Continue walking along the fence line.

4.5 Pass beside a barn to your right, then curve left. Here, the Shillalah Creek Trail leads right. Explore many small outbuildings, part of the greater Willie Gibbons Farm.

4.6 Pass the Gibbons Farm chimney, then leave the open fields of the settlement and join a path entering forest. Gently descend southbound.

4.8 Rock-hop Shillalah Creek. Leave the creek and enter a wide flat with rock ramparts to your left. Reenter Virginia.

5.2 Come underneath Indian Rock, a huge dry rock shelter used by aboriginals. Abruptly descend to meet the Ridge Trail. Turn left on the Ridge Trail and come along the mountain edge. Southward views open through the trees.

5.8 Look for the remains of a pig pen and other wooden structures just before stepping over the upper reaches of Shillalah Creek. Walk uphill, passing a clearing on your left with a crumbled chimney in it.

5.9 Complete the loop portion of the hike. Turn right here, staying with the Ridge Trail. From here it is 3.7 miles back to the trailhead. Backtrack past the campsites to turn right on the Chadwell Gap Trail and carefully descend.

9.6 Reach the Chadwell Gap trailhead, completing the hike.

40 Cumberland Gap

Talk about historic hikes! This trek, at Cumberland Gap National Historical Park, traces the route used by man and beast for millennia, working their way from the East into what became Kentucky. Made famous by Daniel Boone, the passage through Cumberland Gap follows the "Wilderness Road," now restored to its original appearance. You will walk a foot trail, tracing Daniel's steps to and through the actual Cumberland Gap, marked by a memorial. Your return trip leads past Cumberland Furnace, an iron-making operation, as well as Gap Cave, which also figure in the history of this mountainous land where Virginia, Tennessee, and Kentucky come together.

Start: Daniel Boone Visitor Information Center trailhead
Distance: 3.0 miles out and back, with spurs
Hiking time: About 2.5-3 hours
Difficulty: Easy-moderate
Trail surface: Gravel
Best season: Year-round
Other trail users: None
Canine compatibility: Leashed dogs permitted

Land status: National park
Fees and permits: None
Schedule: Open daily year-round
Maps: Cumberland Gap National Historical Park; USGS Middlesboro South
Trail contact: Cumberland Gap National Historical Park, 91 Bartlett Park Rd., Middlesboro, KY 40965; (606) 248-2817; www.nps.gov/cuga

Finding the trailhead: From the town square in Jonesville, take US 58 west for 33.4 miles. Just after you reach Tennessee, turn right at the Historic Area sign. Follow this road 0.1 mile, reentering Virginia, to reach the Daniel Boone Visitor Information Center trailhead on your right. Trailhead GPS: N36 36.105' / W83 39.605'

The Hike

Cumberland Gap is a natural passage in the mountain barrier dividing Kentucky and Virginia. Once fought over by Shawnee and Cherokee Indians, the gap was used to connect the rich—and disputed—hunting grounds of Kentucky with points south. The Indian trail through the gap even had a name: Warriors Path. After European colonists arrived, the mountain barrier of the Appalachians kept them at bay, but it was the Cumberland Gap through which they eventually spilled westward. First came Dr. Thomas Walker in 1750, in search of lands for the Loyal Land Company. He entered what became Kentucky on the Warriors Path, naming the Cumberland River before returning east. He was followed by long hunters through the years, the

Daniel Boone will be forever associated with Cumberland Gap. ▶

Looking toward Kentucky and Tennessee from Gap Cave

most famous of which was Daniel Boone. Employed by a different land speculator, Judge Thomas Henderson, Boone made a foray from his home in the Yadkin Valley of North Carolina, beyond the Cumberland Gap, returning with a haul of furs.

This Kentucky region intrigued him, and in 1775 Boone hacked out a rough road from the Holston River's Long Island in Tennessee (near present-day Kingsport) to and through the Cumberland Gap and on to the Kentucky River. This became the famous Wilderness Road, through which thousands eventually came, establishing Kentucky as the fifteenth state in the Union in 1792. Cumberland Gap remained an important passageway between east and west. During the Civil War both North and South vied for control of the passage. Although it changed hands during the conflict, there were no major battles fought here, though Civil War fort sites remain.

After the Civil War the natural resources of the region brought attention back to the area where Virginia, Kentucky, and Tennessee come together. An iron forge was established just below the gap. Coal mining rose to prominence, resulting in the founding of Middlesboro, Kentucky, just north of Cumberland Gap. The gap became a rutty, mired mess. Eventually, an auto highway was run through the passage, altering its historical appearance. By the 1930s a movement was afoot to establish a national park here, and today we have Cumberland Gap National Historical Park. The highway has since been removed (it now tunnels its way through Cumberland Mountain) and Cumberland Gap has been restored to its original appearance. It isn't often that a trail becomes a road and then returns again to trail.

▶ The iron forge along this hike operated from the 1820s to the 1880s and was known as the Newlee Iron Furnace.

Today, you can absorb loads of history at the elaborate trailhead and walk the Wilderness Road to and through the gap, visiting the pyramid monument. Explore

Cumberland Gap National Historical Park

Notice how the word *historical* is included in this national park's name. It is no accident. The combination of natural beauty and a significant past made Cumberland Gap a great choice for a preserve. In the 1920s local boosters in the Tri-State area—Virginia, Kentucky, and Tennessee—began working with their local congressmen to establish a national park. However, the movement stalled in congressional committees. Finally, in 1939 a park bill passed congressional muster and was signed by President Franklin D. Roosevelt. Purchasing land and establishing the park took another two decades. By this time the park was 20,000 acres in size. On July 4, 1959, Cumberland Gap National Historical Park was finally dedicated. It not only preserves this important passageway in American history but also natural features such as the Pinnacle, White Rocks, Sand Cave, and Skylight Cave, historical trails like Cumberland Gap, Chadwell Gap, Civil War forts McCook and Lyon, the Hensley Settlement—a preserved village—and still other jewels. Even today, lands are being added to the park, increasing its umbrella of preservation to 24,000 acres and growing.

Approximately 70 miles of hiking trails run through the park, visiting many of the scenic sites. Backcountry campsites are situated along the crest of Cumberland Mountain. The linear hike along the park spine makes for a visually and historically rewarding endeavor. The park also has an auto-accessible campground, with hot showers and some electric sites. It provides an ideal base camp for exploring this national treasure shared by Virginia, Kentucky, and Tennessee.

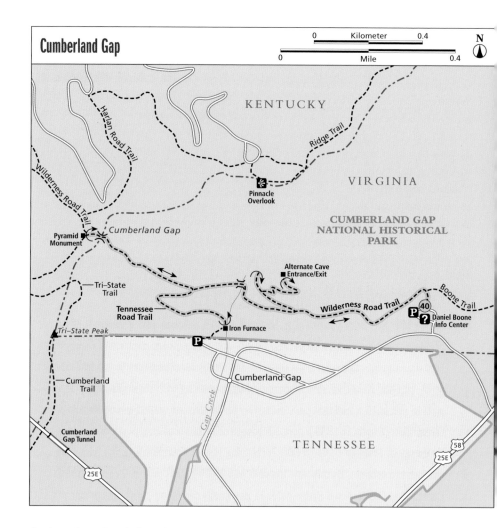

the iron forge just below the gap in a scenic setting along Gap Creek. Visit Gap Cave and its nearby alternate entrance (cave entrance allowed only on park tours). This cave provided shelter and water for passersby and later became a popular cave tour destination when illuminated with electric lights in 1934. Tours were expanded when a tunnel was dug, linking other caves to Gap Cave. Later, the cave was damaged and vandalized, but it was restored to its natural state with the gap restoration.

Enlightening interpretive information is scattered throughout the hike. While here, be mindful of those who came before—the buffalo that made the trail, the Indians that followed, the long hunters, the future Kentuckians, the Civil War soldiers, the coal miners, the iron forgers, the tourists of the twentieth century, and the national park visitors of the twenty-first century. It is truly a walk through the footsteps of history.

Miles and Directions

0.0 Start by passing under the breezeway of the Daniel Boone Visitor Information Center trailhead. Walk just a short distance. Go left with the Wilderness Road Trail, as the Boone Trail splits right. Walk a wide track westerly in mixed woods.

0.1 Open to the restored segment of Cumberland Gap. The area of old US 25E is now grassy and growing up with trees. The trail continues westerly. The hamlet of Cumberland Gap, Tennessee, lies below.

0.4 A spur path leads right to Gap Cave. For now, stay straight on the Wilderness Road Trail.

0.5 Cross Gap Creek on a wooden log bridge. The stream flows out of Gap Cave. This stream was mentioned in the journals of Dr. Thomas Walker, who passed through here in 1750. The stream also provided drinking water for Civil War soldiers stationed at Cumberland Gap, and the throngs who passed through this break in Cumberland Mountain.

0.6 The Tennessee Road Trail leaves left to the iron forge and the town of Cumberland Gap, Tennessee. Stay straight with the Wilderness Road Trail. Mountains rise all around you.

0.9 Reach the actual Cumberland Gap after a short steep section. The gap was dug out when the highway ran through but is now at its original elevation. At this point the Wilderness Road descends into Kentucky. Turn left, joining the Tri-State Trail up wood-and-earth steps to reach the stone pyramid, commemorating passages through the gap. This is also the beginning of the Cumberland Trail, a footpath running south along the Cumberland Plateau to near Chattanooga, Tennessee. Backtrack on the Wilderness Road toward the trailhead.

1.2 Join the Tennessee Road Trail, switchbacking downhill through woods toward the iron furnace.

1.5 Reach the furnace on your left. Steps lead to the open interior of the former forge that made iron. Its bellows were powered by nearby Gap Creek. Another trailhead lies below, just over the Tennessee state line. Backtrack to the Wilderness Trail.

2.0 Turn left on the Gap Cave Trail. You are following the route of old US 25E. Ahead, the trail splits right to an alternate cave entrance/exit. Keep straight for Gap Cave.

2.1 Reach Gap Cave. Today, ranger-led, lantern-lit cave tours are run by the national park service. Backtrack, then walk up to the other cave entrance/exit. This arched cave entrance is also barred. Gap Cave has six known entrances. Backtrack to the Wilderness Road Trail. Trace the Wilderness Trail easterly back toward the trailhead.

3.0 Return to the trailhead, completing the hike.

The Art of Hiking

When standing nose to nose with a mountain lion, you're probably not too concerned with the issue of ethical behavior in the wild. No doubt you're just terrified. But let's be honest. How often are you nose to nose with a mountain lion? For most of us, a hike into the "wild" means loading up the SUV with expensive gear and driving to a toileted trailhead. Sure, you can mourn how civilized we've become—how GPS units have replaced natural instinct and Gore-Tex stands in for true-grit—but the silly gadgets of civilization aside, we have plenty of reason to take pride in how we've matured. With survival now on the back burner, we've begun to understand that we have a responsibility to protect, no longer just conquer, our wild places: that they, not we, are at risk. So please, do what you can. The following section will help you understand better what it means to "do what you can" while still making the most of your hiking experience. Anyone can take a hike, but hiking safely and well is an art requiring preparation and proper equipment.

Trail Etiquette

Leave no trace. Always leave an area just like you found it—if not better than you found it. Avoid camping in fragile, alpine meadows and along the banks of streams and lakes. Use a camp stove versus building a wood fire. Pack up all of your trash and extra food. Bury human waste at least 100 feet from water sources under 6 to 8 inches of topsoil. Don't bathe with soap in a lake or stream—use prepackaged moistened towels to wipe off sweat and dirt, or bathe in the water without soap.

Stay on the trail. It's true, a path anywhere leads nowhere new, but purists will just have to get over it. Paths serve an important purpose; they limit impact on natural areas. Straying from a designated trail may seem innocent but it can cause damage to sensitive areas—damage that may take years to recover, if it can recover at all. Even simple shortcuts can be destructive. So, please, stay on the trail.

Leave no weeds. Noxious weeds tend to overtake other plants, which in turn affects animals and birds that depend on them for food. To minimize the spread of noxious weeds, hikers should regularly clean their boots, tents, packs, and hiking poles of mud and seeds. Also brush your dog to remove any weed seeds before heading off into a new area.

Keep your dog under control. You can buy a flexi-lead that allows your dog to go exploring along the trail, while allowing you the ability to reel him in should another hiker approach or should he decide to chase a rabbit. Always obey leash laws and be sure to bury your dog's waste or pack it in resealable plastic bags.

*Stony Man Mountain offers open ▶
bluffs and dramatic views.*

Respect other trail users. Often you're not the only one on the trail. With the rise in popularity of multiuse trails, you'll have to learn a new kind of respect, beyond the nod and "hello" approach you may be used to. First investigate whether you're on a multiuse trail, and assume the appropriate precautions. When you encounter motorized vehicles (ATVs, motorcycles, and 4WDs), be alert. Though they should always yield to the hiker, often they're going too fast or are too lost in the buzz of their engine to react to your presence. If you hear activity ahead, step off the trail just to be safe. Note that you're not likely to hear a mountain biker coming, so be prepared and know ahead of time whether you share the trail with them. Cyclists should always yield to hikers, but that's little comfort to the hiker. Be aware. When you approach horses or pack animals on the trail, always step quietly off the trail, preferably on the downhill side, and let them pass. If you're wearing a large backpack, it's often a good idea to sit down. To some animals, a hiker wearing a large backpack might appear threatening. Many national forests allow domesticated grazing, usually for sheep and cattle. Make sure your dog doesn't harass these animals, and respect ranchers' rights while you're enjoying yours.

Getting into Shape

Unless you want to be sore—and possibly have to shorten your trip or vacation—be sure to get in shape before a big hike. If you're terribly out of shape, start a walking program early, preferably eight weeks in advance. Start with a fifteen-minute walk during your lunch hour or after work and gradually increase your walking time to an hour. You should also increase your elevation gain. Walking briskly up hills really strengthens your leg muscles and gets your heart rate up. If you work in a storied office building, take the stairs instead of the elevator. If you prefer going to a gym, walk the treadmill or use a stair machine. You can further increase your strength and endurance by walking with a loaded backpack. Stationary exercises you might consider are squats, leg lifts, sit-ups, and push-ups. Other good ways to get in shape include biking, running, aerobics, and, of course, short hikes. Stretching before and after a hike keeps muscles flexible and helps avoid injuries.

Preparedness

It's been said that failing to plan means planning to fail. So do take the necessary time to plan your trip. Whether going on a short day hike or an extended backpack trip, always prepare for the worst. Simply remembering to pack a copy of the *U.S. Army Survival Manual* is not preparedness. Although it's not a bad idea if you plan on entering truly wild places, it's merely the tourniquet answer to a problem. You need to do your best to prevent the problem from arising in the first place. In order to survive—and to stay reasonably comfortable—you need to concern yourself with the basics: water, food, and shelter. Don't go on a hike without having these bases covered. And don't go on a hike expecting to find these items in the woods.

Water. Even in frigid conditions, you need at least two quarts of water a day to function efficiently. Add heat and taxing terrain and you can bump that figure up to one gallon. That's simply a base to work from—your metabolism and your level of conditioning can raise or lower that amount. Unless you know your level, assume that you need one gallon of water a day. Now, where do you plan on getting the water?

Preferably not from natural water sources. These sources can be loaded with intestinal disturbers, such as bacteria, viruses, and fertilizers. *Giardia lamblia,* the most common of these disturbers, is a protozoan parasite that lives part of its life cycle as a cyst in water sources. The parasite spreads when mammals defecate in water sources. Once ingested, Giardia can induce cramping, diarrhea, vomiting, and fatigue within two days to two weeks after ingestion. Giardiasis is treatable with prescription drugs. If you believe you've contracted giardiasis, see a doctor immediately.

Treating water. The best and easiest solution to avoid polluted water is to carry your water with you. Yet, depending on the nature of your hike and the duration, this may not be an option—one gallon of water weighs eight-and-a-half pounds. In that case, you'll need to look into treating water. Regardless of which method you choose, you should always carry some water with you in case of an emergency. Save this reserve until you absolutely need it.

There are three methods of treating water: boiling, chemical treatment, and filtering. If you boil water, it's recommended that you do so for ten to fifteen minutes. This is often impractical because you're forced to exhaust a great deal of your fuel supply. You can opt for chemical treatment, which will kill Giardia but will not take care of other chemical pollutants. Another drawback to chemical treatments is the unpleasant taste of the water after it's treated. You can remedy this by adding powdered drink mix to the water. Filters are the preferred method for treating water. Many filters remove Giardia, organic and inorganic contaminants, and don't leave an aftertaste. Water filters are far from perfect as they can easily become clogged or leak if a gasket wears out. It's always a good idea to carry a backup supply of chemical treatment tablets in case your filter decides to quit on you.

Food. If we're talking about survival, you can go days without food, as long as you have water. But we're also talking about comfort. Try to avoid foods that are high in sugar and fat like candy bars and potato chips. These food types are harder to digest and are low in nutritional value. Instead, bring along foods that are easy to pack, nutritious, and high in energy (e.g., bagels, nutrition bars, dehydrated fruit, gorp, and jerky). If you are on an overnight trip, easy-to-fix dinners include rice mixes with dehydrated potatoes, corn, pasta with cheese sauce, and soup mixes. For a tasty breakfast, you can fix hot oatmeal with brown sugar and reconstituted milk powder topped off with banana chips. If you like a hot drink in the morning, bring along herbal tea bags or hot chocolate. If you are a coffee junkie, you can purchase coffee that is packaged like tea bags. You can prepackage all of your meals in heavy-duty resealable plastic bags to keep food from spilling in your pack. These bags can be reused to pack out trash.

Shelter. The type of shelter you choose depends less on the conditions than on your tolerance for discomfort. Shelter comes in many forms—tent, tarp, lean-to, bivy sack, cabin, cave, etc. If you're camping in the desert, a bivy sack may suffice, but if you're above the treeline and a storm is approaching, a better choice is a three- or four-season tent. Tents are the logical and most popular choice for most backpackers as they're lightweight and packable—and you can rest assured that you always have shelter from the elements. Before you leave on your trip, anticipate what the weather and terrain will be like and plan for the type of shelter that will work best for your comfort level (see Equipment later in this section).

Finding a campsite. If there are established campsites, stick to those. If not, start looking for a campsite early—around 3:30 or 4:00 p.m. Stop at the first decent site you see. Depending on the area, it could be a long time before you find another suitable location. Pitch your camp in an area that's level. Make sure the area is at least 200 feet from fragile areas like lakeshores, meadows, and stream banks. And try to avoid areas thick in underbrush, as they can harbor insects and provide cover for approaching animals.

If you are camping in stormy, rainy weather, look for a rock outcrop or a shelter in the trees to keep the wind from blowing your tent all night. Be sure that you don't camp under trees with dead limbs that might break off on top of you. Also, try to find an area that has an absorbent surface, such as sandy soil or forest duff. This, in addition to camping on a surface with a slight angle, will provide better drainage. By all means, don't dig trenches to provide drainage around your tent—remember you're practicing zero-impact camping.

If you're in bear country, steer clear of creekbeds or animal paths. If you see any signs of a bear's presence (i.e., scat, footprints), relocate. You'll need to find a campsite near a tall tree where you can hang your food and other items that may attract bears such as deodorant, toothpaste, or soap. Carry a lightweight nylon rope with which to hang your food. As a rule, you should hang your food at least 20 feet from the ground and 5 feet away from the tree trunk. You can put food and other items in a waterproof stuff sack and tie one end of the rope to the stuff sack. To get the other end of the rope over the tree branch, tie a good size rock to it, and gently toss the rock over the tree branch. Pull the stuff sack up until it reaches the top of the branch and tie it off securely. Don't hang your food near your tent! If possible, hang your food at least 100 feet away from your campsite. Alternatives to hanging your food are bear-proof plastic tubes and metal bear boxes.

Lastly, think of comfort. Lie down on the ground where you intend to sleep and see if it's a good fit. For morning warmth (and a nice view to wake up to), have your tent face east.

First Aid

I know you're tough, but get 10 miles into the woods and develop a blister and you'll wish you had carried that first-aid kit. Face it, it's just plain good sense. Many companies produce lightweight, compact first-aid kits. Just make sure yours contains at least the following:

- adhesive bandages
- moleskin or duct tape
- various sterile gauze and dressings
- white surgical tape
- an Ace bandage
- an antihistamine
- aspirin
- Betadine solution
- a first-aid book
- antacid tablets
- tweezers
- scissors
- antibacterial wipes
- triple-antibiotic ointment
- plastic gloves
- sterile cotton tip applicators
- syrup of ipecac (to induce vomiting)
- thermometer
- wire splint

Here are a few tips for dealing with and hopefully preventing certain ailments.

Sunburn. Take along sunscreen or sun block, protective clothing, and a wide-brimmed hat. If you do get a sunburn, treat the area with aloe vera gel, and protect the area from further sun exposure. At higher elevations, the sun's radiation can be particularly damaging to skin. Remember that your eyes are vulnerable to this radiation as well. Sunglasses can be a good way to prevent headaches and permanent eye damage from the sun, especially in places where light-colored rock or patches of snow reflect light up in your face.

Blisters. Be prepared to take care of these hike-spoilers by carrying moleskin (a lightly padded adhesive), gauze and tape, or adhesive bandages. An effective way to apply moleskin is to cut out a circle of moleskin and remove the center—like a doughnut—and place it over the blistered area. Cutting the center out will reduce the pressure applied to the sensitive skin. Other products can help you combat blisters. Some are applied to suspicious hot spots before a blister forms to help decrease friction to that area, while others are applied to the blister after it has popped to help prevent further irritation.

Insect bites and stings. You can treat most insect bites and stings by applying hydrocortisone 1% cream topically and taking a pain medication such as ibuprofen or acetaminophen to reduce swelling. If you forgot to pack these items, a cold compress or a paste of mud and ashes can sometimes assuage the itching and discomfort. Remove any stingers by using tweezers or scraping the area with your fingernail or a knife blade. Don't pinch the area as you'll only spread the venom.

Some hikers are highly sensitive to bites and stings and may have a serious allergic reaction that can be life threatening. Symptoms of a serious allergic reaction can include wheezing, an asthmatic attack, and shock. The treatment for this severe type of reaction is epinephrine. If you know that you are sensitive to bites and stings, carry a pre-packaged kit of epinephrine, which can be obtained only by prescription from your doctor.

Ticks. Ticks can carry diseases such as Rocky Mountain spotted fever and Lyme disease. The best defense is, of course, prevention. If you know you're going to be hiking through an area littered with ticks, wear long pants and a long sleeved shirt. You can apply a permethrin repellent to your clothing and a Deet repellent to exposed skin. At the end of your hike, do a spot check for ticks (and insects in general). If you do find a tick, grab the head of the tick firmly—with a pair of tweezers if you have them—and gently pull it away from the skin with a twisting motion. Sometimes the mouth parts linger, embedded in your skin. If this happens, try to remove them with a disinfected needle. Clean the affected area with an antibacterial cleanser and then apply triple antibiotic ointment. Monitor the area for a few days. If irritation persists or a white spot develops, see a doctor for possible infection.

Poison ivy, oak, and sumac. These skin irritants can be found most anywhere in North America and come in the form of a bush or a vine, having leaflets in groups of three, five, seven, or nine. Learn how to spot the plants. The oil they secrete can cause an allergic reaction in the form of blisters, usually about twelve hours after exposure. The itchy rash can last from ten days to several weeks. The best defense against these irritants is to wear clothing that covers the arms, legs and torso. For summer, zip-off cargo pants come in handy. There are also nonprescription lotions you can apply to exposed skin that guard against the effects of poison ivy/oak/sumac and can be washed off with soap and water. If you think you were in contact with the plants, after hiking (or even on the trail during longer hikes) wash with soap and water. Taking a hot shower with soap after you return home from your hike will also help to remove any lingering oil from your skin. Should you contract a rash from any of these plants, use an antihistamine to reduce the itching. If the rash is localized, create a light bleach/water wash to dry up the area. If the rash has spread, either tough it out or see your doctor about getting a dose of cortisone (available both orally and by injection).

Snakebites. Snakebites are rare in North America. Unless startled or provoked, the majority of snakes will not bite. If you are wise to their habitats and keep a careful eye on the trail, you should be just fine. When stepping over logs, first step on the log, making sure you can see what's on the other side before stepping down. Though your chances of being struck are slim, it's wise to know what to do in the event you are.

If a *nonpoisonous* snake bites you, allow the wound to bleed a small amount and then cleanse the wounded area with a Betadine solution (10% povidone iodine). Rinse the wound with clean water (preferably) or fresh urine (it might sound ugly, but it's sterile). Once the area is clean, cover it with triple antibiotic ointment and a clean bandage. Remember, most residual damage from snakebites, poisonous or otherwise, comes from infection, not the snake's venom. Keep the area as clean as possible and get medical attention immediately.

If somebody in your party is bitten by a poisonous snake, follow these steps:

1. Calm the patient.
2. Remove jewelry, watches, and restrictive clothing, and immobilize the affected limb. Do not elevate the injury. Medical opinions vary on whether the area should be lower or level with the heart, but the consensus is that it should not be above it.
3. Make a note of the circumference of the limb at the bite site and at various points above the site as well. This will help you monitor swelling.
4. Evacuate your victim. Ideally he should be carried out to minimize movement. If the victim appears to be doing okay, he can walk. Stop and rest frequently, and if the swelling appears to be spreading or the patient's symptoms increase, change your plan and find a way to get your patient transported.
5. If you are waiting for rescue, make sure to keep your patient comfortable and hydrated (unless he begins vomiting).

Snakebite treatment is rife with old-fashioned remedies: You used to be told to cut and suck the venom out of the bite site or to use a suction cup extractor for the same purpose; applying an electric shock to the area was even in vogue for a while. Do not do any of these things. Do not apply ice, do not give your patient painkillers, and do not apply a tourniquet. All you really want to do is keep your patient calm and get help. If you're alone and have to hike out, don't run—you'll only increase the flow of blood throughout your system. Instead, walk calmly.

Dehydration. Have you ever hiked in hot weather and had a roaring headache and felt fatigued after only a few miles? More than likely you were dehydrated. Symptoms of dehydration include fatigue, headache, and decreased coordination and judgment. When you are hiking, your body's rate of fluid loss depends on the outside temperature, humidity, altitude, and your activity level. On average, a hiker walking in warm weather will lose four liters of fluid a day. That fluid loss is easily replaced by normal consumption of liquids and food. However, if a hiker is walking briskly in hot, dry weather and hauling a heavy pack, he or she can lose one to three liters of water an hour. It's important to always carry plenty of water and to stop often and drink fluids regularly, even if you aren't thirsty.

Heat exhaustion is the result of a loss of large amounts of electrolytes and often occurs if a hiker is dehydrated and has been under heavy exertion. Common symptoms of heat exhaustion include cramping, exhaustion, fatigue, lightheadedness, and nausea. You can treat heat exhaustion by getting out of the sun and drinking an electrolyte solution made up of one teaspoon of salt and one tablespoon of sugar dissolved in a liter of water. Drink this solution slowly over a period of one hour. Drinking plenty of fluids (preferably an electrolyte solution/sports drink) can prevent heat exhaustion. Avoid hiking during the hottest parts of the day, and wear breathable clothing, a wide-brimmed hat, and sunglasses.

Hypothermia is one of the biggest dangers in the backcountry, especially for day hikers in the summertime. That may sound strange, but imagine starting out on a hike in midsummer when it's sunny and 80 degrees out. You're clad in nylon shorts and a cotton T-shirt. About halfway through your hike, the sky begins to cloud up, and in the next hour a light drizzle begins to fall and the wind starts to pick up. Before you know it, you are soaking wet and shivering—the perfect recipe for hypothermia. More advanced signs include decreased coordination, slurred speech, and blurred vision. When a victim's temperature falls below 92 degrees, the blood pressure and pulse plummet, possibly leading to coma and death.

To avoid hypothermia, always bring a windproof/rainproof shell, a fleece jacket, long underwear made of a breathable, synthetic fiber, gloves, and hat when you are hiking in the mountains. Learn to adjust your clothing layers based on the temperature. If you are climbing uphill at a moderate pace you will stay warm, but when you stop for a break you'll become cold quickly, unless you add more layers of clothing.

If a hiker is showing advanced signs of hypothermia, dress him or her in dry clothes and make sure he or she is wearing a hat and gloves. Place the person in a sleeping bag in a tent or shelter that will protect him or her from the wind and other elements. Give the person warm fluids to drink and keep him awake.

Frostbite. When the mercury dips below 32 degrees, your extremities begin to chill. If a persistent chill attacks a localized area, say, your hands or your toes, the circulatory system reacts by cutting off blood flow to the affected area—the idea being to protect and preserve the body's overall temperature. And so it's death by attrition for the affected area. Ice crystals start to form from the water in the cells of the neglected tissue. Deprived of heat, nourishment, and now water, the tissue literally starves. This is frostbite.

Prevention is your best defense against this situation. Most prone to frostbite are your face, hands, and feet, so protect these areas well. Wool is the traditional material of choice because it provides ample air space for insulation and draws moisture away from the skin. Synthetic fabrics, however, have made great strides in the cold weather clothing market. Do your research. A pair of light silk liners under your regular gloves is a good trick for keeping warm. They afford some additional warmth, but more importantly they'll allow you to remove your mitts for tedious work without exposing the skin.

If your feet or hands start to feel cold or numb due to the elements, warm them as quickly as possible. Place cold hands under your armpits or bury them in your crotch. If your feet are cold, change your socks. If there's plenty of room in your boots, add another pair of socks. Do remember, though, that constricting your feet in tight boots can restrict blood flow and actually make your feet colder more quickly. Your socks need to have breathing room if they're going to be effective. Dead air provides insulation. If your face is cold, place your warm hands over your face, or simply wear a head stocking.

Should your skin go numb and start to appear white and waxy, chances are you've got or are developing frostbite. Don't try to thaw the area unless you can maintain the warmth. In other words, don't stop to warm up your frostbitten feet only to head back on the trail. You'll do more damage than good. Tests have shown that hikers who walked on thawed feet did more harm, and endured more pain, than hikers who left the affected areas alone. Do your best to get out of the cold entirely and seek medical attention—which usually consists of performing a rapid rewarming in water for twenty to thirty minutes.

The overall objective in preventing both hypothermia and frostbite is to keep the body's core warm. Protect key areas where heat escapes, like the top of the head, and maintain the proper nutrition level. Foods that are high in calories aid the body in producing heat. Never smoke or drink when you're in situations where the cold is threatening. By affecting blood flow, these activities ultimately cool the body's core temperature.

Altitude sickness (AMS). High lofty peaks, clear alpine lakes, and vast mountain views beckon hikers to the high country. But those who like to venture high may become victims of altitude sickness (also known as Acute Mountain Sickness—AMS). Altitude sickness is your body's reaction to insufficient oxygen in the blood due to decreased barometric pressure. While some hikers may feel lightheaded, nauseous, and experience shortness of breath at 7,000 feet, others may not experience these symptoms until they reach 10,000 feet or higher.

Slowing your ascent to high places and giving your body a chance to acclimatize to the higher elevations can prevent altitude sickness. For example, if you live at sea level and are planning a weeklong backpacking trip to elevations between 7,000 and 12,000 feet, start by staying below 7,000 feet for one night, then move to between 7,000 and 10,000 feet for another night or two. Avoid strenuous exertion and alcohol to give your body a chance to adjust to the new altitude. It's also important to eat light food and drink plenty of nonalcoholic fluids, preferably water. Loss of appetite at altitude is common, but you must eat!

Most hikers who experience mild to moderate AMS develop a headache and/or nausea, grow lethargic, and have problems sleeping. The treatment for AMS is simple: stop heading uphill. Keep eating and drinking water and take meds for the headache. You actually need to take more breaths at altitude than at sea level, so breathe a little faster without hyperventilating. If symptoms don't improve over twenty-four to forty-eight hours, descend. Once a victim descends about 2,000 to 3,000 feet, his signs will usually begin to diminish.

Severe AMS comes in two forms: High Altitude Pulmonary Edema (HAPE) and High Altitude Cerebral Edema (HACE). HAPE, an accumulation of fluid in the lungs, can occur above 8,000 feet. Symptoms include rapid heart rate, shortness of breath at rest, AMS symptoms, dry cough developing into a wet cough, gurgling sounds, flu-like or bronchitis symptoms, and lack of muscle coordination. HAPE is life threatening so descend immediately, at least 2,000 to 4,000 feet. HACE usually occurs above 12,000 feet but sometimes occurs above 10,000 feet. Symptoms are similar to HAPE but also include seizures, hallucinations, paralysis, and vision disturbances. Descend immediately—HACE is also life threatening.

Hantavirus Pulmonary Syndrome (HPS). Deer mice spread the virus that causes HPS, and humans contract it from breathing it in, usually when they've disturbed an area with dust and mice feces from nests or surfaces with mice droppings or urine. Exposure to large numbers of rodents and their feces or urine presents the greatest risk. As hikers, we sometimes enter old buildings, and often deer mice live in these places. We may not be around long enough to be exposed, but do be aware of this disease. About half the people who develop HPS die. Symptoms are flu-like and appear about two to three weeks after exposure. After initial symptoms, a dry cough and shortness of breath follow. Breathing is difficult. If you even think you might have HPS, see a doctor immediately!

Natural Hazards

Besides tripping over a rock or tree root on the trail, there are some real hazards to be aware of while hiking. Even if where you're hiking doesn't have the plethora of poisonous snakes and plants, insects, and grizzly bears found in other parts of the United States, there are a few weather conditions and predators you may need to take into account.

Lightning. Thunderstorms build over the mountains almost every day during the summer. Lightning is generated by thunderheads and can strike without warning, even several miles away from the nearest overhead cloud. The best rule of thumb is to start leaving exposed peaks, ridges, and canyon rims by about noon. This time can vary a little depending on storm buildup. Keep an eye on cloud formation and don't underestimate how fast a storm can build. The bigger they get, the more likely a thunderstorm will happen. Lightning takes the path of least resistance, so if you're the high point, it might choose you. Ducking under a rock overhang is dangerous as you form the shortest path between the rock and ground. If you dash below treeline, avoid standing under the only or the tallest tree. If you are caught above treeline, stay away from anything metal you might be carrying. Move down off the ridge slightly to a low, treeless point and squat until the storm passes. If you have an insulating pad, squat on it. Avoid having both your hands and feet touching the ground at once and never lay flat. If you hear a buzzing sound or feel your hair standing on end, move quickly as an electrical charge is building up.

Flash floods. On July 31, 1976, a torrential downpour unleashed by a thunderstorm dumped tons of water into the Big Thompson watershed near Estes Park. Within hours, a wall of water moved down the narrow canyon killing 139 people and causing more than $30 million in property damage. The spooky thing about flash floods, especially in western canyons, is that they can appear out of nowhere from a storm many miles away. While hiking or driving in canyons, keep an eye on the weather. Always climb to safety if danger threatens. Flash floods usually subside quickly, so be patient and don't cross a swollen stream.

Bears. Most of the United States (outside of the Pacific Northwest and parts of the Northern Rockies) does not have a grizzly bear population, although some rumors exist about sightings where there should be none. Black bears are plentiful, however. Here are some tips in case you and a bear scare each other. Most of all, avoid surprising a bear. Talk or sing where visibility or hearing are limited, such as along a rushing creek or in thick brush. In grizzly country especially, carry bear spray in a holster on your pack belt where you can quickly grab it. While hiking, watch for bear tracks (five toes), droppings (sizable with leaves, partly digested berries, seeds, and/or animal fur), or rocks and roots along the trail that show signs of being dug up (this could be a bear looking for bugs to eat). Keep a clean camp, hang food or use bearproof storage containers, and don't sleep in the clothes you wore while cooking. Be especially careful to avoid getting between a mother and her cubs. In late summer and fall bears are busy eating to fatten up for winter, so be extra careful around berry bushes and oakbrush. If you do encounter a bear, move away slowly while facing the bear, talk softly, and avoid direct eye contact. Give the bear room to escape. Since bears are very curious, it might stand upright to get a better whiff of you, and it may even charge you to try to intimidate you. Try to stay calm. If a black bear attacks you, fight back with anything you have handy. If a grizzly bear attacks you, your best option is to "play dead" by lying face down on the ground and covering the back of your neck and head with your hands. Unleashed dogs have been known to come running back to their owners with a bear close behind. Keep your dog on a leash or leave it at home.

Mountain lions. Mountain lions appear to be getting more comfortable around humans as long as deer (their favorite prey) are in an area with adequate cover. Usually elusive and quiet, lions rarely attack people. If you meet a lion, give it a chance to escape. Stay calm and talk firmly to it. Back away slowly while facing the lion. If you run, you'll only encourage the cat to chase you. Make yourself look large by opening a jacket, if you have one, or waving your hiking poles. If the lion behaves aggressively throw stones, sticks, or whatever you can while remaining tall. If a lion does attack, fight for your life with anything you can grab.

Moose. Because moose have very few natural predators, they don't fear humans like other animals. You might find moose in sagebrush and wetter areas of willow, aspen, and pine, or in beaver habitats. Mothers with calves, as well as bulls during mating season, can be particularly aggressive. If a moose threatens you, back away slowly and talk calmly to it. Keep your pets away from moose.

Other considerations. Hunting is a popular sport in the United States, especially during rifle season in the cooler months. Hiking is still enjoyable in those months in many areas, so just take a few precautions. First, learn when the different hunting seasons start and end in the area in which you'll be hiking. During this time frame, be sure to wear at least a blaze orange hat, and possibly put an orange vest over your pack. Don't be surprised to see hunters in camo outfits carrying bows or rifles around during their season. If you would feel more comfortable without hunters around, hike in national parks and monuments or state and local parks where hunting is not allowed.

Navigation

Whether you are going on a short hike in a familiar area or planning a weeklong backpack trip, you should always be equipped with the proper navigational equipment—at the very least a detailed map and a sturdy compass.

Maps. There are many different types of maps available to help you find your way on the trail. Easiest to find are Forest Service maps and BLM (Bureau of Land Management) maps. These maps tend to cover large areas, so be sure they are detailed enough for your particular trip. You can also obtain National Park maps as well as high quality maps from private companies and trail groups. These maps can be obtained either from outdoor stores or ranger stations.

U.S. Geological Survey topographic maps are particularly popular with hikers—especially serious backcountry hikers. These maps contain the standard map symbols such as roads, lakes, and rivers, as well as contour lines that show the details of the trail terrain like ridges, valleys, passes, and mountain peaks. The 7.5-minute series (1 inch on the map equals approximately ⅔ mile on the ground) provides the closest inspection available. USGS maps are available by mail (U.S. Geological Survey, Map Distribution Branch, PO Box 25286, Denver, CO 80225), or at mapping.usgs.gov/esic/to_order.html.

If you want to check out the high-tech world of maps, you can purchase topographic maps on CD-ROM. These software-mapping programs let you select a route on your computer, print it out, then take it with you on the trail. Some software mapping programs let you insert symbols and labels, download waypoints from a GPS unit, and export the maps to other software programs.

The art of map reading is a skill that you can develop by first practicing in an area you are familiar with. To begin, orient the map so the map is lined up in the correct direction (i.e., north on the map is lined up with true north). Next, familiarize yourself with the map symbols and try and match them up with terrain features around you such as a high ridge, mountain peak, river, or lake. If you are practicing with a USGS map, notice the contour lines. On gentler terrain these contour lines are spaced farther apart, and on steeper terrain they are closer together. Pick a short loop trail, and stop frequently to check your position on the map. As you practice map reading, you'll learn how to anticipate a steep section on the trail or a good place to take a rest break, and so on.

Compasses. First off, the sun is not a substitute for a compass. So, what kind of compass should you have? Here are some characteristics you should look for: a rectangular base with detailed scales, a liquid-filled housing, protective housing, a sighting line on the mirror, luminous alignment and back-bearing arrows, a luminous north-seeking arrow, and a well-defined bezel ring.

You can learn compass basics by reading the detailed instructions included with your compass. If you want to fine-tune your compass skills, sign up for an orienteering class or purchase a book on compass reading. Once you've learned the basic skills of using a compass, remember to practice these skills before you head into the backcountry.

If you are a klutz at using a compass, you may be interested in checking out the technical wizardry of the GPS (Global Positioning System) device. The GPS was developed by the Pentagon and works off twenty-four NAVSTAR satellites, which were designed to guide missiles to their targets. A GPS device is a handheld unit that calculates your latitude and longitude with the easy press of a button. The Department of Defense used to scramble the satellite signals a bit to prevent civilians (and spies!) from getting extremely accurate readings, but that practice was discontinued in May 2000, and GPS units now provide nearly pinpoint accuracy (within 30 to 60 feet).

There are many different types of GPS units available and they range in price from $100 to $400. In general, all GPS units have a display screen and keypad where you input information. In addition to acting as a compass, the unit allows you to plot your route, easily retrace your path, track your travelling speed, find the mileage between waypoints, and calculate the total mileage of your route.

Before you purchase a GPS unit, keep in mind that these devices don't pick up signals indoors, in heavily wooded areas, on mountain peaks, or in deep valleys. Also, batteries can wear out or other technical problems can develop. A GPS unit should be used in conjunction with a map and compass, not in place of those items.

Pedometers. A pedometer is a small, clip-on unit with a digital display that calculates your hiking distance in miles or kilometers based on your walking stride. Some units also calculate the calories you burn and your total hiking time. Pedometers are available at most large outdoor stores and range in price from $20 to $40.

Trip Planning

Planning your hiking adventure begins with letting a friend or relative know your trip itinerary so they can call for help if you don't return at your scheduled time. Your next task is to make sure you are outfitted to experience the risks and rewards of the trail. This section highlights gear and clothing you may want to take with you to get the most out of your hike.

Day Hikes

- bear repellent spray (if hiking in grizzly country)
- camera
- compass/GPS unit
- pedometer
- daypack
- first-aid kit
- food
- guidebook
- headlamp/flashlight with extra batteries and bulbs
- hat
- insect repellent
- knife/multipurpose tool
- map
- matches in waterproof container and fire starter
- fleece jacket
- rain gear
- space blanket
- sunglasses
- sunscreen
- swimsuit and/or fishing gear (if hiking to a lake)
- watch
- water
- water bottles/water hydration system

Overnight Trip

- backpack and waterproof rain cover
- backpacker's trowel
- bandanna
- bear repellent spray (if hiking in grizzly country)
- bear bell
- biodegradable soap
- pot scrubber
- collapsible water container (2–3 gallon capacity)
- clothing—extra wool socks, shirt and shorts
- cook set/utensils

- ditty bags to store gear
- extra plastic resealable bags
- gaiters
- garbage bag
- ground cloth
- journal/pen
- nylon rope to hang food
- long underwear
- permit (if required)
- rain jacket and pants
- sandals to wear around camp and to ford streams
- sleeping bag
- waterproof stuff sack
- sleeping pad
- small bath towel
- stove and fuel
- tent
- toiletry items
- water filter
- whistle

Equipment

With the outdoor market currently flooded with products, many of which are pure gimmickry, it seems impossible to both differentiate and choose. Do I really need a tropical-fish-lined collapsible shower? (No, you don't.) The only defense against the maddening quantity of items thrust in your face is to think practically—and to do so before you go shopping. The worst buys are impulsive buys. Since most name brands will differ only slightly in quality, it's best to know what you're looking for in terms of function. Buy only what you need. You will, don't forget, be carrying what you've bought on your back. Here are some things to keep in mind before you go shopping.

Clothes. Clothing is your armor against Mother Nature's little surprises. Hikers should be prepared for any possibility, especially when hiking in mountainous areas. Adequate rain protection and extra layers of clothing are a good idea. In summer, a wide-brimmed hat can help keep the sun at bay. In the winter months the first layer you'll want to wear is a "wicking" layer of long underwear that keeps perspiration away from your skin. Wear long underwear made from synthetic fibers that wick moisture away from the skin and draw it toward the next layer of clothing, where it then evaporates. Avoid wearing long underwear made of cotton as it is slow to dry and keeps moisture next to your skin.

The second layer you'll wear is the "insulating" layer. Aside from keeping you warm, this layer needs to "breathe" so you stay dry while hiking. A fabric that provides insulation and dries quickly is fleece. It's interesting to note that this one-of-a-kind fabric is made out of recycled plastic. Purchasing a zip-up jacket made of this material is highly recommended.

The last line of layering defense is the "shell" layer. You'll need some type of waterproof, windproof, breathable jacket that will fit over all of your other layers. It should have a large hood that fits over a hat. You'll also need a good pair of rain pants made from a similar waterproof, breathable fabric. Some Gore-Tex jackets cost as much as $500, but you should know that there are more affordable fabrics out there that work just as well.

Now that you've learned the basics of layering, you can't forget to protect your hands and face. In cold, windy, or rainy weather you'll need a hat made of wool or fleece and insulated, waterproof gloves that will keep your hands warm and toasty. As mentioned earlier, buying an additional pair of light silk liners to wear under your regular gloves is a good idea.

Footwear. If you have any extra money to spend on your trip, put that money into boots or trail shoes. Poor shoes will bring a hike to a halt faster than anything else. To avoid this annoyance, buy shoes that provide support and are lightweight and flexible. A lightweight hiking boot is better than a heavy, leather mountaineering boot for most day hikes and backpacking. Trail running shoes provide a little extra cushion and are made in a high-top style that many people wear for hiking. These running shoes are lighter, more flexible, and more breathable than hiking boots. If you know you'll be hiking in wet weather often, purchase boots or shoes with a Gore-Tex liner, which will help keep your feet dry.

When buying your boots, be sure to wear the same type of socks you'll be wearing on the trail. If the boots you're buying are for cold weather hiking, try the boots on while wearing two pairs of socks. Speaking of socks, a good cold weather sock combination is to wear a thinner sock made of wool or polypropylene covered by a heavier outer sock made of wool or a synthetic/wool mix. The inner sock protects the foot from the rubbing effects of the outer sock and prevents blisters. Many outdoor stores have some type of ramp to simulate hiking uphill and downhill. Be sure to take advantage of this test, as toe-jamming boot fronts can be very painful and debilitating on the downhill trek.

Once you've purchased your footwear, be sure to break them in before you hit the trail. New footwear is often stiff and needs to be stretched and molded to your foot.

Hiking poles. Hiking poles help with balance, and more importantly take pressure off your knees. The ones with shock absorbers are easier on your elbows and knees. Some poles even come with a camera attachment to be used as a monopod. And heaven forbid you meet a mountain lion, bear, or unfriendly dog, the poles can make you look a lot bigger.

Backpacks. No matter what type of hiking you do you'll need a pack of some sort to carry the basic trail essentials. There are a variety of backpacks on the market, but let's first discuss what you intend to use it for. Day hikes or overnight trips?

If you plan on doing a day hike, a daypack should have some of the following characteristics: a padded hip belt that's at least 2 inches in diameter (avoid packs with only a small nylon piece of webbing for a hip belt); a chest strap (the chest strap helps stabilize the pack against your body); external pockets to carry water and other items that you want easy access to; an internal pocket to hold keys, a knife, a wallet, and other miscellaneous items; an external lashing system to hold a jacket; and, if you so desire, a hydration pocket for carrying a hydration system (which consists of a water bladder with an attachable drinking hose).

For short hikes, some hikers like to use a fanny pack to store just a camera, food, a compass, a map, and other trail essentials. Most fanny packs have pockets for two water bottles and a padded hip belt.

If you intend to do an extended, overnight trip, there are multiple considerations. First off, you need to decide what kind of framed pack you want. There are two backpack types for backpacking: the internal frame and the external frame. An internal frame pack rests closer to your body, making it more stable and easier to balance when hiking over rough terrain. An external frame pack is just that, an aluminum frame attached to the exterior of the pack. Some hikers consider an external frame pack to be better for long backpack trips because it distributes the pack weight better and allows you to carry heavier loads. It's often easier to pack, and your gear is more accessible. It also offers better back ventilation in hot weather.

The most critical measurement for fitting a pack is torso length. The pack needs to rest evenly on your hips without sagging. A good pack will come in two or three sizes and have straps and hip belts that are adjustable according to your body size and characteristics.

When you purchase a backpack, go to an outdoor store with salespeople who are knowledgeable in how to properly fit a pack. Once the pack is fitted for you, load the pack with the amount of weight you plan on taking on the trail. The weight of the pack should be distributed evenly and you should be able to swing your arms and walk briskly without feeling out of balance. Another good technique for evaluating a pack is to walk up and down stairs and make quick turns to the right and to the left to be sure the pack doesn't feel out of balance. Other features that are nice to have on a backpack include a removable day pack or fanny pack, external pockets for extra water, and extra lash points to attach a jacket or other items.

Sleeping bags and pads. Sleeping bags are rated by temperature. You can purchase a bag made with synthetic insulation, or you can buy a goose down bag. Goose down bags are more expensive, but they have a higher insulating capacity by weight and will keep their loft longer. You'll want to purchase a bag with a temperature rating that fits the time of year and conditions you are most likely to camp in. One caveat: The techno-standard for temperature ratings is far from perfect. Ratings vary from manufacturer to manufacturer, so to protect yourself you should purchase a bag rated 10 to 15 degrees below the temperature you expect to be camping in. Synthetic bags are more resistant to water than down bags, but many down bags are now made with a Gore-Tex shell that helps to repel water. Down bags are also more compressible than synthetic bags and take up less room in your pack, which is an important consideration if you are planning a multiday backpack trip. Features to look for in a sleeping bag include a mummy style bag, a hood you can cinch down around your head in cold weather, and draft tubes along the zippers that help keep heat in and drafts out.

You'll also want a sleeping pad to provide insulation and padding from the cold ground. There are different types of sleeping pads available, from the more expensive self-inflating air mattresses to the less expensive closed-cell foam pads. Self-inflating air mattresses are usually heavier than closed-cell foam mattresses and are prone to punctures.

Tents. The tent is your home away from home while on the trail. It provides protection from wind, rain, snow, and insects. A three-season tent is a good choice for backpacking and can range in price from $100 to $500. These lightweight and versatile tents provide protection in all types of weather, except heavy snowstorms or high winds, and range in weight from four to eight pounds. Look for a tent that's easy to set up and will easily fit two people with gear. Dome type tents usually offer more headroom and places to store gear. Other handy tent features include a vestibule where you can store wet boots and backpacks. Some nice-to-have items in a tent include interior pockets to store small items and lashing points to hang a clothesline. Most three-season tents also come with stakes so you can secure the tent in high winds. Before you purchase a tent, set it up and take it down a few times to be sure it is easy to handle. Also, sit inside the tent and make sure it has enough room for you and your gear.

Cell phones. Many hikers are carrying their cell phones into the backcountry these days in case of emergency. That's fine and good, but please know that cell phone coverage is often poor to nonexistent in valleys, canyons, and thick forest. More importantly people have started to call for help because they're tired or lost. Let's go back to being prepared. You are responsible for yourself in the backcountry. Use your brain to avoid problems, and if you do encounter one, first use your brain to try to correct the situation. Only use your cell phone, if it works, in true emergencies. If it doesn't work down low in a valley, try hiking to a high point where you might get reception.

Hiking with Children

Hiking with children isn't a matter of how many miles you can cover or how much elevation gain you make in a day; it's about seeing and experiencing nature through their eyes.

Kids like to explore and have fun. They like to stop and point out bugs and plants, look under rocks, jump in puddles, and throw sticks. If you're taking a toddler or young child on a hike, start with a trail that you're familiar with. Trails that have interesting things for kids, like piles of leaves to play in or a small stream to wade through during the summer, will make the hike much more enjoyable for them and will keep them from getting bored.

You can keep your child's attention if you have a strategy before starting on the trail. Using games is not only an effective way to keep a child's attention, it's also a great way to teach him or her about nature. Quiz children on the names of plants and animals. Pick up a family-friendly outdoor hobby like Geocaching (www.geocaching.com) or Letterboxing (www.atlasquest.com), both of which combine the outdoors, clue-solving, and treasure hunting. If your children are old enough, let them carry their own daypack filled with snacks and water. So that you are sure to go at their pace and not yours, let them lead the way. Playing follow the leader works particularly well when you have a group of children. Have each child take a turn at being the leader.

With children, a lot of clothing is key. The only thing predictable about weather is that it will change. Especially in mountainous areas, weather can change dramatically in a very short time. Always bring extra clothing for children, regardless of the season. In the winter, have your children wear wool socks, and warm layers such as long underwear, a fleece jacket and hat, wool mittens, and good rain gear. It's not a bad idea to have these along in late fall and early spring as well. Good footwear is also important. A sturdy pair of high top tennis shoes or lightweight hiking boots are the best bet for little ones. If you're hiking in the summer near a lake or stream, bring along a pair of old sneakers that your child can put on when he wants to go exploring in the water. Remember when you're near any type of water, always watch your child at all times. Also, keep a close eye on teething toddlers who may decide a rock or leaf of poison oak is an interesting item to put in their mouth.

From spring through fall, you'll want your kids to wear a wide-brimmed hat to keep their face, head, and ears protected from the hot sun. Also, make sure your children wear sunscreen at all times. Choose a brand without Paba—children have sensitive skin and may have an allergic reaction to sunscreen that contains Paba. If you are hiking with a child younger than six months, don't use sunscreen or insect repellent. Instead, be sure that their head, face, neck, and ears are protected from the sun with a wide-brimmed hat, and that all other skin exposed to the sun is protected with the appropriate clothing.

Remember that food is fun. Kids like snacks so it's important to bring a lot of munchies for the trail. Stopping often for snack breaks is a fun way to keep the trail interesting. Raisins, apples, granola bars, crackers and cheese, cereal, and trail mix all make great snacks. Also, a few of their favorite candy treats can go a long way toward heading off a fit of fussing. If your child is old enough to carry her own backpack, let him or her fill it with some lightweight "comfort" items such as a doll, a small stuffed animal, or a little toy (you'll have to draw the line at bringing the ten-pound Tonka truck). If your kids don't like drinking water, you can bring some powdered drink mix or a juice box.

Avoid poorly designed child-carrying packs—you don't want to break your back carrying your child. Most child-carrying backpacks designed to hold a forty-pound child will contain a large carrying pocket to hold diapers and other items. Some have an optional rain/sun hood.

Hiking with Your Dog

Bringing your furry friend with you is always more fun than leaving him behind. Our canine pals make great trail buddies because they never complain and always make good company. Hiking with your dog can be a rewarding experience, especially if you plan ahead.

Getting your dog in shape. Before you plan outdoor adventures with your dog, make sure he's in shape for the trail. Getting your dog into shape takes the same discipline as getting yourself into shape, but luckily, your dog can get in shape with you. Take your dog with you on your daily runs or walks. If there is a park near your house, hit a tennis ball or play Frisbee with your dog.

Swimming is also an excellent way to get your dog into shape. If there is a lake or river near where you live and your dog likes the water, have him retrieve a tennis ball or stick. Gradually build your dog's stamina up over a two- to three-month period. A good rule of thumb is to assume that your dog will travel twice as far as you will on the trail. If you plan on doing a 5-mile hike, be sure your dog is in shape for a 10-mile hike.

Training your dog for the trail. Before you go on your first hiking adventure with your dog, be sure he has a firm grasp on the basics of canine etiquette and behavior. Make sure he can sit, lie down, stay, and come. One of the most important commands you can teach your canine pal is to "come" under any situation. It's easy for your friend's nose to lead him astray or possibly get lost. Another helpful command is the "get behind" command. When you're on a hiking trail that's narrow, you can have your dog follow behind you when other trail users approach. Nothing is more bothersome than an enthusiastic dog that runs back and forth on the trail and disrupts the peace of the trail for others—or, worse, jumps up on other hikers and gets them muddy. When you see other trail users approaching you on the trail, give them the right of way by quietly stepping off the trail and making your dog lie down and stay until they pass.

Equipment. The most critical pieces of equipment you can invest in for your dog are proper identification and a sturdy leash. Flexi-leads work well for hiking because they give your dog more freedom to explore but still leave you in control. Make sure your dog has identification that includes your name and address and a number for your veterinarian. Other forms of identification for your dog include a tattoo or a microchip. You should consult your veterinarian for more information on these last two options.

The next piece of equipment you'll want to consider is a pack for your dog. By no means should you hold all of your dog's essentials in your pack—let him carry his own gear! Dogs that are in good shape can carry 30 to 40 percent of their own weight.

Most packs are fitted by a dog's weight and girth measurement. Companies that make dog packs generally include guidelines to help you pick out the size that's right for your dog. Some characteristics to look for when purchasing a pack for your dog include a harness that contains two padded girth straps, a padded chest strap, leash attachments, removable saddle bags, internal water bladders, and external gear cords.

You can introduce your dog to the pack by first placing the empty pack on his back and letting him wear it around the yard. Keep an eye on him during this first introduction. He may decide to chew through the straps if you aren't watching him closely. Once he learns to treat the pack as an object of fun and not a foreign enemy, fill the pack evenly on both sides with a few ounces of dog food in resealable plastic bags. Have your dog wear his pack on your daily walks for a period of two to three weeks. Each week add a little more weight to the pack until your dog will accept carrying the maximum amount of weight he can carry.

You can also purchase collapsible water and dog food bowls for your dog. These bowls are lightweight and can easily be stashed into your pack or your dog's. If you are hiking on rocky terrain or in the snow, you can purchase footwear for your dog that will protect his feet from cuts and bruises.

Always carry plastic bags to remove feces from the trail. It is a courtesy to other trail users and helps protect local wildlife.

The following is a list of items to bring when you take your dog hiking: collapsible water bowls, a comb, a collar and a leash, dog food, plastic bags for feces, a dog pack, flea/tick powder, paw protection, water, and a first-aid kit that contains eye ointment, tweezers, scissors, stretchy foot wrap, gauze, antibacterial wash, sterile cotton tip applicators, antibiotic ointment, and cotton wrap.

First aid for your dog. Your dog is just as prone—if not more prone—to getting in trouble on the trail as you are, so be prepared. Here's a rundown of the more likely misfortunes that might befall your little friend.

Bees and wasps. If a bee or wasp stings your dog, remove the stinger with a pair of tweezers and place a mudpack or a cloth dipped in cold water over the affected area.

Porcupines. One good reason to keep your dog on a leash is to prevent it from getting a nose full of porcupine quills. You may be able to remove the quills with pliers, but a veterinarian is the best person to do this nasty job because most dogs need to be sedated.

Heat stroke. Avoid hiking with your dog in really hot weather. Dogs with heat stroke will pant excessively, lie down and refuse to get up, and become lethargic and disoriented. If your dog shows any of these signs on the trail, have him lie down in the shade. If you are near a stream, pour cool water over your dog's entire body to help bring his body temperature back to normal.

Heartworm. Dogs get heartworms from mosquitoes which carry the disease in the prime mosquito months of July and August. Giving your dog a monthly pill prescribed by your veterinarian easily prevents this condition.

Plant pitfalls. One of the biggest plant hazards for dogs on the trail are foxtails. Foxtails are pointed grass seed heads that bury themselves in your friend's fur, between his toes, and even get in his ear canal. If left unattended, these nasty seeds can work their way under the skin and cause abscesses and other problems. If you have a long-haired dog, consider trimming the hair between his toes and giving him a summer haircut to help prevent foxtails from attaching to his fur. After every hike, always look over your dog for these seeds—especially between his toes and his ears.

Other plant hazards include burrs, thorns, thistles, and poison oak. If you find any burrs or thistles on your dog, remove them as soon as possible before they become an unmanageable mat. Thorns can pierce a dog's foot and cause a great deal of pain. If you see that your dog is lame, stop and check his feet for thorns. Dogs are immune to poison oak but they can pick up the sticky, oily substance from the plant and transfer it to you.

Protect those paws. Be sure to keep your dog's nails trimmed so he avoids getting soft tissue or joint injuries. If your dog slows and refuses to go on, check to see that his paws aren't torn or worn. You can protect your dog's paws from trail hazards such as sharp gravel, foxtails, lava scree, and thorns by purchasing dog boots.

Sunburn. If your dog has light skin he is an easy target for sunburn on his nose and other exposed skin areas. You can apply a nontoxic sunscreen to exposed skin areas that will help protect him from overexposure to the sun.

Ticks and fleas. Ticks can easily give your dog Lyme disease, as well as other diseases. Before you hit the trail, treat your dog with a flea and tick spray or powder. You can also ask your veterinarian about a once-a-month pour-on treatment that repels fleas and ticks.

Mosquitoes and deer flies. These little flying machines can do a job on your dog's snout and ears. Best bet is to spray your dog with fly repellent for horses to discourage both pests.

Giardia. Dogs can get giardia, which results in diarrhea. It is usually not debilitating, but it's definitely messy. A vaccine against giardia is available.

Mushrooms. Make sure your dog doesn't sample mushrooms along the trail. They could be poisonous to him, but he doesn't know that.

When you are finally ready to hit the trail with your dog, keep in mind that national parks and many wilderness areas do not allow dogs on trails. Your best bet is to hike in national forests, BLM lands, and state parks. Always call ahead to see what the restrictions are.

Forgotten chimney as seen through spring woods ▶

Hike Index

About the Author

Johnny Molloy is a writer and adventurer based in Johnson City, Tennessee, just a few miles south of the Old Dominion. His nonfiction passion started after reading *In Cold Blood* by Truman Capote, which his father had left lying around. After that he delved into all manner of nonfiction reading, from *Strange but True Football Stories* to books about the Mississippi River and his hometown of Memphis, Tennessee. He has since focused his reading on early American history.

His passion for the outdoors started on a backpacking trip in Great Smoky Mountains National Park while attending the University of Tennessee. That first foray unleashed a love of the outdoors that has led Molloy to spending most of his time hiking, backpacking, canoe camping, and tent camping for the past three decades. Friends enjoyed his outdoor adventure stories; one even suggested he write a book. He pursued his friend's idea and soon parlayed his love of the outdoors into an occupation. The results of his efforts are more than fifty guides. His writings include hiking guidebooks, camping guidebooks, paddling guidebooks, comprehensive guidebooks about specific areas, and true outdoor adventure books covering the eastern United States. Molloy writes for various magazines and websites and is a columnist and feature writer for his local paper, the *Johnson City Press*. He continues writing and traveling extensively throughout the United States, endeavoring in a variety of outdoor pursuits. His nonoutdoor interests include serving God as a Gideon and University of Tennessee sports. For the latest on Johnny, please visit johnnymolloy.com.

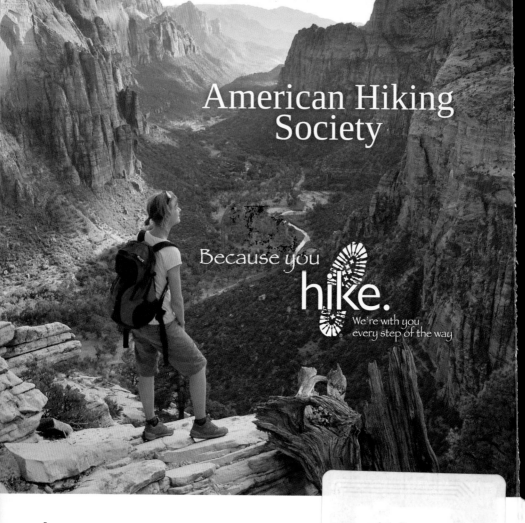

American Hiking Society

Because you hike.

We're with you
every step of the way

As a national voice for hikers, **American Hikin** ...

- Building and maintaining hiking trails
- Educating and supporting hikers by providing ...
- Supporting hiking and trail organizations nati ...
- Speaking for hikers in the halls of Congress a ...

Whether you're a casual hiker or a seasoned ...
become a member of American Hiking Society ...
national hiking community! You'll enjoy great mer ...
and help preserve the nation's hiking trails, so tom ...
is even better than today's. We invite you to join u ...